Pitiful Plaintiffs

Child Welfare Litigation

and the Federal Courts

Susan Gluck Mezey

University of Pittsburgh Press

Published by the University of Pittsburgh Press, Pittsburgh, Pa. 15261

Copyright © 2000, University of Pittsburgh Press
Manufactured in the United States of America

Printed on acid-free paper

10 9 8 7 6 5 4 3 2 1

Library of Congress Cataloging-in-Publication Data

Mezey, Susan Gluck, 1944-

    Pitiful plaintiffs : child welfare litigation and the federal courts / Susan Gluck Mezey.

    p. cm.

    Includes bibliographical references and index.

    ISBN 0-8229-5717-5 (paper : acid-free paper) — ISBN 0-8229-4116-3 (cloth : acid-free paper)

    1. Children—Legal status, laws, etc.—United States.   2. Judicial process—United States.
3. Child welfare—United States. I. Title.

KF3735 . M49 2000

344.73'0327—dc21   99-050679

For My Family

Contents

Preface

This is a book about tens of thousands of pitiful plaintiffs, the abused and neglected children in the United States who enlisted the help of the federal courts to compel state and local governments to fulfill their obligations to them. Hoping the courts would be receptive to the pleas of "one of the largest and most vulnerable minority groups [in the United States]" (Kohler 1977, 217), children's advocates, beginning in the 1970s, attempted to use the power of the federal judiciary to counter the effects of state policymakers who sought to reconcile budgetary shortfalls at the expense of the children.

Their weapons were, for the most part, class action suits that sought widespread reform of entire child welfare systems. The class actions, brought on behalf of abused and neglected children seeking relief from their "bleak and Dickensian" (*B.H. v. Johnson* 1989, 1389) existence, were directed at almost all aspects of the child welfare system, including placements, protective services, foster care, adoption, education, and health care. In adopting a strategy of systemic reform litigation, the advocates were hoping to change the practices of states in which business as usual means, "Unless a death hits the headlines, foster care children are easy to ignore. They are too young to have a political voice . . . and the states responsible for them fear that reform will cost money" (*National Law Journal,* June 27, 1994).

Reflecting a variety of legal and political factors, the litigation spread into most states and localities. According to the National Child Welfare Litigation Docket, compiled by the National Center for Youth Law (1995), seventy-four child welfare cases—most of them class action suits—were filed from 1975 through 1995. By 1995, child welfare suits were pending or had recently been completed against more than thirty-one state and municipal child welfare agencies in the nation, including Washington, D.C. An updated version of the Litigation Docket showed eighty-seven cases (mostly class actions) filed through 1998 (National Center for Youth Law 1998).

As a result of the litigation, federal court judges assumed supervisory responsibility over many of the nation's child welfare systems. Despite the proliferation of lawsuits in the area of child welfare reform and the increasingly important role of the federal judiciary in child welfare policymaking, however, structural reform litigation against child welfare systems has received scant scholarly attention from a political science or public policy perspective.

The literature on child welfare law is found almost exclusively in law reviews and social work journals. Books on the topic tend to be extended versions of these works. The law review pieces primarily present legal analyses of judicial decisions, while the social work journals are largely devoted to assessing the delivery of child welfare services. Although these studies provide valuable insights into the operations of these systems, for the most part they fail to address questions of interest to political scientists or public policy analysts.

Set within the context of the literature on institutional reform litigation, this study examines the role of the federal courts in the child welfare policymaking process and the extent to which the litigation achieved its goal of reforming child welfare systems. It focuses on class action litigation against the Illinois child welfare system, encompassing the vast array of political, social, and legal issues affecting child welfare reform in Illinois. Applying a model of institutional reform litigation that can be used as a framework for future research, this study represents the first systematic analysis of child welfare litigation in the federal courts.

This project arises from my longstanding interest in the role of the federal courts in the U.S. political system and builds on my earlier work on social security disability policy, children's rights policy, and women's rights policy. Each of those projects, however, focused primarily on the end result of the litigation and centered on the interaction among the institutions of the national government and between the state and the federal court. This book is more process oriented, examining the outcome but also seeking to explain how child welfare policy is formulated and how the federal courts have affected that process.

Acknowledgments

Writing this book has been both a painful and pleasurable experience. It was painful because it acquainted me with a segment of life I only vaguely knew existed. As I read the stories of B.H., Joshua, LaShawn, R.C., and the others who were mistreated by the adults around them, I was constantly confronted with the horrors that millions of children are forced to endure. In part, I dedicate this book to the abused and neglected children in the hope that it will lead to the development of policies that will protect them in their homes and in the courts.

The pleasurable part of this project arose from the opportunity it provided for me to meet the sincere and hardworking individuals who are committed to correcting the errors of other adults and improving the lives of the children that desperately need their help. In part, this book is also dedicated to them.

This study was inspired in part by my semester as an Ethics Fellow at Loyola University Chicago when I began to familiarize myself with Illinois abuse and neglect law and the juvenile court system. A research grant and subsequent leave of absence from teaching responsibilities at Loyola allowed me to complete the book in a timely fashion.

During my research on this project, I gained a great deal of respect for the juvenile court judges who are frequently required to make life and death decisions in the cases that come before them. I want to thank those who allowed me to interview them and permitted me to observe their work first-hand. I also grew to respect and admire the men and women—lawyers, judges, policy experts—who played important roles in the child welfare system. I want to thank those who generously spent time explaining the system to me. While grateful to all of them, I want to single out Chuck Golbert, Stacey Platt, and Ben Wolf for their encouragement and interest in the project. By reading and commenting on the chapters on child welfare policy, Chuck and Stacey saved me from committing errors of fact and interpretation. Graduate students Douglas Roscoe, Elizabeth Janairo, and Will Jordan helped by reading and analyzing the large number of cases involved in child welfare law and checking citations. Naturally, however, I assume sole responsibility for any errors contained in these pages.

Although the customary thanks to editors for their help and advice may often be perfunctory and insincere, there is nothing perfunctory or insincere in my thank-you to Niels Aaboe of the University of Pittsburgh Press, who was wonderful to work with throughout. From our first conversation at the American Political Science Association meeting, he expressed support and enthusiasm for the book and for me. I also want to thank *Law & Policy* editor Murray Levine for his helpful comments on the manuscript on child welfare litigation that was ultimately published in the journal. Managing editor Laura Mangan was a pleasure to work with as well. Blackwell Publishers allowed me to reprint material from the article, published in the April 1998 issue of *Law & Policy*. And I'd like to thank Xenia Vieth, a good friend since law school, who has always encouraged my work as an "academic" lawyer.

Last, I want to acknowledge the love and support I continually receive from my family: my husband, Michael, and my children, Jennifer and Jason; thinking of them always served as an antidote to the depressing subjects I encountered in researching and writing on this topic. My mother, Paula Gluck, gave me her strength and determination to succeed. I cannot adequately express all that I owe to them, but I can dedicate this book to them.

Pitiful Plaintiffs

1 Child Welfare Policymaking

EXPLORING THE JUDICIAL ROLE

In the 1970s children's advocates began to look to the federal courts for the dual purpose of vindicating children's rights and effectuating structural changes in flawed child welfare systems.[1] The extent of the nation's child welfare dilemma is indicated by the extensive litigation seeking reform of child welfare agencies. In part these suits to reform child welfare systems, involving the lives of thousands of children and millions of dollars, arose in response to a growing national crisis caused by the "sharp increase in the scope of the problem [of child maltreatment]" (Sedlak and Broadhurst 1996, 3). Characterized as "the hotbed of children's litigation" (*National Law Journal*, June 27, 1994), the campaign for child welfare reform materialized as the evidence mounted that children separated from their biological families were further victimized by government bureaucracies entrusted with the duty of keeping them safe (Mushlin, Levitt, and Anderson 1986; see Colvin 1992).

Children's advocates turned to the federal courts, seeking their assistance to force the government to honor its commitment to these doubly victimized youngsters. As a consequence of the proliferation of lawsuits against child welfare systems, federal court judges have played an important role in the child welfare policymaking process for more than two decades. By March 1996, as a result of reform litigation, child welfare agencies in almost half the states were operating under a form of court supervision, with the District of Columbia under the authority of a court-appointed receiver (*New York Times*, March 17, 1996; see Hansen 1994, 226).

Judicial Policymaking

While the federal judiciary assumed its role in child welfare policymaking relatively recently, the federal courts have long been a preferred arena for systemic reform efforts in a variety of areas. In the 1950s and 1960s litigants obtained federal injunctions to force schools to desegregate, and in the 1970s and 1980s they were able to secure injunctive relief in class actions brought to reform state prisons, mental hospitals, and police departments.

In such highly visible suits as *Wyatt v. Stickney* (1971), *Hobson v. Hansen* (1971), *Ruiz v. Estelle* (1980), and *United States v. City of Parma* (1980), litigants sought to reform mental health institutions, public school systems, correctional institutions, and public housing facilities. Brought in the courtrooms of federal judges such as Frank Johnson, Skelly Wright, William Wayne Justice, and Frank Battisti, these public lawsuits involved sweeping discovery; extensive reliance on expert witnesses; wide-ranging bargaining between the parties, frequently leading to negotiated settlements and consent decrees; retention of jurisdiction by the court to maximize enforceability of the decree; and continual judicial involvement, heightened by the appointment of monitors or masters to oversee compliance with the decree (Chayes 1976).

Not surprisingly, many suits for system-wide reform are brought on behalf of groups with little ability to influence the political process through conventional means (see Vose 1959; Cortner 1968; Kluger 1976). However, although the litigants were almost invariably disadvantaged, because they were commonly represented by attorneys experienced in large-scale litigation efforts, they often enjoyed the advantages of the organizational resources and expertise that accrue to "repeat players" in the courtroom (see Galanter 1974). Moreover, the suits, aimed at reforming public institutions, were facilitated by the growth of public interest law firms; the passage of fee-shifting statutes, especially the 1976 Civil Rights Attorneys' Fee Awards Act; the creation of new statutory rights; the relaxation of standing and class action rules; and expansive interpretations of existing constitutional rights (Horowitz 1983).

Largely brought as class action suits, this "public law litigation" (Chayes 1976), known also as "institutional reform litigation," "remedial decree litigation," "systemic litigation," and "structural reform litigation," is characterized by plaintiffs' seeking relief for the deprivation of constitutional or statutory rights by state or local governments. Because of restrictions imposed by the Eleventh Amendment, plaintiffs were limited to declaratory or injunctive relief rather than money damages (see *Will v. Michigan Department of State Police* 1989).

The litigants' success in obtaining far-reaching orders detailing the number of square feet in prison cells, enumerating the number of psychiatrists required in state hospitals, designating specified numbers of low-income housing units, and ordering equalization of public school teachers' salaries and the integration of public schools spawned a debate among scholars over the role of litigation in social policy decisionmaking and the ability of federal judges to make sound policy decisions. In large part the opponents of judicial involvement in social policymaking argued that social reform litigation resulted in judicial decisionmaking that ignored practical budgetary constraints and imposed unrealistic demands on government institutions.

Some judicial scholars (for example, Graglia 1976; Berger 1977) castigated the U.S. Supreme Court for inappropriately engaging in policymaking by expanding constitutional rights. Other critics, such as Donald Horowitz (1977; see also Glazer 1975, 1978; Rabkin 1989), argued that the real danger of judicial overreaching arises because federal court judges lack the capacity to intervene in the administration of public institutions and by exercising power over public bureaucracies, they engage in questionable and inappropriate uses of judicial authority. In this view, generalist judges in the federal courts do not possess the expertise to make effective decisions governing the operation of complex institutions when adjudicating systemic reform cases. Additionally, the critics' objections to structural reform litigation in the federal trial courts stem from their belief that it encourages judicial intrusion into state legislative and administrative policymaking, including, at times, decision-making about the public fisc.[2] Commenting on the trial court's conduct in prison reform litigation, Alexander Williams (1991, 565–66), a state's attorney in Maryland's Prince George's County, argued that the federal judiciary's tendency to intervene on behalf of the prison population inappropriately usurped political responsibility for deciding budgetary priorities. He charged that courts "often take no account of fiscal considerations" in ordering additional resources for prisons and urged judges to "recognize that when they require increased expenditures on prisons, another segment of society must suffer the loss of those funds."

Contending that his goal was to move beyond the normative debate over the legitimacy of judicial policymaking, Horowitz presented a series of case studies that, he asserted, provided empirical evidence of the court's inability to determine public policy. Defenders of the judiciary (see, for example, Fiss 1979; Eisenberg and Yeazell 1980), however, were not persuaded by these claims. They argued that the charges of judicial incapacity by Horowitz and others merely cloaked disapproval of judicial decisionmaking on behalf of politically powerless litigants against the state. Judges, they insisted, are capable of adjudicating systemic reform cases and, with the assistance of experts, are competent to issue remedial orders. With most judges urging settlement, they added, a substantial number of cases resulted in consent decrees in which the parties themselves negotiated and helped shape the terms of the final agreement. Moreover, the proponents of social reform litigation maintained, courts do not seek out institutional reform litigants; rather, the courts have no choice about the role they play in social policymaking because they are constitutionally and statutorily bound to adjudicate legal issues that are properly brought before them.

Entering the debate more recently, Charles Haar (1996, 133) assessed the effectiveness of the litigation against exclusionary zoning regulations in New

Jersey. In his view, the state supreme court's role in the landmark Mount Laurel litigation demonstrated that "the scathing charge that courts lack the competence, the ability, even the patience to implement social policies over time is not borne out by the New Jersey experience."

Lately another dimension has been added to the controversy over litigation and judicial capacity by scholars who question the wisdom of reformers' seeking social change through litigation, particularly at the Supreme Court level. From this perspective, the inquiry initially appears to be less concerned with the normative debate over whether the *courts* should engage in social policy decisionmaking; rather, the debate revolves around the question of whether *litigants* should bring social policy issues to the courts. However, even though the terms of this debate over the court's role in the political system differ from the terms in the debate precipitated by Horowitz, the questions remain substantially the same: *can* and *should* the courts adjudicate in social policy reform cases?

One side of the controversy, advanced by Gerald Rosenberg (1991), contended that because of institutional constraints placed on them, the federal courts are largely ineffectual in producing social policy reform—perhaps even counterproductive—and litigators turn to them at their peril. He offered two competing models of the Supreme Court's ability to effect social policy change, a "dynamic" and a "constraint" model, arguing that the latter more accurately depicts the Court's role in social policy reform and explains why it is unable to produce the results envisioned by hopeful litigators. Given the (three) constraints acting on it, he argued, the Court is incapable of producing social reform unless a number of conditions (four), such as the intervention of outside agencies or the existence of market forces, are present.

Rosenberg devoted most of his attention to assessing the impact of *Brown v. Board of Education* (1954) and *Roe v. Wade* (1973) on school desegregation and abortion reform, respectively. He argued that these opinions did not mobilize public support for the changes that occurred in these policy arenas and that the Court is given too much credit for producing those changes. Pointing to decisions in sex discrimination, apportionment, and criminal procedure cases as additional support for his position, he concluded that "U.S. courts can *almost never* be effective producers of significant social reform" (Rosenberg 1991, 338; emphasis in the original). In a rebuttal to critics who challenged his conclusions, Rosenberg (1998, 278) reiterated his view that social reform litigators simply do not understand that courts are "constrained from helping them."

This negative evaluation of judicial efficacy is vulnerable to a number of criticisms. First, although the title of Rosenberg's book suggests that his critique encompasses the entire federal court system, the analysis is limited to the Supreme Court and omits significant policymaking activity by the lower courts. Another problem with Rosenberg's position that litigation is ineffective in achieving "significant social reform" is that his perception of litigation is too narrow. Although he distinguishes between "litigation aimed at changing the way a single bureaucracy functions" and "litigation attempting to change the functioning of a whole set of bureaucracies or institutions nationwide" (Rosenberg 1991, 4), he overlooks the catalytic effect of litigation on public policy. Studies have shown that litigation that succeeds in changing the policy of a single bureaucracy often serves as a stimulus to further litigation that can result in changes in bureaucratic policy in multiple jurisdictions (see Mezey 1988; Schultz and Gottlieb 1998).

In his case study of pay equity reform litigation, Michael McCann (1994, 290) examined some of the premises of these "'gap' studies of judicial impact"; that is, studies such as Rosenberg's that "typically find a large gap between the promise and achievement of court victories." He concluded that the disparaging view of courts offered by such "neo-legal realists" does not adequately consider the multifaceted transformative effects of legal advocacy on the participants and on the larger population. He believes that such scholars, by limiting their scope to the narrow study of judicial impact and using a court-centered perspective that equated impact with compliance, lose sight of the possibility of indirect effects of judicial actions and "secondary tactical use of litigation by movement activists."[3]

Viewing the role of litigation and its outcomes more broadly in exploring the effects of pay equity litigation in the lower federal courts, McCann came to a different conclusion about legal mobilization and judicial efficacy. He discovered that the early legal victories of the pay equity movement helped mobilize support among a variety of potential adherents including feminists, lawyers, and, perhaps most important, union leaders and union members. The results of these legal tactics, he found, gave pay equity advocates the necessary "leverage" to wrest concessions from noncourt actors. Although this power gradually diminished as employers learned to fight back and the courts became less hospitable to the claims of the pay equity proponents, the litigation played an important role in furthering movement activity.

McCann's carefully nuanced representation of litigation, one substantially echoed by other public law scholars (see, for example, Canon 1998; Schultz and Gottlieb 1998; Zalman 1998), suggests that Rosenberg's constricted view of judicial capacity or "impotence" (Canon 1998), like Horowitz's, is too narrow.

In addition to McCann, others challenged some of Rosenberg's claims. For example, Joel Handler (1978), Stuart Scheingold (1981), and Susan Gluck Mezey (1988) had argued, before Rosenberg's critique, that although the litigation by itself may not always produce immediate and sweeping results, it can function as part of an effective political strategy for achieving social reform. Handler (1978) contended that evaluating the success of social reform litigation requires consideration of the increased publicity and consciousness-raising that results from the litigation as well as the greater access to the policymaking process by traditionally unrepresented groups.

Scheingold (1981) believes that litigation can be used effectively to exert influence against public institutions and that the attendant publicity arising out of such suits can sway public opinion, serving as a weapon in subsequent political battles to achieve the goals of the litigation. Additionally, the eventual success of the social security disability litigation, in gradual circuit-by-circuit victories, is also testimony to the power of litigation. The accumulated effect of judicial reversals of the Social Security Administration's termination of disability benefits and its accompanying media publicity soon brought the issue to congressional attention and led to passage of reform legislation that constrained the agency's efforts to terminate recipients' benefits (Mezey 1988).

These analyses suggest that those who view litigation more realistically, seeing it as part of a broader strategy for social reform, are more likely to perceive the courts in a positive light, especially when evaluating the results of adjudication in the lower federal courts.

Seeking to avoid the continual debate over the legitimacy and capacity of federal court decisionmaking and the discussion over the wisdom of litigators' turning to the federal courts, other scholars have adopted an approach to the study of social reform litigation that examines the litigation process in its entirety—from onset to outcome—paying particular attention to the changes in the legal and political environments occasioned by the litigation (see, for example, Yarbrough 1981; Anderson 1986; Stein 1987; Cooper 1988; Yackle 1989; Crouch and Marquart 1989; Kemerer 1991; Chilton 1991; Welsh 1995).

Centered almost entirely on public law litigation in the lower federal courts, these studies highlighted lawsuits brought by politically powerless groups, primarily inmates in state and county prisons. By scrutinizing the interactions between the court and the litigants, the studies assessed the role of the court in the litigation process as well as the impact of the litigation on the parties involved in it. Viewing litigation as a long-term process affected by factors outside as well as inside the courtroom, they evaluated the results of the litigants' efforts, including the extent to which they were able to effect changes in the conditions that precipitated the litigation.

These examinations of social reform litigation devoted little time to appraising the court's capability to adjudicate such cases, nor to assessing the legitimacy of its decisionmaking. Instead, by directing their inquiries at the means through which litigants attempted to create significant social change by persuading the courts to impose reform on public bureaucracies, they created a new level of understanding of the court's role in effecting social policy reform.

A Case Study of Child Welfare Litigation

Child welfare litigation shares some of the characteristics of the earlier attempts to achieve social reform through litigation. Like the litigation to reform prisons and jails, child welfare litigation involves a long-term campaign for systemic reform by a politically powerless group. Moreover, child welfare reform is primarily confined to the lower federal courts, with only an occasional opinion by the Supreme Court. There are some differences, however. Unlike prisoners, abused children are the quintessential pitiful plaintiffs, readily able to garner sympathy from the public, especially when confronting a highly unpopular state agency. Most politicians can support efforts to ameliorate the harsh conditions of the child welfare system without much concern for jeopardizing their political careers—in contrast to the financial and political costs of voting for improvements in prison conditions. Since a quest for systemic reform of a public bureaucracy is fought on political as well as legal grounds and ultimately requires political support for a successful outcome, it is likely that the more appealing image of the child welfare plaintiffs—in the eyes of both the public and political leaders—can positively affect the outcome of the litigation.

To add to the empirical literature on systemic reform litigation against public institutions and shed more light on how courts function in social policy reform cases, this study focuses on class action litigation against the Illinois Department of Children and Family Services (DCFS), an agency with an annual budget of $1.3 billion and a staff of approximately 4,500 that is responsible for the safety and well-being of thousands of abused and neglected children committed to the state's custody.

Following the examples of scholars whose books on institutional reform litigation traced the development of lawsuits within the geographic boundaries of one state (see, for example, Crouch and Marquart 1989, in Texas; Yackle 1989, in Alabama; Chilton 1991, in Georgia; Welsh 1995, in California; and Haar 1996, in New Jersey), this analysis focuses on the path-breaking remedial decree case known in Illinois simply as *B.H.*

B.H., a class action suit involving tens of thousands of plaintiffs and hundreds of millions of dollars, was brought on behalf of Illinois children forced to live outside their familial home because of abuse or neglect. The complaint against DCFS alleged deficiencies in a number of areas, including protective services, placement and supervision in substitute care, and health care.[4] Underlying the complaint was a vast array of political, social, and legal problems that affected the reform of the Illinois child welfare system.

While case studies may have limited generalizability, one of their undeniable strengths is, as Phillip Cooper (1988, 6) notes, that "they have the virtue of on-site long-term access to documentary and interview sources as well as a perspective on local politics that cannot be equaled by an outside investigator in the absence of an extended visit to the community." The modified case-study approach used in this analysis combines the advantages of the in-depth analysis afforded by a case study with the benefits of a broad-based perspective on national child welfare litigation activity. It presents a picture of child welfare litigation in one state, within the context of a national campaign for child welfare reform, thus minimizing the potential limitations of a single-case approach. To assess the role of the federal courts in social reform policymaking more generally, it evaluates the degree to which abused and neglected children are able to use the authority of the courts to reform the system that governs much of their lives.

A Model of Child Welfare Litigation

Because of the extensive reliance on litigation to achieve social reform, scholars have formulated models to analyze the role of the court in public policymaking and to illustrate the way in which the court and litigants interact with each other within the larger political and social environment. The model of the institutional reform litigation process used as the framework for analysis for this study is derived from a number of sources.

Cooper (1988, chap. 1) emphasizes the importance of viewing remedial decree litigation as a continuous process, involving interaction among plaintiffs, the defendants, the courts, and public officials. His model of social policy litigation is an excellent starting point for this analysis of child welfare litigation. Adopting an empirical approach to the litigation process, Cooper argues that the normative debates over "remedial decree litigation"—focusing on the court's capacity to fashion and implement a remedy and the legitimacy in doing so—largely miss the point. What is required, he insists, is an understanding of the way in which such cases actually proceed through the courts. He attempts to provide a "picture of the process by which remedial decree cases develop and are resolved" (Cooper 1988, 16). The picture Cooper draws is of a dynamic model divided into four stages: 1) the trigger phase (the political, economic, and legal circumstances in which the suit arises); 2) the liability phase (the determination of the nature and degree of the violation); 3) the remedy crafting phase (the process of negotiation and formal decisionmaking);

and 4) the post-decree phase (the implementation and evaluation of the decree). Characterizing these four phases as "analytic categories" rather than chronological stages in the litigation, Cooper applies his model to a diverse set of structural reform suits against schools, public housing sites, prisons, police departments, and mental health facilities. His case studies suggest that remedial decree litigation must be viewed as a dynamic rather than a static process and that interaction among the actors plays an important role, not only in the outcome of the lawsuit, but also in any policy changes that may result from it.

In his discussion preceding a collection of case studies of social policy litigation, Robert Wood (1990, 9–10) is broadly concerned with judicial enforcement of remedies following litigation against government agencies. Seeking to structure the comments of participants in a colloquium on public law litigation, he presents a model of the remedial law process in which the level of judicial involvement in reform of public institutions was based on three key factors: "the extent of the violations (broad or narrow); the capability of the target agency to institute and administer the remedy (high or low); and the disposition of the political culture (supportive or hostile)." Intended to include cases involving reform of schools, prisons, and public housing, an eight-celled table developed by Wood shows a range of judicial relief from receivership in cases with broad constitutional violations, an agency of low organizational capacity, and a hostile political culture to a consent decree in situations with narrow constitutional violations, an agency with a high organizational capacity, and a supportive political culture. Implicit in his analysis is the understanding that in the battle to reform a public institution, occasional clashes between the court and the agency involved will break out. Although Wood warns that the model is not predictive, he argues that it helps explain why remedial law cases are often unable to achieve the goals envisioned for them.

Wayne Welsh's (1995, 18–19) study of court-ordered reform of the California county jail system attempts to integrate several earlier models. He creates a model that included key variables in each analytic category marking the progress of the litigation. Adapting Cooper's model, he adds a fifth stage of the litigation process, the "impact" stage. Welsh includes such variables as: the political and legal environment in the trigger stage; the nature of the violations and the bases for legal claims in the liability stage; the nature of the remedies and the negotiations in the remedy stage; the duration of the lawsuit and judicial methods in the post-decree stage; and system-wide impacts and changes in institutional conditions in the impact stage.

These models provide useful frameworks for analysis, in large part because they are applicable to a variety of types of social policy reform litigation and help explain relationships among the factors shaping the litigation process. Yet, for different reasons, each falls short of presenting a total picture. Wood's model focuses primarily on the end product of the litigation rather than on the process; Cooper's does not fully encompass the influence of nonlitigants in the litigation process and tends to underemphasize the implementation stage of the litigation; and Welsh's understates the political implications of judicial intervention in public policymaking.

To counter these omissions, the model used in this study, illustrated in figure 1, blends the three approaches, viewing the federal trial court as a participant in a series of colloquies with individuals directly and indirectly involved in the litigation throughout the entire process. It divides the structural reform litigation process into five phases: stimulus, accountability, adjudication, implementation, and response, with each phase containing key analytic variables. A number of the variables in this litigation model are derived from these earlier models; when appropriate, they are supplemented by others that help reveal a more comprehensive picture of the dynamics of the child welfare litigation.

Like the other models, this model of the litigation process is intended to highlight the key variables in each stage without conforming to strict chronological boundaries. As figure 1 indicates, the stimulus phase, during which conditions for systemic reform litigation develop, contains the variables system-wide failure, prior litigation, media attention, and the legal players.

The variables in the accountability phase, during which the parameters of the state's responsibility to the plaintiffs are determined, are the parties to the litigation, the claims made, and the state's constitutional and statutory duties.

Included as variables in the adjudication phase, during which the plaintiffs' claims are evaluated and a strategy for reform develops, are the court's preliminary rulings, the conditions of settlement, the role of expert testimony, and the final decree.

The variables in the implementation phase, in which the agency's efforts to comply with the decree assume center stage, consist of the culture of the agency—specifically, factors affecting its compliance with the decree; developments in child welfare law and policy; judicial oversight of the implementation process; and the role of the monitor.

The response phase, somewhat akin to Welsh's impact stage, interjects an explicit political dimension into the litigation process and is the stage during which the policy effects of the litigation become most apparent. The most complex phase of the litigation, the response phase spans the entire litigation process. It chronicles reactions to the litigation from individuals and groups who appeared in the earlier phases of the litigation process: child welfare authorities, comprising DCFS and juvenile court officials; state political lead-

Figure 1. The Five Phases of Litigation

Stimulus	Accountability	Adjudication	Implementation	Response
System-wide failure	Parties to the litigation	Preliminary rulings	Agency culture	Political leaders
Previous litigation	Claims made	Conditions of settlement	Legal developments	Children's advocates
Media attention	Constitutional duty	Expert testimony	Judicial oversight	The media
Legal players	Statutory duty	The consent decree	The monitor	Child welfare authorities

ers; advocates from the child welfare community; and the media. These individuals represent a subset of the actors described by Canon and Johnson (1999) in their study of the impact of judicial policies: the implementing population and the secondary population. While DCFS officials represent the implementing population, it is more difficult to categorize the juvenile court authorities, who are not directly charged with implementing the decision but whose actions (or inactions) directly affect its implementation. Individuals in the last three groups generally fall within the secondary population.

Although not intended to conform strictly to chronological time frames, each of the first four phases of the *B.H.* litigation can be divided roughly into four unequal time periods marked by discrete events. The stimulus phase is the longest and provides the background for this study; it begins with the development of the child welfare system and DCFS's creation in 1964 and ends in 1988, when *B.H.* was filed. The accountability phase lasts approximately one year—between the time the complaint was filed and 1989, stopping short of the district court's ruling on the state's motion to dismiss the case; it includes, however, an analysis of the relevant caselaw going back several decades. The adjudication period begins with the court's ruling on the state's motion and concludes with the formulation and signing of the consent decree almost three years later. The implementation phase covers approximately five years, beginning in 1991 with the court's approval of the consent decree and ending with the monitor's resignation in 1996. And the response phase, the least time-bound, while encompassing and reflecting on events occurring throughout the preceding four phases, also extends the analysis to the present.

The purpose of this model is to illustrate the effect of systemic litigation on reform of the Illinois child welfare system, while highlighting the role of the federal court in the policymaking process. Dividing the litigation process into five phases, or categories, makes it possible to separate analytically events that may occur simultaneously; paradoxically, the separation produces a clearer picture of the litigation process as a whole, and the focused lens of the case study approach provides the kind of rich detail necessary to explicate each stage of the litigation.

In applying the institutional reform model to the *B.H.* litigation process, this study also places *B.H.* within the context of a wider-ranging national campaign to achieve child welfare reform, largely through litigation. To this end, it includes examples of other struggles to produce child welfare reform through litigation, in Illinois as well as beyond the boundaries of the state. And by examining child welfare litigation as a subset of institutional reform litigation, the study also seeks to explore the efficacy of litigation in producing social policy reform.

Why Illinois?

A recent examination of child welfare justifies its focus on Chicago by asking rhetorically: "Where else [should one study child welfare policy] but in that urban crucible of social service ferment that earlier produced the likes of Jane Addams and Hull House, Healy and Bronner, and the juvenile court?" (Whittaker in Schuerman, Rzepnicki, and Littell 1994, xi).

Extending the inquiry beyond the borders of the city to the state, one can ask, albeit more prosaically, where else should one study child welfare policy but in the state with the third highest substitute care population in the nation (after California and New York) and one of the five states in the nation that are responsible for almost half the total number of children in substitute care (along with California, New York, Texas, and Michigan) (Goerge, Wulczyn, and Harden 1996, 13)?[5]

Where else should one study child welfare but in the state with a higher proportionate number of children in substitute care than either New York or California? According to data compiled by Conna Craig and Derek Herbert (1997, 9) of the National Center for Policy Analysis, 17 out of every 1,000 Illinois children were living in substitute care in 1996, compared with 11 per 1,000 in California and 12 per 1,000 in New York. And although the District of Columbia led the nation with 22 children in substitute care per 1,000 children in the population in 1995, there were only about 2,500 children in the entire D.C. foster care system.

Finally, where else should one study child welfare but in the state that was second in the nation in the growth of the number of children in foster care between 1990 and 1995? According to the Children's Defense Fund *Yearbook* (1998, 122), the number of Illinois children in foster care increased 130.6 percent from the last day of 1990 to the last day of 1995; the average increase in the nation during this time was 19 percent. In comparison, California's foster care population rose only 21.6 percent during these five years, while there was a decrease in Washington, D.C., and New York. And although the largest jump in the nation was in Wyoming's substitute care population, which increased 363 percent, it had grown only from 484 children in 1990 to 2,241 children in 1995.[6]

Responsible for the lives of tens of thousands of emotionally and physically battered children within its jurisdiction, the state, not surprisingly, often fails to meet its obligations. In Illinois and elsewhere, "when economic constraints require tradeoffs in a state's budget, children's services are usually the first to go—after all, the children cannot fight back. Abused children must depend upon child activists to voice their concerns and call attention to their plight" (Colvin 1992, 531).

In part because of the magnitude and reach of its responsibilities, DCFS has been a perennial target of criticism by child welfare advocates. Inspired perhaps by examples of institutional reform litigation around the nation, in the 1970s, Illinois children's activists sought to enlist the power of the federal courts to reform a system that seemed destined for self-destruction absent intervention of some kind. Over time, Illinois became one of the most popular venues for federal class action child welfare litigation as children's advocates tried to change the conditions under which DCFS functioned, hoping to improve the lives of the children whose futures depended on it.

Characterized by its critics as "the worst system in the country" (*Chicago Tribune*, December 22, 1997), DCFS by 1995 had earned the dubious distinction of being the most frequently named defendant in federal child welfare lawsuits (National Center for Youth Law, 1995).[7] The lawsuits against DCFS included a case involving an interpretation of federal child welfare law that resulted in a Supreme Court decision that had implications for national child welfare policy; the other was *B.H.*, the suit for systemic reform that led to a child welfare consent decree that was the nation's most comprehensive in its scope and breadth.

Illinois is an excellent site for a case study of child welfare litigation for a number of other reasons as well. Because of *B.H.* and the persistence of its attorneys and other child welfare advocates, Illinois offers an opportunity to examine all five phases of the litigation process. The Illinois federal courts have largely been hospitable to child welfare advocates, and a substantial body of caselaw exists. Illinois has an active child welfare bar with measurable success in securing judgments and consent decrees that govern most of the state's child welfare programs. Illinois has a substantial number of child welfare advocacy groups—such as Voices for Illinois Children, Illinois Action for Children, the Citizens Committee on the Juvenile Court, and Cook County Court

Appointed Special Advocates—that oversee the operations of the child welfare system, including the juvenile courts and DCFS. Cook County, with responsibility for three-quarters of Illinois children in substitute care,[8] has the largest government-funded public guardian's office in the nation, and the public guardian, with a staff of 150 lawyers and 75 other professionals, plays a significant role in shaping Illinois child welfare policy.[9] Because DCFS is a frequent subject of media attention, there is a high level of public awareness about the department's work. Finally, as a government agency with "inexorable . . . problems pressing in on" it (Kingdon 1984, 17), DCFS occupies a prominent place on the state's public policy agenda.

Research Design and Method

This study is based on a variety of data sources. The core of the research consists of in-depth open-ended interviews with individuals involved in the Illinois child welfare system, focusing particularly on those engaged in the litigation process. Fifty-seven respondents, most of them key players in the Illinois child welfare system, were personally interviewed over a span of approximately two years.

The interview net was widely cast. In addition to the parties directly involved in *B.H.* and other child welfare litigation, interviews with public officials and members of DCFS and juvenile court watchdog groups were also conducted; when respondents suggested other individuals who should be interviewed, their names were added to the list as well. This modified "snowball" technique resulted in interviews with the most significant actors—public and private—in the Illinois child welfare litigation process and the child welfare system more generally.[10]

Most respondents were attorneys, including nine federal court judges; with one or two exceptions, the remainder held advanced social work or public policy degrees. The questions were open-ended and modified when necessary to accommodate the roles of the respondents in the child welfare system; respondents were encouraged to go beyond the bounds of the questions and provide any information they thought relevant. The interviews ranged from thirty-five minutes to two hours, with most lasting over an hour. No interviews were taped; extensive notes were taken during the interviews.

Because DCFS reform is a highly politicized subject in Illinois, respondents were assured they could designate any or all of their remarks as off the record and that their permission would be sought before they were quoted. For confidentiality, respondents' views are often presented in a summary fashion, and quotes are frequently not attributed to individuals by name or title. When confidentiality is not compromised, respondents are identified by their titles or positions in the litigation. Notwithstanding the sensitivity of the issues involved, the respondents were willing to share their information and opinions once they were told of the confidentiality ground rules.

The study is also based on responses to interviews conducted in 1993 and 1994 with seventeen attorneys and senior staffers at public interest law firms and public policy groups in Washington, D.C., San Francisco, Chicago, and New York as well as a senior official in the Department of Health and Human Services.[11] These respondents all worked to expand children's rights—primarily through federal court litigation, with most concentrating their efforts on class action lawsuits against state and local child welfare agencies. These subjects were also asked to respond to a semi-structured set of questions. Each interview lasted approximately one hour, and extensive notes were taken.[12]

Additionally, to learn more about the social and legal environment within which DCFS functioned, in 1995, personal interviews with nineteen juvenile court judges were conducted, and numerous hours were spent observing juvenile court proceedings in abuse and neglect cases in the Chicago metropolitan area, including Cook County and four of the five "collar" counties.[13] The information gathered in these three rounds of interviews was supplemented by analysis of legal documents, including court papers, published and unpublished opinions, parties' briefs and memoranda; government reports and publications; statistical data; and scholarly writings. Local and national newspaper databases, spanning almost two decades, were searched by computer; they frequently yielded information that was unavailable elsewhere. In addition to providing distinct pieces of information, these data sources combined to present as complete a picture of the Illinois child welfare system as an outside observer could achieve.

Outline of the Book

Chapter 2 presents the history of child welfare policy in the United States. It discusses the nationalization of the policymaking process beginning in 1974 with the passage of the Child Abuse Prevention and Treatment Act, followed shortly by the Adoption Assistance and Child Welfare Act of 1980. With these statutes, the national government became an important actor in child welfare policymaking, not least of which was the involvement by the federal courts as children's advocates attempted to correct the deficiencies of child welfare systems through litigation. The chapter shows that, as reform efforts continued, children's advocates began to debate conflicting theories of the government's role in maintaining the family unit and that one of the consequences of this debate was the passage of the Adoption and Safe Families Act of 1997.

Using the framework of the model shown above, chapters 3 to 7 explicate the five phases of the litigation process. Chapter 3 presents the stimuli giving rise to the *B.H.* suit, focusing on the manifest failure of the Illinois child welfare system to protect children in state custody. It traces the history of the state's involvement in child welfare and introduces the institutions and actors within the child welfare system, detailing the forces that generated the impetus for the *B.H.* lawsuit: an active child welfare community; widespread systemic failures; and negative media attention.

Chapter 4 discusses the basis of DCFS's legal liability in *B.H.*, analyzing the federal child welfare caselaw that was used to determine the parameters of the state's responsibility for protecting children in custody. It shows the federal courts' increasing willingness to hold states constitutionally liable for the safety and well-being of children in custody. It also reveals the consensus among the federal courts that the 1980 act conferred at least some enforceable rights on children in state care; the consensus broke down, however, as the courts could not agree on whether states could be liable if they failed to comply with specified provisions of the act.

Chapter 5 discusses the adjudication phase of *B.H.*, beginning with the court's ruling against DCFS's motion to dismiss the suit. It shows that the court did not attempt to impose relief on the parties and maintained a relatively low profile during the settlement process, largely guiding the parties toward a mutually acceptable settlement agreement. Additionally, it suggests that conditions within the agency and legal developments both within and outside Illinois also induced DCFS to enter into a consent decree and shows how the court indirectly influenced the outcome of the settlement by appointing expert witnesses to set the adjudicatory framework. The chapter concludes by presenting the *B.H.* decree, listing a wide array of agency duties and containing DCFS's pledge to take better care of the children in state custody.

Chapter 6 details the implementation phase, demonstrating the difficulty of implementing a consent decree arising from social reform litigation, largely because compliance with the decree requires changing the culture of the agency and the behavior of its personnel. The chapter shows that internal problems within the agency were enhanced by a mounting abuse and neglect caseload and state budgetary turmoil; moreover, it suggests that implementation was hindered by other litigants' demands for DCFS reform in the federal courts and, less directly, by developments in child welfare law outside Illinois. It discusses the judge's role in implementation, including his appointment of a monitor, and presents evidence that DCFS had not achieved full compliance with the decree within the time limit ordered and that the parties' attempt to modify the decree was, in part, a recognition of this failure.

Chapter 7, presenting the response phase of the litigation process, sorts out the multiplicity of reactions to the lawsuit, the most dramatic being the sharp rise in DCFS's budget. Not surprisingly, however, state legislators, resenting judicial interference with their constitutional duty to appropriate state funds and set agency standards, displayed antipathy to the court as well as DCFS. Also during this phase, some of the Illinois child welfare advocates, divided by conflicts over personalities and legal strategy, traded charges of failing to represent the children. The media's persistence in drawing attention to the agency's lack of compliance with the decree, including its failure to prevent the death of a three-year-old just released to the custody of his mother, focused all eyes on DCFS's deficiencies.

The chapter ends, however, by presenting evidence of recent reform within the Illinois child welfare system. To maintain some degree of suspense about the success of the litigation, I leave the details for the end of the book.

Chapter 8 summarizes the story of the *B.H.* litigation and returns to the questions raised earlier in this chapter, namely, whether federal courts can achieve social policy reform and, if so, whether they can accomplish it without transgressing the constitutional boundaries of their judicial role or acting beyond their administrative skills and knowledge. The answers to these questions, signaled throughout the telling of this story, also await fuller explication at the end of the book.

2 Child Welfare in the United States

COMBATING ABUSE AND NEGLECT

A survey of the past four decades of child welfare policymaking shows that since the 1960s the United States has experienced a continual rise in reported accounts of child abuse and neglect. Using statistics collected by the American Humane Association, Patricia Tjaden and Nancy Thoennes (1992, 807) calculated that reported incidents of child abuse and neglect increased by an astonishing 1,233 percent between 1963 and 1986.

A recent survey on child abuse and neglect reporting, conducted by the Child Welfare League of America, shows that the number of children reported as abused or neglected increased from 33 per 1,000 in the population in 1986 to 42 per 1,000 in the population in 1995, an increase of 27 percent (Petit and Curtis 1997, 3). And in 1996, of the 3.1 million abuse and neglect reports, almost one million (969,000) were confirmed (Children's Defense Fund 1998, 64).

The National Child Abuse and Neglect Data System (NCANDS), compiled by the National Center on Child Abuse and Neglect (NCCAN), an agency within the Department of Health and Human Services (HHS), serves as one of the leading sources of information on abused and neglected children known to state child protective services agencies. In 1997, NCCAN issued a report entitled *Child Maltreatment 1995*, based on statistics compiled from state child protective services (CPS) in forty-nine states. The report showed that of the more than one million victims of abuse or neglect, more than half (52.3 percent) suffered from neglect and a quarter (24.5 percent) from physical abuse, with sexual and emotional abuse and medical neglect together accounting for most of the rest.[1] An "other" category of 14.4 percent included additional types of maltreatment such as abandonment or congenital drug addiction, acts that would almost certainly constitute neglect in many states. According to these data, about one quarter of the victims were three years old or younger; more than half were under eight (U.S. Department of Health and Human Services 1997a, 2–7, 2–8). With CPS agencies in forty-five states reporting, the NCANDS data show 996 deaths resulting from abuse or neglect, most occurring among children three or under. On the basis of these calculations, it was estimated that there were approximately 100 fatalities per 100,000 victims of maltreatment (U.S. Department of Health and Human Services 1997a, 2–10).

Another source of information about child abuse and neglect is the National Incidence Study (NIS), the latest of which is the third, the NIS-3. Conducted by the NCCAN, as mandated by Congress, the NIS is based on a nationally representative sample of more than 5,600 professionals in 842 agencies serving 42 counties. The data in the National Incidence Study are more comprehensive than the NCANDS because, in addition to statistics on children known to CPS agencies, the NIS data also contain information on abused and neglected children known by community professionals that was not reported to CPS or was screened out by CPS agencies without investigation. Authors of the NIS-3 report claim this study is the "single most comprehensive source of information about the current incidence of child abuse and neglect in the United States" (Sedlak and Broadhurst 1996, v).

Using the narrower "harm" standard—as opposed to a more inclusive "endangerment" standard—the NIS-3 shows that, compared with the NIS-2 report published in 1988 (which was based on data collected in 1986 and 1987), there were significant increases in the estimates of children sexually abused (an 83 percent rise); physically neglected (a 102 percent increase); emotionally neglected (a 333 percent increase); and physically abused (a 42 percent rise). Perhaps most startling was the 299 percent increase in the estimated number of seriously injured children between 1986 and 1993 (Sedlak and Broadhurst 1996, 4).

The rise in the incidence of child abuse and neglect has led to a concomitant increase in the number of children entering the nation's child welfare system. Entrusted with the task of protecting children, child welfare agencies are commanded to combat the pervasive effects of poverty, homelessness, and inadequate health care. More recently, pressures on child welfare agencies have intensified as a result of drug and alcohol abuse and the prevalence of HIV and AIDS (English and Freundlich 1997).

Child welfare experts disagree about the relationship between child maltreatment and the social and economic characteristics of the families in which it occurs. A 1980 nationwide study showed that neglect tended to be more closely linked with socioeconomic status, while physical abuse was more closely associated with variables related to family structure, such as marital status (Fryer 1993, chap. 4).[2] More specifically, Bruce Boyer (1996, 1646) cites studies showing the relationship between poverty and the particular types of harm associated with neglect. Other studies show that the single most important factor associated with child abuse and neglect is poverty, with most documenting higher rates of child maltreatment in poor families (see Vondra 1993; Dorne 1997; Sedlak and Broadhurst 1996). Summarizing earlier work on child abuse, Garbarino and Kostelny (1993, 285) report that in contrast to European nations, "Social class/low income is a very powerful predictor of the amount of child abuse and neglect in neighborhoods within American cities."

Scholars have also examined the relationship between racial and ethnic status and child maltreatment. The vast majority of the child abuse and neglect cases in Cook County, for example, involved African American and Hispanic children, far more than their proportion of the population (Murphy 1997, 95). Statewide data in Illinois confirm that more minority children are reported as abused and neglected. In fiscal 1992, although only about 19 percent of the children in Illinois were African American, 42 percent of all children reported as abused or neglected were African American (Illinois Department of Children and Family Services 1992, 3; see also Illinois Department of Children and Family Services 1998a, table 3).

Scholars suggest that the higher number of reports and the higher incidence of child maltreatment in lower socioeconomic, minority, and single parent families are largely explained by their greater visibility to social welfare agencies and less privacy in their living conditions so that episodes of abuse in such families are more likely to be seen and reported. And some argue that because of societal biases, child protection agencies "target hundreds of thousands of mothers who are disproportionately poor and of color" (Appell 1997, 578).

Rejecting this analysis, Richard Wexler (1995b, chap. 3) debunks the myth of "classlessness" as a fabrication that perpetuates the notion that child abuse occurs equally among all classes. According to him, "the gap in the rate of abuse and neglect between rich and poor is simply too great to be explained away as an artifice of the reporting system" (Wexler 1995b, 69). Similarly, Boyer (1996, 1645) cites studies showing a "correlation between child maltreatment and poverty for all forms of neglect and abuse, including for serious categories of harm where the greater susceptibility of poor people to public scrutiny cannot easily explain disparities in the income of reported families."

Whether the statistical findings reflect biases in the system or are accurate indications of higher levels of child maltreatment, it is undisputed that children of the poor, children from single-parent families, and children of color are most commonly found in the foster care ranks (English and Freundlich 1997, 111; Appell 1997, 578; Murphy 1997, 157–58; Barth 1998, 223). In Illinois, for example, according to Cook County Public Guardian Patrick Murphy (1997, 155), about 88 percent of Cook County children in state custody are African American, while only about a third of the county's residents are African American.

In protecting abused and neglected children from the horrors that confront them, the child welfare system commonly removes them from their homes and places them in substitute care—typically, a foster home.[3] For a variety of reasons, foster care has become the preferred approach for child welfare agencies, although studies often show that children are removed from their homes too readily and not returned quickly enough (see Lindsey 1994, chap. 3).

Data compiled by the American Public Welfare Association (Tatara 1997, 1–2) indicate that nationwide 483,000 children were in substitute care in 1995. On the basis of these data, the association's report estimated that on an average day in 1996, as many as 502,000 children were in foster care. Viewed retrospectively, the substitute care population had increased by 91.6 percent during the fourteen years between 1982 and 1996.

"Foster care is intended to provide a temporary, safe haven for children whose parents are unable to care for them" (Mushlin 1984, 188). By removing children from their homes and placing them in a foster care setting, the state assumes a great deal of responsibility for their welfare. However, as many have noted, foster care frequently fails to live up to its promise. In speaking of his own state, a Massachusetts federal court judge deplored the fact that "children [in the foster care system] have suffered unspeakable injuries to body and spirit . . . because of circumstances beyond the reach of the most benign and effective protection any government has ever afforded. But, as well, children have suffered because state officials charged with protecting them have fallen short of what they undertook to do" (*Lynch v. King* 1982, 327).

Indeed, Wexler (1995b, 167) argues that "for thousands of abused and neglected children . . . foster care is not the happy ending, it is the tragic beginning. It is not where the nightmare ends. It is where it starts." However, Richard Barth (1998, 223–24), presenting an opposing view, reports that children placed in foster families "function better than those similarly situated children who remain at home; that is, foster care per se is not responsible for the later problems of foster children and, generally, does provide some benefit." He acknowledges, however, the likely damage to children subjected to multiple short-term foster placements. Occupying a middle—and possibly more realistic—ground, child welfare expert Douglas Besharov (1984, 196) notes that "more often than we would like to admit, children are abused or neglected while in foster homes, shelters, or residential institutions" (see also Kearse 1996).

Perhaps the most serious flaw in the foster care system is that, for too many children, it represents a long-term sentence rather than a short-term respite. As early as the 1950s, studies identified the problem of "foster care drift," that is, children becoming lost in the foster care system—transferred from one foster care setting to another, never attaining permanency either with their own families or in adoptive homes. An American Bar Association

(1993, 50) report entitled *America's Children at Risk* documented the dimensions of foster care drift: in 1988, almost one-half (48 percent) of children in foster care were shifted around to as many as five foster homes.

Child Welfare Policy

Children entering the child welfare system are a "tragic class of people—children of alcohol and drug addicts, children victimized by severe domestic violence, children who are abused in unimaginable ways, children who are malnourished, sick and neglected" (*Artist M. v. Johnson* 1990, 996). The system purportedly aims at providing a safe environment for the nation's abused and neglected children; yet at the same time it can, and often does, inflict grievous harm on those it is charged with protecting. According to Marcia Robinson Lowry (1988, 266), executive director of the New York–based Children's Rights, Inc., and one of the nation's leading child welfare litigators, "Child welfare is a system designed to do good. It is a public response to thousands of private crises and tragedies."[4] The response, however, is often insufficient or, at the least, untimely. In a profile of the problems and challenges facing the child welfare system, Schuerman (1997, 5) explained:

> Child welfare social workers labor under the burden of caseloads that are too
> large, impossible demands on their time, inadequate training and supervi-
> sion, and inadequate resources of many kinds. In recent years, there has been
> an explosion in the number of allegations reported to child protective
> services. Judges and lawyers are required to process too many cases in too
> little time and have little opportunity for considered deliberation of decisions
> with profound consequences.

Perhaps because of the immensity of its tasks, the deficiencies of the child welfare system are staggering. And even with federal constitutional and statutory requirements ostensibly maintaining some measure of consistency in the system, the quality of care offered to children across the nation varies greatly (see Robison 1990). The nation's "discovery" of child abuse and its transformation into a major societal issue became possible once the blinders of governmental laissez-faire were removed and the curtain of familial privacy was lifted. The interest in child abuse was sparked by a 1962 article entitled "The Battered-Child Syndrome," in the *Journal of the American Medical Association* (Kempe and others 1962). This article was a culmination of research in pediatric radiology during the 1940s and 1950s that showed that X-rays could detect evidence of abuse in situations in which parents falsely represented their children's injuries as accidents. Child abuse was placed on the public policy agenda when these findings became linked to clinical observations by pediatricians and general practitioners (Dorne 1997, chap. 3).

Citing the far-reaching dimensions of the issue, the Kempe article urged medical professionals to take a more active role in combating child abuse, a problem that had largely remained invisible to that point. Shortly thereafter, a national conference on child abuse convened by the U.S. Children's Bureau (an agency created by Congress in 1912) led to a model child maltreatment–reporting statute with provisions for reporting suspected abuse and for civil and criminal immunity from liability for the reporter (Dorne 1997, chap. 4). Other groups, such as the American Humane Association and the American Medical Association, also proposed model legislation in the early 1960s. By 1964 all states had enacted laws specifying that various types of professionals were required to report the suspected incidence of abuse or neglect under threat of criminal penalties or civil damages (Gordon 1994; Myers 1992).

In a clear example of policy flowing from the bottom up, Congress then entered into the child welfare policymaking arena by enacting its own child maltreatment legislation in 1974, the Child Abuse Prevention and Treatment Act (CAPTA)—Public Law 93-247—sponsored by Senator Walter Mondale (D-Minn.) and Representative Patricia Schroeder (D-Col.). Congress's earlier attempt to legislate child welfare was a bill to mandate reporting of suspected abuse cases in the District of Columbia, enacted in 1966 after an unsuccessful introduction in 1964. In 1969 Representative Mario Biaggi (D-N.Y.) introduced reporting legislation as an amendment to the Social Security Act. Although it failed, it had piqued the federal government's interest in child abuse reporting legislation (Dorne 1997, chap. 4).

CAPTA was largely aimed at exhorting states, with the lure of federal financial assistance, to create "demonstration programs for the prevention, identification, and treatment of child abuse and neglect." Section 5102 of the act broadly defined child abuse and neglect as "the physical or mental injury, sexual abuse, negligent treatment, or maltreatment of any child under the age of eighteen by a person who is responsible for the child's welfare under circumstances which indicate the child's health or welfare is harmed or threatened thereby . . ." (Nelson 1984, 14).

The act also established the National Center on Child Abuse and Neglect within HHS to serve as a clearinghouse for research and information on child protection activities. To assist states in meeting their responsibilities, it authorized grants for research, demonstration projects, and data collection on child maltreatment (Dorne 1997, chap. 4).

The federal government's involvement in child abuse policy was expanded in 1980 with the enactment of the Adoption Assistance and Child Welfare Act, commonly known as Public Law (P.L.) 96-272.[5] As the Second Circuit later noted, Congress enacted P.L. 96-272 "to provide states with financial incentives to encourage a more active and systematic monitoring of children in the foster care system" (*Vermont Department of Social and Rehabilitation Services v. United States Department of Health and Human Services* 1986, 59).

Reflecting the prevailing view of child welfare experts, the phrase summarizing the spirit of P.L. 96-272 was "permanency planning."[6] The law aimed at "lessen[ing] the emphasis on foster care placement and encourag[ing] greater efforts to find permanent homes . . . either by making it possible to return [children] to their families or by placing them in adoptive homes." With federal dollars as an incentive, the act's supporters wanted to diminish the state's reliance on foster care (Allen, Golubock, and Olson 1983; Pine 1986; Stein and Comstock 1987). In the words of Senator Alan Cranston (D-Cal.), P.L. 96-272 was intended to counteract the pattern of "far too many children and families . . . [being] broken apart when they could have been preserved with a little effort." In his view, P.L. 96-272 emphasized the principle that "foster care ought to be a last resort rather than the first" (*Congressional Record*, June 13, 1980, S6942).[7]

The bill was signed into law on June 17, 1980, at a time when it was reported that nearly 100,000 children had been in foster homes for more than six years (*Congressional Quarterly Weekly*, June 21, 1980, 1731). Senator Daniel Patrick Moynihan (D-N.Y.) applauded the passage of P.L. 96-272, calling it the "first significant piece of social welfare legislation to pass the Congress since the inauguration of President Carter." He went on to say, "This is reform legislation of the best and most honorable kind" (*Congressional Record*, June 13, 1980, S14765).

The goal of P.L. 96-272 was to redirect the energies of the nation's child welfare system. Based on the principle that children are benefited most by permanency in their lives, the law sought to reduce reliance on long-term foster care, thus diminishing, if not eliminating, foster care drift, and to provide safe placements for children, with a preference for reunification with the biological family, followed by adoption as the second choice (Herring 1995, 187). Representative Dan Rostenkowski (D-Ill.) expressed the hope that "with the passage of H.R. 3434 [P.L. 96-272], instead of being faced with a rootless insecurity, these children can now be assured a more stable and more permanent family setting" (*Congressional Record*, August 2, 1979, H7097).

A cooperative federal-state child welfare and assistance program, P.L. 96-272 contains a set of interrelated substantive requirements and financial inducements that provide a national framework for foster care and adoption policy. It attempts to formalize the child welfare process by spelling out the obligations and rights of the various actors in the system: government, parents, and children (Testa 1985, 25). As in other Social Security Act programs, participation is voluntary, yet if a state opts to participate, it must comply with the requirements of the act.

Similar to other grant-in-aid programs, Congress empowered HHS to cut off federal funding to states that refused to comply with the statutory provisions and administrative regulations. But, as with most federal-state cooperative funding arrangements, cutting funds "is an extremely drastic remedy [that] will likely help no one and at the same time will destroy the program . . . [and therefore] is rarely, if ever, invoked" (Key 1996, 292). Throughout the next decade, the courts would struggle to determine whether Congress intended to limit the remedy for a state's failure to comply with the statute to the termination of federal funds to the state.

P.L. 96-272 amended the existing Child Welfare Services Program, Title IV-B of the Social Security Act, authorizing federal funds for a range of child welfare services—including foster care prevention and family reunification services. In an effort to restrict spending on foster care and curtail its use, the act requires that money made available to states under the IV-B program be directed to family support services rather than to foster care.

To receive their allotment of federal dollars, states must adopt a plan meeting certain requirements. Incentive funds are also available if the state satisfies additional requirements such as instituting a case plan and review system—as specified in Title IV-E—for children in state supervised foster care; inventorying children in the child welfare system; creating statewide information systems; and establishing preventive and reunification services programs. Unlike its companion, Title IV-E, Title IV-B applies to *all* children in state-supervised foster care, not merely to children receiving public welfare benefits.

The need for reform was self-evident; many of the requirements, the case plan, for example, had existed under previous federal law but were seldom enforced. During hearings preceding passage of P.L. 96-272, Congress learned that states rarely conducted reviews of children in the foster care system, and in some states it was reported that officials were even unaware of the number of children in the system (Stein 1991).

P.L. 96-272 created a new title, IV-E—the Foster Care and Adoption Assistance Program—to replace the old Title IV-A of the Social Security Act of 1935 in which the federal government provided unlimited matching funds to states for foster care expenses. With no funding for programs aimed at keeping families together, and no constraints on the length of time children remained in the foster care system, Title IV-A had created a disincentive for states to reduce long-term foster care. In contrast, the new IV-E, in an effort to lessen foster care drift, created a presumption in favor of keeping families together or, failing that, of preparing children for adoption.

Title IV-E is an open-ended entitlement that reimburses states on a percentage basis (up to 75 percent) for foster care maintenance and administrative expenses for children eligible for public welfare benefits before the foster care placement. It also contains an entitlement program to encourage the adoption of hard-to-place children, that is, children with special needs (Bussiere 1985).

As a condition of receiving federal IV-E funds, states are required to have HHS-approved plans; the act specified that states were required to have the approved plans in place by October 1, 1983. To gain approval from HHS, the state plans must comply with section 671(a) of the act, which provides, among other things, that the plans specify provisions for individual case plans and periodic reviews for children in foster care, contain procedures for reporting child abuse and neglect to appropriate authorities, and establish and apply standards for foster care settings. Section 671(a)(15) requires each state plan to provide "that in each case, reasonable efforts will be made (A) prior to the placement of a child in foster care, to prevent or eliminate the need for removal of the child from his [or her] home, and (B) to make it possible for the child to return to his [or her] home."[8] Section 671(b) authorizes the secretary of HHS to cut off funds to a state that has substantially failed to comply with its approved plan.

Congress intended Titles IV-E and IV-B to be mutually reinforcing: fulfilling the reasonable efforts requirement for the individual child depends on the existence of statewide preventive service programs. IV-E contained an explicit quid pro quo to the states: absent a showing of "reasonable efforts" made before a particular child is placed in foster care, a state does not receive federal matching funds for the child's stay in care.[9]

Neither the statute nor its subsequent regulations defined reasonable efforts or provided a means for assessing whether the agency's efforts to preserve the family were reasonable. HHS did, however, issue a regulation indicating examples of reasonable efforts states might include in their state plans. Among the efforts considered reasonable by HHS were: day care, counseling, emergency shelters, drug and alcohol counseling, and homemaker services. In the absence of more explicit direction, it was largely left to state legislatures or judges to determine the contours of the standard of reasonableness. Although not all have legislatively defined reasonableness, currently thirty states, including Illinois, have incorporated the federal "reasonable efforts" requirement into their state juvenile court acts (Bufkin 1996/1997, 361–62).

Elaborating on the case plan and review requirements in Title IV-B, Title

IV-E requires the state plan to provide for the development of a case plan and review system for each child receiving foster care maintenance payments. Caseworkers must file written case plans, indicating the type and appropriateness of the placement and services, for each child in federally reimbursed foster care. Furthermore, there must be a review procedure that ensures that each child has a "case plan designed to achieve placement in the least restrictive (most family-like) and most appropriate setting available and in close proximity to the parents' home, consistent with the best interest and special needs of the child." States are required to assess the child's status at least once every six months (either by a court or by an administrative review body) and hold a "dispositional hearing" within eighteen months of the child's removal from home to decide on the child's permanent placement—return home or termination of parental rights and adoption, or, at times, even long-term foster care, the last considered the least desirable.

Seeking to avoid the prospect of long-term foster care, the law emphasized three principles: reasonable efforts, permanency, and placement in the least restrictive environment (Schuerman 1997). Although return home was not the exclusive method of achieving permanency for the child, because of the legislation the family assumed a preeminent status that it had not had before 1980 (see Murphy 1997). For while the law envisioned the possibility of adoption or guardianship or even long-term foster care, it clearly manifested a preference for reunifying the family. Consequently, for most children, the aim of P.L. 96-272 became embodied in the goal of "family preservation," a policy based on two fundamental assumptions: that children are better off when raised by their biological parents and that, with appropriate services and resources, parents guilty of abuse or neglect will be able to care for their children (Lowe 1996).

Politically, family preservation was popular on both ends of the ideological spectrum. According to Richard Gelles (1996, chap. 5), an expert on child welfare and family violence, conservatives found it attractive because it focused on the family and restricted governmental interference with it; liberals applauded it because it sought to support families by providing government services. And as Goerge (1990, 424) notes, parental rights and societal norms favor reunification and show concern about the potential psychological damage to children in foster care; moreover, states favor reunification because it is less expensive than foster care and lessens the need for adoptions that are difficult to accomplish.

Despite the act's rhetorical commitment to containing the growth of foster care and the emphasis on sustaining the family, federal funding for Titles IV-B and IV-E has varied greatly, often straying from the articulated purposes of the law. Annual congressional appropriations for IV-B services were by no means secure, the program having to compete with a vast array of domestic activities, including other child welfare programs. By fiscal 1991, IV-B funding was just $273 million, compared with Title IV-E's expenditures for foster care (excluding adoption assistance) of almost $1.8 billion, with adoption assistance expenses almost $190 million (*Congressional Quarterly Weekly*, March 30, 1991, 798–99).

Not surprisingly, with fewer federal dollars available for preventive and reunification services, states committed fewer resources to them. For example, in 1989, more than eight times as much money was spent on foster care as on keeping children out of foster care (Wexler 1995b, 207).[10] Thus, notwithstanding the articulated goals of P.L. 96-272, the realities of federal funding under P.L. 96-272 often encouraged state agencies to direct their limited funds to the foster care system instead of spending money on family preservation efforts (Costin, Karger and Stoesz 1996, 154).

By the late 1980s the number of children in foster care, which had somewhat declined during the decade, had risen to new heights, renewing fears about systemic overload. Too often, in many jurisdictions, the courts and agencies were becoming "overwhelmed by the enormity of their respective tasks" (Boyer 1995, 377).

A number of children's advocates became increasingly critical of the contradictory policy of providing unlimited funds for foster care and only limited funding for preventive and reunification services. A 1989 report by the House Select Committee on Children, Youth, and Families criticized the child welfare system, with committee chair George Miller (D-Cal.) characterizing its problems: "Skyrocketing reports of child abuse, new conditions resulting from crack cocaine and alcohol abuse, and homelessness among families with children are driving an increasing number of children into costly out-of-home placements with inadequate services and accountability" (*Washington Post*, December 12, 1989).

The success of P.L. 96-272 depends, in part, on the ability of social welfare agencies and juvenile courts, both of which serve as "institutional substitute parent[s]" (Boyer 1995, 379), to work in tandem to guarantee a child's safety as well as to provide permanency.[11] To do so, agency workers and juvenile court judges must make informed, reasoned decisions about each child's future and ensure that the family is furnished necessary services so that the child can be safely returned home. Overloaded beyond capacity, the system thus fails because the "institutional parents," the courts and the agencies, frequently lack sufficient time and resources to designate and achieve an appropriate goal for each child.

The mounting number of child abuse and neglect reports and increases in rates of poverty, substance abuse, and homelessness contributed to the steadily growing sense that the child welfare system was unable to cope with the demands on it. On the basis of these factors, a consensus seemed to develop that, despite its stated goals, P.L. 96-272 was failing to achieve either permanency or family preservation (Sheldon 1997).

In the early 1990s reports published by HHS, the Children's Defense Fund, the Child Welfare League of America, the American Public Welfare Association, and the North American Council on Adoptable Children broadly attacked the nation's child welfare system (Kelly 1994). Charles Gershenson, former chief of research and evaluation at the Children's Bureau, characterized the system as "a basket case," adding, "I've been in the field for 40 years, and I've never seen it in worse shape than it is now" (*Washington Post*, March 31, 1991).

Similarly, Gregory Coler, chair of the American Public Welfare Association's project on child welfare and family preservation and former head of Florida's welfare agency under Republican governor Bob Martinez, depicted it as "underresourced and outgunned." David Liederman, executive director of the Child Welfare League of America, also called for added resources, saying that "we need billions, not millions"; and Eileen Pasztor of the Child Welfare League, declared: "We are serving 1990s children in an 1860s model" (*Congressional Quarterly Weekly*, March 30, 1991, 796–801).

In 1990 Congress had begun to react to concerns about the child welfare system by considering proposals to place greater emphasis on preventive efforts and family preservation services. Caught in the turmoil of presidential politics revolving around disputes over urban riots and tax surcharges on millionaires, several bills cleared Congress to be vetoed by President George Bush for reasons unrelated to child welfare. Then, in March 1993, President Bill Clinton announced proposals to strengthen family services programs. Ultimately the Family Preservation and Support Act, part of the Omnibus Budget Reconciliation Act of 1993, was approved by Congress on August 6 and signed by Clinton on August 10 (*Congressional Quarterly Weekly*, September 18, 1993, 2482).

The law amended Title IV-B by adding a new subpart 2, entitled Family Preservation and Support Services. The legislation was intended to divert children from foster care by offering preventive community-based services to avoid children's entry into the child welfare system and providing resources to at-risk families to help alleviate crisis situations. Enacted partly to infuse the child welfare system with new federal dollars, the law created a capped entitlement of $930 million over a five-year period to fund family preservation services to families with children at risk or in crisis; states were required to contribute a 25 percent match to the federal funds (*Congressional Quarterly Weekly*, September 4, 1993, 2321). According to figures released by the Ad ministration for Children and Families, a division within HHS, yearly funding for Family Preservation and Support Services programs was $240 million in FY 1997 and $255 million in FY 1998. As a means of comparison, foster care funding was $3.8 billion in FY 1997 and $3.2 billion in FY 1998; the foster care amounts did not include funds for adoption assistance and independent living (U.S. Department of Health and Human Services, 1997b, 2).

Despite the statutory reforms and the additional funding, the numbers of children in foster care continued to grow, and so did the reports of the devastating physical and emotional harms to which many were subjected. Concomitantly, attacks on Title IV-E's "reasonable efforts" mandate and its underlying ideology, family preservation, also escalated. The attacks reflected a growing disenchantment with family preservation with critics demanding reassessment of the wisdom of the policy, claiming it favored the interests of the family over the interests of the child.

One source of opposition to the family preservation principle came from Richard Gelles, the director of the Family Violence Research Program of the University of Rhode Island. Although once committed to family preservation, Gelles claims that mandating that child welfare authorities use reasonable efforts to preserve families leads to a greater number of children being hurt by their parents. He believes that there has been an "overmarketing of family preservation" and that some families are simply incapable of being rehabilitated (Gelles 1996, 142). Consequently, in his view, too many children are injured, or even killed, in situations where preserving the family is not a realistic possibility (Lowe 1996, 20–21). In his book chronicling the short life of fifteen-month-old David Edwards, who was killed by his mother, Gelles (1996, 9) argues that the baby's death "can be traced to the doctrine that requires social service agencies . . . to make 'reasonable efforts' to keep or reunite abused and neglected children with their biological parents."

Similarly, Patrick Murphy, the Cook County public guardian, is not convinced about the wisdom of a family preservation policy. He noted that after P.L. 96-272 was enacted, "a lot more kids [were] staying home" because of family preservation, and he does not believe their lives were improved (Murphy 1997, chap. 3). In his view, the principle of family preservation is ill-conceived because the child welfare system is unable to distinguish between parents whose children should be removed and those who should be given another opportunity to care for their children safely.

Individuals disparagingly called "child savers" by the adherents of family preservation led the charge against family preservation policy. Wexler (1995b, 28), however, depicts "child savers" as committed to "destroying children in order to save them." In his view, the child savers refuse to give families any benefit of the doubt in cases of suspected abuse and neglect, generally believing that removing children is preferable to working with the family (see also Golden 1997).

In the debate over reasonable efforts and family preservation, some (see Golden 1997, chap. 2; Wexler 1995b, chap. 8) charge that attempts by child welfare agencies to keep families intact whenever possible are more rhetorical than real. They argue that true family preservation programs absorb more financial and personnel resources than agencies are able or willing to commit (Shotton 1990).

Susan Notkin of the Edna McConnell Clark Foundation notes that an authentic family preservation program "offers a variety of services, operates with very light caseloads, lasts four to six weeks and puts the caseworker in the family's home frequently, often daily, and on call 24 hours a day" (*New York Times*, July 30, 1995). In their analysis of family preservation policies, Schuerman and Littell (1995, 15–16) conclude that the problem with most existing programs can be traced in part to the fact that "the federal government has not provided adequate funds to the states to meet the mandate and most states have failed to implement family preservation programs on a wide scale or with adequate resources." The irony is, however, according to Golden (1997, 50) that family preservation efforts cost less than foster care settings or residential treatment centers.

The model for the family preservation program, known as Homebuilders, was developed by two Tacoma, Washington, psychologists in 1974.[12] Homebuilders reflected the belief that intensive, short-term, home-based attention prevents placement in substitute care and saves the state money as well by containing costs (Gelles 1996, 123).[13] After its inception, a number of states, including Illinois, adopted versions of the Homebuilders program during the 1980s (Tucker and Blatt 1994).[14] Early reports on the effectiveness of such family preservation programs, measured by the percentage of families remaining intact after receiving services, were very positive, but more recently a debate has arisen over whether such programs actually prevent out-of-home placement.

Presenting the results of their comprehensive study of the Illinois Family First program, Schuerman, Rzepnicki, and Littell (1994, chap. 2) cited concerns over the methodology used in earlier studies that reported on the success of programs using the intensive home-based services; they specifically commented on the questionable use of experimental and control groups in the research. Moreover, they declared that the reports on whether such programs prevented further occurrences of child maltreatment were quite mixed. Using an experimental design in which they compared Illinois families receiving Family First services with families receiving regular services from the Department of Children and Family Services (DCFS), they found that "overall the Family First program had no effect on the type or duration of placements" and that it "had no substantial effect on subsequent maltreatment of children" (Schuerman, Rzepnicki, and Littell 1994, 187). Their data showed that rather than saving money, the Family First program may have cost the state slightly more in foster care expenses.

Although the controversy will likely continue over whether the delivery of family preservations services or programs through the Homebuilders model is the best approach to fulfilling the goals of the child welfare system, there is widespread agreement that the task of deciding whether to leave children at home or remove them from their families is "much more complicated [than rocket science]" (Barth 1998, 222). Arguing for a carefully nuanced policy that balances the opposing concerns of removal versus preservation, child welfare advocate (and cocounsel in *B.H.*) Benjamin Wolf of the American Civil Liberties Union stressed, "You have to weigh the risks in *both* instances" (*Chicago Tribune*, November 16, 1997; emphasis added). Indeed, Wolf and Boyer, the latter of Northwestern University's Children and Family Justice Center, reject the simplistic portrayal of the family preservation issue as one of child versus parent. Interviewed for an article in a *Chicago Tribune* (November 16, 1997) series on the child welfare system, Boyer stated that he "see[s] a commonality of interests [between parent and child]. There may be some divergence of interests when parents fall down on the job, but when you're trying to figure out what's right for a child, it's not so different from what's right for a family." In the same article, Wolf agreed, pointing out that "good child welfare policy and practice is family oriented."

Although Wexler and others, for example Golden (1997), emphasize the deficiencies of the foster care system and stress the harm it does to children, the child savers feel vindicated when there are reports that children who are returned home suffer tragic consequences. Such a situation occurred in the highly publicized death of three-year-old Joseph Wallace of Chicago in April 1993, following the court's decision to return him to his mentally ill mother for the third time (Wexler 1995a).

National media attention to the Wallace case contributed to the public's disaffection with family preservation; horror at the child's death became translated into a greater propensity for child welfare agencies to remove children from their homes and keep them away. As Boyer (*Chicago Tribune*, November 16, 1997) explained, caseworkers may be "held personally and professionally accountable for physical harm to the child who remains at home." However, he continued, the individual caseworker generally escapes liability when children are injured in foster care, even when the agency is sued. Thus, anxious to avoid individual responsibility for a child's death at the hands of a parent, child welfare workers not surprisingly become more inclined to remove children from their homes and less willing to allow them to return home (Sheldon 1997; see Barth 1998).

Underlying the difficulty of adhering to a family preservation policy amid widespread public scrutiny is the juvenile court judge's reluctance to decide to return the child home, because of the attendant risk of harm (Herring 1995; Sheldon 1997). The Wallace case left many Cook County judges filled with doubt about the wisdom of sending children home to their parents. Consequently, judges seemed to take longer to adjudicate cases and were more cautious about declaring parents fit (Merry and others 1997, 15 n. 23). According to a report issued by a commission created to investigate the Wallace case, many judges feared "that they will be unfairly tried in the press if a child they return home subsequently dies" (McMurray 1995, 121). After all, as one attorney put it, headlines rarely shout, "Judge slow to reunify family" (*Chicago Tribune*, July 26, 1996).

With a growing number of children being abused or even killed by their parents, the nation collectively recoiled from family preservation in the mid-1990s, with a number of states enacting laws to remove obstacles to the termination of parental rights (Sheldon 1997). And by 1997 the pendulum had swung against the preference for family preservation and reasonable efforts, as evidenced by the passage of the Adoption and Safe Families Act of 1997 (ASFA), amending P.L. 96-272. Introduced by Representative David Camp (R-Mich.) and Barbara Kennelly (D-Conn.), the ASFA, which was signed into law on November 19, 1997, was described as "the most significant change in federal child-protection policy in almost two decades" (*Washington Post*, January 18, 1998).

The act was aimed at reducing the steadily rising number of children in foster care—about half a million at the time. Its passage was accompanied by the same rhetoric that had appeared in 1980 during legislative debate on P.L. 96-272. In language reminiscent of 1980, Senator John Chafee (R-R.I.) stated: "Too often, children who cannot return to their parents wait for years in foster care before they are adopted" (*Congressional Record*, November 13, 1997, S12675).

By inserting the language "in making . . . reasonable efforts, the child's health and safety shall be the paramount concern" and emphasizing the benefits of adoption for children removed from home, the ASFA was intended to refocus the energies of the child welfare system. Although it reiterated the "reasonable efforts" language and reauthorized the 1993 Family Preservation and Family Support Services Program (renamed the Promoting Safe and Stable Families Program) through FY 2001, it provided that such efforts are not required if they are determined to be "inconsistent with the permanency plan for the child" or in situations of chronic abuse or abandonment. Moreover, it allowed states to make efforts to place a child for adoption concurrently with its attempts to reunify the family.[15]

Remarks on the Senate floor indicate that the legislative intent behind the ASFA was to reverse the preference for family preservation that had been inherent in P.L. 96-272. As seen in the statement of Senator Larry Craig (R-Id.): "Currently to obtain federal funds, states are required to use 'reasonable efforts' to keep families together. While this sounds like a goal we can all support, this requirement has resulted in states using extraordinary efforts to keep children in what may be abusive or unsafe situations. . . . *Our bill will change this.* It requires that the child's health and safety must be the paramount concerns in any decisions made by the state on behalf of that child" (*Congressional Record*, November 13, 1997, S12673; emphasis added).

The legislation constituted a shift away from the preference for family preservation. Courts were now required to hold dispositional hearings to set permanency goals within twelve (rather than eighteen) months after a child came into care, thus effectively reducing the time for parental rehabilitation to one year. At the dispositional hearing, courts had to determine whether and when the child will be returned home or placed for adoption. In most cases, states were required to petition for the termination of parental rights for children who were in foster care for fifteen of the past twenty-two months. To encourage adoption of children in substitute care, the ASFA provided approximately $100 million in federal funding for states that increase their rate of adoption over their previous records. Eligible states would receive a $4,000 bonus for each child adopted and $6,000 for each adoption of a child with special needs. Finally, foster parents, preadoptive parents, and relative caretakers were also given the right to be notified of hearings and given an opportunity to present information to the court, thus diminishing the preference for the child's immediate family and providing further evidence of a shift away from the family preservation philosophy.

As a result of the act, although family preservation remained the stated goal of the system, it was no longer considered virtually synonymous with permanency. When signing the bill into law, the president applauded the new legislation for "help[ing] us meet the goal of doubling, by the year 2002, the number of children who are adopted or permanently placed each year" (Clinton 1997, 2). Based on the administration's *Adoption 2002* report, the law set the goal of doubling the number of adoptions, from 27,000 in 1997 to 54,000 by 2002.[16] These changes made it appear that adoption is as acceptable a goal as return home for children in substitute care (Slater 1998).

Early Child Welfare Litigation

With authority over child welfare policy traditionally left to the states, the federal government played a relatively limited policymaking role until the mid-1970s. In the 1980s the federal judiciary became a pivotal actor in the nation's child welfare system as children's advocates sought systemic remedies for the deficiencies of child welfare agencies in the courts. The "mission [of foster care litigation is] to save children from bureaucracies that . . . place them in abusive and otherwise inappropriate foster homes; trap them in destructive 'foster care drift'; and help destroy biological families that, with aid, might have been preserved" (*National Law Journal*, June 27, 1994).

According to a report by the National Commission on Child Welfare and Family Preservation (formed by the American Public Welfare Association in 1988), child welfare agencies are typically subjected to "hiring freezes and other budgetary constraints, staff turnover, unappropriated funds, and recruitment and retention difficulties due to low salaries and high caseloads" (Tucker and Blatt 1994, 179). Not surprisingly, under these conditions, agencies are increasingly unable to fulfill their responsibilities to the children in their care. As recently as a decade ago, Lowry (1988, 288) characterized state child welfare agencies as "almost universally . . . marked by totally unreliable information systems, inadequate training, high caseloads, Byzantine procedures, and administrative paralysis."

Children's advocates began to file lawsuits, alleging that the combination of rising caseloads, underfunding, and inadequate staffing resulted in the agencies' systematic failure to provide for the abused and neglected children committed to their custody. Actions brought in state court to redress the grievances of children harmed in foster care most commonly charged the placement agency with negligence in selecting and supervising the foster parents (Kieffer 1984). In the federal lawsuits, many of which were class actions advanced by attorneys in public interest law firms, advocates broadly claimed that state and county child welfare agencies were not fulfilling their constitutional obligations to shield children from harm (Sinden 1994).

On the federal level, the major difficulty in pursuing such cases was in convincing the courts that, among other things, the state has a constitutional duty to protect children in custody and that its failure to ensure their safety amounts to a federal constitutional violation. And in both state and federal court plaintiffs had to overcome obstacles presented by governmental immunity doctrines.

The early federal class action lawsuits, offering the possibility of furthering the interests of thousands of children in substitute care, were brought in such diverse states as New York, Missouri, and New Mexico. According to

Lowry, the lawsuit was the "2-by-4 that we [attorneys] have been using to beat the mule over the head to get him to change direction . . ." (*National Law Journal*, June 27, 1994).

Focusing on two early New York cases, *Child v. Beame* (1976) and *Black v. Beame* (1976), both litigated by the Children's Rights Project of the New York Civil Liberties Union, Lowry (1988, 279–80) wrote that the "early attempts at system-wide reform litigation were greeted with incredulity by the courts, outrage by defendants, and a large number of procedural and jurisdictional hurdles to overcome."

In one case, attorneys for the five children in the Child family (a fictitious name) alleged that the defendants, including the City of New York, kept the children in foster care and failed to find adoptive homes for them, contravening their constitutional right to permanency in a stable family environment. The plaintiffs claimed they represented a class of more than 5,000 children and a subclass of nonwhite children who, because of their race, were more likely to be deprived of this right than white children. In the other action, Mrs. Frances Black's nine children, four of whom were in state custody, claimed they had a right to an intact family and appropriate counseling services to keep them together.

Acknowledging that the rights sought by the children in these actions were important, the judge in each case dismissed on the grounds that the plaintiffs had failed to state valid constitutional claims. Their reactions illustrated the judiciary's unwillingness at the time to hold the state to its responsibility to foster care children as well as its reluctance to impose federal court oversight on the delivery of child welfare services.

Perhaps reflecting a changing legal environment, a 1977 lawsuit filed by attorneys from Legal Aid of Western Missouri and the Children's Rights Project of the New York Civil Liberties Union against Jackson County's Division of Family Services led to extensive reform of that county's foster care system. Relying on Eighth and Fourteenth Amendment theories, the attorneys sued on behalf of five named plaintiffs and the approximately 1,200 children housed in foster care facilities. The children named in the suit, ranging in age from three to fifteen years, claimed they suffered from numerous disabilities and had not received appropriate services from the child welfare agency. In addition to presenting evidence on the named plaintiffs, the attorneys for the children cited data from a study they had commissioned of the county foster care system.

The parties settled shortly before the trial began, with Chief Judge Russell G. Clark of Kansas City approving a forty-four page consent decree specifying reform in fourteen areas, including licensing foster homes and training foster parents, providing adequate medical care, ensuring children's physical safety, and limiting workers to caseloads of twenty-five children each.

According to the children's attorneys, this case was an important milestone in the federal court's involvement in child welfare policymaking, representing the first time a federal judge approved a consent decree encompassing reform of a child welfare system. "The G.L. [v. Zumwalt (1983)] decree," they stress, "marks a—perhaps dramatic, perhaps evolutionary—change from past judicial noninvolvement in this area that has important implications for the child welfare community" (Mushlin, Levitt, and Anderson 1986, 142).

Four months after the G.L. decree was approved, another federal consent decree was issued in a class action suit brought by attorneys in Albuquerque, New Mexico, together with the New York Civil Liberties Union's Children's Rights Project against the New Mexico Department of Human Services. Filed in July 1980, on behalf of a class of about 500 New Mexican children in foster care who had no relationship to their biological parents and no hope of being returned to them, the suit sought statewide systemic reform of the child welfare agency. The named plaintiffs, siblings Joseph and Josephine A., were 7 and 8 years old at the time the complaint was filed; they had been in custody since they were 6 months and 1-1/2 years old, respectively. Like these two, the other named plaintiffs in the suit, as well as the rest of the class, claimed that although they were eligible for adoption, the agency made little or no attempt to find adoptive parents for them nor to free them for adoption.

Although the district court dismissed most of the plaintiffs' constitutional claims (*Joseph and Josephine A. v. New Mexico Department of Human Services* 1982), the parties entered into settlement talks and, as a result of an agreement approved by Judge Juan Burciaga in September 1983, the department committed itself to reforming its staffing and training programs to facilitate permanency planning for the children. The decree "acknowledged that children in the custody of the Human Services Department have rights to fair, reasonable and timely decision-making with regard to access to adoption, and to fair, reasonable and adequate procedures and practices necessary to insure access to permanent adoptive homes" (*Joseph and Josephine A. v. New Mexico Department of Human Services* 1983, 1). In addition to permanency planning, the decree set caseload limits and provided for a citizen review board and a monitor to oversee compliance.

Eventually decrees such as G.L. and *Joseph and Josephine A.* would be replicated in other class action suits around the nation. By the end of the 1980s, when the Illinois child welfare advocates filed B.H., seeking systemic changes in DCFS, they were aided by significant developments in child welfare law.

During the decade of the 1980s, the federal judiciary, for the most part, had become more receptive to the child welfare litigants, largely abandoning its posture of "noninvolvement" and adopting a willingness to hold state and local governments accountable in federal court for the delivery of child welfare services.

3 Stimulus

RIPENING CONDITIONS FOR A LAWSUIT

 The nation's child welfare systems, David Herring (1995, 199) contends, are in crisis because of inadequate judicial enforcement of "reasonable efforts," ineffective use of case plans to provide appropriate services and monitor their use, and failure to return children home in a timely manner. The difficulties confronting state and local governments in trying to cope with these systemic deficiencies are compounded by the changing population of children in care today: they are "younger, are more damaged, and have greater mental health and education problems, and, indeed, there are more of them" (Preston 1996, 1655).

System-Wide Failure

Commenting generally on the state of child welfare in the nation during the 1980s, Fred Wulczyn of the New York State Department of Social Services and Robert Goerge of the Chapin Hall Center for Children of the University of Chicago (1992, 278) noted that since passage of the 1980 Adoption Assistance and Child Welfare Act, "Poverty among families with children has remained stubbornly high, calls to child abuse hotlines have skyrocketed, drug abuse among childbearing women has spread, and foster care caseloads around the county have jumped in size."

Illinois was not exempt from this national trend. The problems encountered in investigating abuse and neglect reports and the difficulty of contending with the growing number of victims of abuse and neglect strained all parts of the child welfare system, most notably the juvenile courts and the Illinois child welfare agency, the Department of Children and Family Services (DCFS). In the two years preceding June 29, 1988, when *B.H.* was filed, the Illinois system became overwhelmed with cases and was increasingly unable to cope with its responsibilities. The steadily deteriorating conditions within the system provided the stimuli that made *B.H.*, or a case like it, almost inevitable.

As appendix table 1 indicates, the Illinois Central Register received more than 200,000 calls between July 1, 1987 and June 30,

1988 (FY 1988), encompassing the year *B.H.* was filed; this represents an increase of more than 20,000 calls from the previous year and almost double the number of calls from the fiscal year ending June 30, 1982 (FY 1982) (Illinois Department of Children and Family Services 1992, 7).[1]

Because hotline calls include requests for information, a better measure of the incidence of child maltreatment in Illinois is the number of actual reports of child abuse and neglect to the authorities. Appendix table 2 shows that almost 100,000 children were reported as suspected victims of abuse or neglect from July 1, 1987, to June 30, 1988, representing a more than 30 percent increase in the number of children reported over the previous two years (Illinois Department of Children and Family Services 1998a). Following investigation of the reports by child welfare workers, as illustrated in appendix table 3, in FY 1988, slightly more than 40,000 children were "indicated" for abuse or neglect, that is, credible evidence of abuse or neglect was found; this represented a 20 percent increase over the preceding two years of reporting (Illinois Department of Children and Family Services 1998a).[2] Not surprisingly, the increased reporting led to a concomitant growth in the number of children placed in substitute care, adding to the burden on the system's limited resources.

Further complicating the problems of the system was an inability to close cases. There had been a relative balance between discharges and admissions from 1983 until mid-1986 (Wulczyn and Goerge 1992, 282–83; Murphy 1997, 132). After 1986, there was a sharp rise in the number of children placed in care and a decline in the number of children discharged from care, creating a significant growth in the caseload. Increasing the strain on the system, the largest growth area of placements was in the homes of relatives, which "tend to last longer than regular foster care placements" (Wulczyn and Goerge 1992, 287).

Other data also confirmed the state's mounting difficulty in struggling with its responsibilities to the children in its custody. A study of children discharged from the system (Goerge and Wulczyn 1990, 19–20) showed that in 1981, the percentage of children discharged after spending less than a year in care began to decrease and the percentage of children discharged after spending more than three years in care began to increase. By 1988 the mean length of time of a child's first placement in the state as a whole was 24 months, up from 14.9 months in 1977, and 29.6 months for children in Cook County, up from 19.1 months in 1977 (Goerge and Wulczyn 1990, 48–49). Moreover, despite the greater length of time children were spending in care, in 1986 almost one-third of them were reentering the system after being discharged (Goerge and Wulczyn 1990, 31).

The Department of Child and Family Services

DCFS began operations on January 1, 1964.[3] Of the several social welfare agencies to serve the needs of Illinois children, DCFS has the broadest mandate: aside from the direct services it provides to abused and neglected children and their families, it "funds, licenses and monitors" public and private providers of day care, foster care, adoption services, and preventive and family support services; it has jurisdiction over homeless children, status offenders, delinquent youngsters under thirteen, and teen parents (Kulla and Richards 1991, 11).

Although the history of child welfare involvement by the state dates all the way back to the post–Civil War era, relatively little attention had been paid to providing direct social services to children. The majority of state dollars were funneled to the few state institutions, with an emphasis on industrial training and reform schools. Most dependent and neglected children were served by voluntary agencies, which, among other deficiencies, largely ignored the needs of children from minority families (Silberman 1991; see also Illinois Department of Children and Family Services 1998b).

In 1962 the Illinois Commission on Children recommended that the state fund a public child welfare agency, and in legislation enacted on June 4, 1963, DCFS was given the mandate to "provide social services to children and their families, to operate children's institutions, and to provide certain other rehabilitative and residential services. . . ."[4]

A year after the agency was established, Illinois enacted the Abused Child Act of 1965, which required medical professionals to report suspected cases of abuse to a central registry and granted them immunity from suit resulting from the reports.[5] The department's caseload grew in 1972, when it was given responsibility for children who had formerly been arrested and brought under the authority of the Department of Corrections as status offenders—that is, children considered runaways, incorrigibles, or truants. A year later, DCFS was also assigned jurisdiction over juveniles under age thirteen convicted of delinquency.[6] Thus, during its early years DCFS's jurisdiction expanded as it assumed increasing responsibility for many of the troubled children and families in Illinois. During those early years, however, funding seemed to keep pace with the growth in responsibilities: the state increased the department's budget from $14 million in 1964 to $84 million in 1974 (Silberman 1991, 32).

The Abused Child Act of 1965 was amended by the Abused and Neglected Child Reporting Act of 1975, which expanded the definition of abuse to include neglect, sexual abuse, and psychological harm and conferred immunity on voluntary, that is, nonmandated, reporters making good-faith reports. The 1975 act, subsequently amended several times, serves as the basis for all child protection policies in the state.

The increased emphasis on reporting suspected cases of abuse and neglect led to even larger numbers of children placed in state custody. By the middle 1970s, however, although the agency was under greater pressure to provide services, the state legislature had slashed its budget because of strains on the economy caused by the oil crisis.

Given the immensity of its tasks and the limited resources it had to carry them out, it is not surprising that the department often failed to fulfill the needs of the state's maltreated children. Subject to increasing criticism and legal actions for its failures, and troubled by the bureaucratic culture in which the department was mired as well as the often poor quality of its own leadership, DCFS had become an agency under stress by the time it was a decade old.

A 1980 amendment to the act required the Child Protective Service (CPS) Unit of DCFS to begin investigations of abuse or neglect within twenty-four hours of a report—sooner for a child in imminent danger—and allowed CPS workers, if necessary, to take a child into temporary custody, that is, to remove the child from the parent's custody. In an effort to make reporting more accessible, the state created a toll-free twenty-four-hour hotline to receive reports of suspected abuse and neglect.

Despite the state's growing attention to the problem of child abuse, some child welfare professionals considered the reporting laws ineffectual and even counterproductive. Undoubtedly reflecting the fact that child abuse had become a political issue, the criticism was divided along ideological fault lines. The left charged that by focusing on abuse and neglect, politicians were able to gain favorable media attention as child advocates, yet avoid dealing with underlying societal causes of abuse and neglect such as poverty. Those on the right complained that child abuse laws unduly invaded familial privacy. As a partial consequence of encouraging increased reporting, they argued, the system was deluged with unfounded reports that overwhelmed caseworkers and obscured real instances of abuse. Moreover, regardless of political ideology, both sides worried about the effects of removing children from their homes and placing them in foster care (Gittens 1994, chap. 3).

The Juvenile Court

With the passage of P.L. 96-272, Congress had intended to diminish the autonomy of state and local child welfare officials by placing them under the oversight of the juvenile court system. The jurisdiction of the Illinois juvenile court system is defined by the Juvenile Court Act of 1987; this act, representing an amalgam of Illinois laws, the Child Abuse Prevention and Treatment Act (CAPTA), and P.L. 96-272, establishes the parameters of the court's involvement in the child welfare system.

The child welfare process typically begins with an abuse and neglect report to the state central register through its hotline, followed by an investigation to determine whether circumstances require taking the child into protective custody.[7] After investigation (and, as indicated above, the decision to investigate, although subject to guidelines, is ultimately left to the discretion of the intake worker), the caseworker characterizes the report as "unfounded," "indicated" (that is, "founded" or "substantiated"), or "undetermined." Most investigations result in a verdict of "unfounded."

Nationally, the figure for unfounded reports is 60 percent; in Illinois, it is a little higher, at about 66 percent. Even when a case is "indicated," that is, credible evidence exists that abuse or neglect has occurred, the child may be left at home and the family offered in-home services. In Illinois only about 17 percent of the "founded" or "indicated" cases lead to children's removal from home and placement in substitute care (Schuerman, Rzepnicki, and Littell 1994, 4).

If DCFS takes protective custody of the child, a caseworker presents evidence of the abuse or neglect to the state's attorney for screening, allowing the latter to decide if sufficient evidence exists to file a petition with the court.[8] If the state's attorney files the petition, there must be a temporary custody hearing before a juvenile court judge within forty-eight hours of the child's being taken into custody.

At the temporary custody hearing, the court must first determine if there is "probable cause to believe that the minor is abused, neglected, or dependent." If the court finds probable cause, it must determine whether "it is a matter of immediate and urgent necessity" to take temporary custody and order the child removed from home. Finally, the court must make a finding on whether the agency used reasonable efforts in the case; that is, it must find "that reasonable efforts have been made or that, in the best interests of the minor, no efforts can reasonably be made to prevent or eliminate the necessity of removal of the minor from his or her home."

In 1993, largely spurred by the horrifying death of little Joseph Wallace, the Illinois General Assembly amended the Juvenile Court Act to incorporate the "best interests of the minor" language into the law to make it clear that the courts must consider the health and safety of the child over the goal of family preservation in determining the child's placement.[9]

Implemented within months after Joseph's death, the amendments also clarified the duties of Denise Kane, whom Governor Jim Edgar had appointed to the post of inspector general for a four-year term. Kane was essentially empowered to serve as a watchdog over DCFS, assisted by a new hotline for a foster parent to report suspected abuse or neglect by a parent or to report any instances of DCFS misconduct. She was given wide-ranging "authority to conduct investigations into allegations of or incidents of possible misconduct, misfeasance, malfeasance, or violations of rules, procedures, or laws by any employee, foster parent, service provider, or contractor of the Department of Children and Family Services."[10]

If a court finds probable cause (and it most often does), but no "urgent and immediate necessity," the judge can order DCFS to provide services to the family and keep the child at home, likely under a protective order. In either event, the court will set a date for the adjudicatory hearing, or "trial," to determine whether the child had been abused or neglected at the time the petition was filed.

The temporary custody hearing is rather informal; the court allows ordinarily inadmissible evidence, such as hearsay testimony, and the state's burden of proof is easily met (Hartnett 1991). Despite this informality, attorneys play an important role in the juvenile court process, with all parties typically represented by counsel.

A minimum of three attorneys are in attendance at Cook County abuse and neglect proceedings; there may even be more depending on the facts of the case. The lead player, representing the people of Illinois, is the state's attorney, who must prove the circumstances of abuse or neglect described in the petition. Typically, at least in Cook County, the parent is represented by the public defender. When there is a conflict between the parents, the court appoints a private attorney to represent one of them. Also present in the courtroom is a guardian *ad litem* to represent the best interests and wishes of the child.[11] Under the 1987 Juvenile Court Act, guardians *ad litem* are empowered to gather information, present evidence to the court, and cross-examine witnesses. The guardians are not required to be attorneys, but if they are not, they must be represented by counsel. In Cook County, an assistant public guardian serves as counsel and guardian *ad litem* for the child; outside Cook County, it is more common for guardians to be lay people represented by counsel.[12] Additionally, an attorney serving as a liaison between DCFS and the juvenile court may be present in the courtroom.[13] Finally, there may also be a court-appointed special advocate, usually a nonlawyer volunteer, who monitors the case and attempts to provide the court with an independent source of information about the child and the conditions of the substitute care placement.[14]

Although some juvenile court observers argue that the adversarial process and the presence of attorneys in the courtroom are counterproductive, for the most part the juvenile court judges seem to welcome their presence there, at least those attorneys representing the parties. The interviews with the nineteen juvenile court judges in the Chicago metropolitan area revealed a general consensus on the usefulness of attorneys in the juvenile court system. The judges variously mentioned that the lawyers helped the process by clarifying legal procedures, gathering necessary information, facilitating the expression of diverse views, negotiating agreements, helping parents accept the court's decisions, and, more broadly, relieving tensions and lowering the emotional temperature of the courtroom. One or two judges cautioned that some attorneys, who sought to promote their professional advancement, unnecessarily contested issues and looked for "little victories" on minor procedural matters. Only one Cook County judge disagreed with the others, arguing that attorneys created an adversarial environment that impeded the court's decisionmaking process (Mezey 1995).

The adjudication, or trial, must take place within ninety days after the petition is filed.[15] Here, the rules of evidence are stricter, although the state is only held to a preponderance of the evidence standard. If the accusations are proven, the court must set a date within thirty days for a dispositional hearing.[16]

At the dispositional hearing the court determines, among other things, whether it is in the best interests of the child to be declared a ward of the court.[17] In deciding whether to remove the child from home (or to keep him or her away from home), the court must find that the parents are "unfit, or are unable, for reasons other than financial circumstances alone, to care for . . . the minor, or are unwilling to do so, and that it is in the best interest of the minor to take him [or her] from the custody of his [or her] parents, guardian or custodian."[18] To diminish the primacy of family preservation, in 1993 the state legislature removed the requirement that the court must find "that appropriate services aimed at family preservation and family reunification have been unsuccessful in rectifying the conditions which have led to a finding of unfitness or inability to care for . . . the minor."

If the court concludes that the child should be placed in substitute care, it has several options. The most common substitute care arrangement is placement of the child with his or her relatives, a practice known as kinship care. Other options are placement in a licensed foster care family, a group home, or a residential shelter.

To implement permanency planning, DCFS must conduct an administrative case review (ACR) every six months and specify the permanency goal for the child and how it will be met. During the post-dispositional phase, the court must hold a permanency review hearing no later than twelve months after the child is taken into temporary custody, and at least once every six months thereafter, until it determines that the plan and the goal have been achieved.[19] At the permanency review hearings, the juvenile court judge or hearing officer reviews the appropriateness of the goal and the plan devised to achieve it, including the services in the plan.

In an effort to expedite the work of the court, the Juvenile Court Act was amended in 1995 to allow hearing officers to conduct permanency hearings.[20] The hearing officers are required to be attorneys with at least three years of experience in the areas of child abuse and neglect or permanency planning. A hearing, more informal than the court proceeding, results in a recommendation to the court, which can accept it or hold additional hearings.

Because adoption is considered the second most desirable goal after "return home,"[21] the court must also determine whether there are grounds to terminate parental rights to prepare the child for adoption. If the state's attorney or the juvenile court judge believes that termination is appropriate, a termination screening process involving the state's attorney, the Office of the Public Guardian (OPG), and DCFS, is set in motion. If these parties agree, the state's attorney files a petition for termination of parental rights. The court must decide, based on clear and convincing evidence, if the parent is "unfit" and if it is in the child's best interests to terminate the parent's rights. Even if the court finds the parent unfit, if there is no prospect for adoption, it may decide that termination is not in the child's best interests.

Although the law governing the juvenile court clearly spells out its duties and responsibilities, the act has not solved the problems the court faces of overcrowding and understaffing. When juvenile court judges must decide "the best interests of the child" in abuse and neglect cases, they are forced to gauge the physical and emotional status of each child coming before them, with too little time to assimilate the information given them and often too little confidence in the source of the information.

Most juvenile court judges have responsibility for too many cases, a situation that leads to delays and errors and contributes to the deficiencies of the child welfare system in Illinois. A study by Illinois Action for Children, reported in the *Chicago Tribune* (October 9, 1986), characterized the state's child welfare system as having "critical flaws, including . . . a sluggish judicial system which cannot respond to children's unmet needs." The report cited delays in adjudicatory hearings in Cook County that averaged 14.4 months (instead of the requisite 120 days), some delays lasting as long as three years.

Almost a decade later it was reported that each juvenile court judge in Cook County had responsibility for approximately 3,800 cases. Leonard Edwards, a well-known juvenile court judge in San Jose, California, characterized the Illinois juvenile court system as "one of the most under-resourced and disappointing juvenile courts in the country" (*Chicago Tribune*, December 21, 1993). His observation was undoubtedly based in part on this statistic.

The "disappointing" operation of the juvenile court system, added to the deficiencies of the child welfare agency, meant that children in Illinois, especially those in Cook County, were more likely to be consigned to foster care, likelier to stay in care longer, and less likely to achieve the permanency that state and federal law (and their proper development) require.

Guardian *ad Litem*

In Cook County the guardian *ad litem* (GAL) also shares responsibility for the welfare of abused and neglected children. Created by the state in 1965, the Cook County GAL is publicly funded and considered an arm of the juvenile court. In counties outside Cook, the guardian *ad litem* is usually a private individual and not necessarily an attorney. As with the other parts of the child welfare system, the GAL's office was in a state of disarray in the years immediately preceding the filing of *B.H.*

As reported in *Crain's Chicago Business News* (August 10, 1987), in November 1985, attorneys from the Legal Assistance Foundation of Chicago (LAF) began to investigate the office of the GAL, charging its eleven attorneys with ineffectually representing its clients and complaining that the office was understaffed and underfunded. Six months later, the LAF filed a complaint against the GAL with the Attorney Registration and Disciplinary Commission of the Illinois Supreme Court, accusing the lawyers, who worked only part-time, in the GAL's office of "incompetence and chronic neglect" (*Chicago Tribune*, October 9, 1986). Harry Comerford, the chief judge of the circuit court, asked the public guardian, Patrick Murphy, to conduct his own investigation of the GAL's office.

Meanwhile the LAF filed a lawsuit against the GAL and the Cook County Board of Commissioners, charging them with legal malpractice. At the same time Murphy's report, which concurred with the LAF's assessment, was submitted to the chief judge. By March 1987 Comerford had asked Murphy to assume the responsibilities of the GAL, combining them with his work as public guardian.

Once appointed, in addition to assuming representation of approximately 18,000 abused and neglected children a year (*Chicago Tribune*, June 9, 1987), Murphy seemed intent on unsettling the child welfare establishment. In an effort to strike back, DCFS appealed to the chief judge, claiming there was a statutory bar to appointing the public guardian as the GAL.

Meanwhile, not shy about offering criticism publicly, the newly appointed guardian *ad litem* charged in the *Crain's* story (August 10, 1987) that of the 13,000 children under DCFS supervision who were legally required to have hearings, only 946 had received them in 1986. Considering a suit to force DCFS to hold the requisite hearings, Murphy felt it preferable instead to use the resources of the GAL's office to sue DCFS on behalf of individual children in damage suits, asserting, "In these situations, it's better to hit DCFS in the pocketbook. . . " (*Crain's Chicago Business News*, August 10, 1987). However, although they believed damage suits were more potent, the attorneys in his office also explored filing federal and state class action suits for injunctive relief.

Each of the individual components of the child welfare system was operating under severe deficits; not surprisingly, as a consequence, the system as a whole was unable to fulfill its responsibilities to the children in its care. The breadth of the system's failures, from placement to discharge, ultimately provided the impetus for the child welfare advocates in Illinois to seek systemic relief in the federal courts.

Previous Litigation

Although there had been individual damage suits against DCFS in the past, class action suits became increasingly popular in the late 1970s, setting the stage for *B.H.* By the time *B.H.* was filed, Illinois child welfare advocates had already entered into consent decrees with DCFS in two major federal class action suits.[22]

Burgos

Burgos v. DCFS, filed on November 20, 1975, was one of the first major class action suits against DCFS. It charged the department with discriminating against Puerto Rican–born American citizens with limited English speaking ability and causing "progressive linguistic and cultural separation between themselves and their children" (*Burgos v. DCFS* 1975, 9–10).

The federal court certified the class as "all persons who were born in Puerto Rico and are now residing in the Chicago metropolitan area whose children have been, are, or will be placed under the guardianship and/or custody of the Illinois Department of Children and Family Services without accommodating the national origin of the parents" (*Burgos v. DCFS* 1977, 2).

Leopoldo and Iris Burgos, two of the named plaintiffs, sued on behalf of Spanish-speaking parents with children in DCFS custody. Their complaint stated that their two children, under the guardianship of DCFS (nine other children remained with them), had been placed with non-Spanish-speaking foster families, that DCFS had not assigned a Spanish-speaking worker to their case, and that DCFS failed to communicate with them in their own language about their children. Because their children had been placed in English-speaking foster care, they argued, they had become estranged from them, diminishing the likelihood of their returning home.

Represented by the LAF, the plaintiffs alleged that at least 80 percent of the approximately 1,000 children with Spanish surnames in DCFS custody had been placed in foster homes where Spanish was not spoken or known, that DCFS had only a single employee in the Chicago metropolitan area to locate Spanish-speaking foster families, and that DCFS assigned non-Spanish-speaking social workers to 92 percent of parents with children in DCFS custody (*Burgos v. DCFS* 1975, 7–8).

They claimed that the department's lack of Spanish-speaking staff and foster families and its failure to offer counseling, services, and information in Spanish discriminated against them on the basis of race and national origin, violating Title VI of the 1964 Civil Rights Act and the equal protection and due process clauses of the Fourteenth Amendment as well as Illinois law.[23] DCFS statistics showed that in 1974 the agency serviced 960 Latino families, with more than a third speaking only Spanish or with Spanish as their primary language (*Burgos v. DCFS* 1976, 2).

The parties entered into settlement negotiations, resulting in a consent decree approved by federal district court Judge Thomas McMillen on January 14, 1977. The decree, made applicable to all Hispanic families, stated that by March 31, 1977, DCFS would identify its Hispanic clients and ensure that all Spanish-speaking children would be placed with Spanish-speaking foster families and social workers (*Burgos v. DCFS* 1977). It also required DCFS as well as its private contractors to provide clients with appropriate Spanish-language documents by this date and to increase the number of bilingual employees in its Chicago area offices by April 30, 1977. DCFS was permitted to place children in English-only foster homes, if necessary, for a maximum of eighty days.

DCFS compliance with the *Burgos* consent decree was problematic from the outset. In April 1979, two years after the deadline for conforming to the decree's mandate, the plaintiffs' lawyers moved to hold DCFS in contempt, citing numerous violations of the decree, including the agency's failure to place Spanish-speaking children with Spanish-speaking foster parents and to distribute Spanish language informational material.

In March 1982 the plaintiffs agreed to withdraw the motion after DCFS promised to recruit more Spanish-speaking foster parents and to exert greater effort to monitor its vendors' compliance with the decree. Five years later, in January 1987, still unsatisfied with DCFS's performance and citing its continued failure to comply with the decree, the LAF filed another motion for contempt with similar charges. The lawyers argued that by failing to identify Hispanic clients, to place Hispanic children in Spanish-speaking foster families, and to provide appropriate Spanish-language documents, DCFS had not fulfilled its obligations under either the decree or the 1982 agreement (*Burgos v. DCFS* 1987).

As a result of the threatened contempt citation, with a hearing to show cause why the department should not be held in contempt scheduled before federal court Judge Susan Getzendanner on June 30, 1987, DCFS director Gordon Johnson announced a series of reforms, including the recruitment of more bilingual foster families and caseworkers and the appointment of a co-ordinator of Hispanic affairs. In a *Chicago Tribune* (June 3, 1987) article report-ing the agreement, Johnson said, "We are in a crisis situation." And conced-ing that DCFS had violated the court order, he committed to a $4.1 million spending program, which he said he would be able to accomplish by shifting funds around. There was no clear indication from where the money would come, however; although the $4.1 million represented only a small part of DCFS's budget, the department's 1987 budget request of $304 million had already been cut to $285 million (*Chicago Tribune*, June 2, 1987).

Although Johnson characterized the initiative as a "good-faith effort," LAF attorney Diane Redleaf declared, "They are not moving forward and, if any-thing, they have been moving backward. This sounds like too little too late" (*Chicago Tribune*, June 3, 1987).

DCFS continued to attempt to recruit more Spanish-speaking foster fami-lies, but in September Johnson again admitted the agency was in violation of the decree. He maintained, however, that the department was "in 98 percent compliance from a foster placement point of view, which was a priority" (*Chi-cago Tribune*, September 22, 1987). Commenting positively on the department's efforts, community leaders pointed to lack of funds as the main source of the problem. One stated: "I wouldn't say the funding is enough, but I don't think you can blame DCFS" (*Chicago Tribune*, September 22, 1987).

Bates

Bates v. Johnson, another federal class action suit brought by the LAF, also demonstrated the difficulty of securing DCFS's compliance with a consent decree.

The *Bates* class consisted of "all parents and non-parental guardians of children who . . . are or will be in the temporary custody of DCFS, or are or will be under the guardianship of DCFS, when the DCFS service plan for such children establishes a goal of returning them to the custody of their parents or guardian" (*Bates v. Johnson* 1986, 3). The named plaintiffs in the case, filed in November 1984, were Gail Bates and Deborah Saunders.

Bates's two children, ages two and four, lived with their aunt—Bates's sister—under DCFS guardianship. Saunders's twenty-one month old son was in the temporary custody of DCFS and lived with her estranged husband's aunt. Although the permanency goal for all three children was "return home," in accordance with its normal policy DCFS limited their mothers to one su-pervised visit a month. The plaintiffs claimed that DCFS's visitation policy violated P.L. 96-272 and federal regulations as well as the First, Ninth, and Fourteenth amendments (*Bates v. Johnson* 1984).

The agency asserted that its official policy for children with a permanency plan of "return home" was to encourage weekly parental visits, adding that it was in compliance with this policy. Despite this, DCFS nevertheless entered into a consent decree with the plaintiffs. The decree, affecting an estimated 9,000 parents and legal guardians, was signed by the parties in April 1986 and, following the fairness hearing, approved by Judge Paul Plunkett two months later.

Paragraph Three of the Agreed Order, the heart of the decree, began by stating: "DCFS visitation policy prior to the filing of this suit and at the time of this agreement is as follows: parents and guardians of children under DCFS temporary custody, or under DCFS guardianship with a goal of return home are expected and encouraged to visit their children weekly unless there is documentation to the contrary in the case/record" (*Bates v. Johnson* 1986, 3).

The agreement also provided that the visits, which were to lengthen gradually, would normally take place in the parent's home, with DCFS responsible for facilitating transportation between the parents and their children. Additionally, DCFS agreed to establish visitation plans within three days of placement (ten days for emergency placements) and to begin the visits within the child's first two weeks in temporary custody or guardianship. The agency also promised to distribute three sets of notices to all class members, informing them of the policy and their right to appeal, and to remind all caseworkers under DCFS supervision (including those in private agencies) of their obligations under the agreement. In the notice to caseworkers informing them of the decree, the department reiterated that the specified procedures did not involve a change in official DCFS rules and regulations (*Bates v. Johnson* 1986, 3–5).

Although DCFS committed to keep the policy in effect for at least two years, the decree provided that the state had the right to modify it within that time subject to the rules of the Illinois Administrative Procedure Act (IAPA), after providing advance notice to the court. If, following the public notice and comment procedure of the IAPA, the state succeeded in having the decree modified, the plaintiffs would be given an opportunity to relitigate.

The attorneys for the families faced a formidable task in securing DCFS's compliance with the decree. As early as December 1986, only six months after the decree was entered into, the LAF began pointing out areas of noncompliance, and in March 1987 it filed a motion for contempt (*Bates v. Johnson*, 1987). Over the next several years, amid complex legal proceedings, DCFS admitted it was out of compliance with the decree, and indeed that it had never been in compliance. The agency claimed that the decree never actually required it to provide weekly visits to all the parents in the class. Arguing over appropriate sanctions for contempt, the plaintiffs proposed a new order as part of the remedy for the department's contempt of the 1986 decree.

In 1989, appearing before the court, the state refused to enter into a new consent decree, arguing that such an action would negatively affect other litigation pending against it and that it had simply modified the decree according to the procedures provided in the original 1986 decree.

Characterizing the department's legal claims as "wrong-headed," with "thin support," the court proclaimed itself "extremely disturbed by the position Defendant has taken," and stated that it "can only conclude that Defendant entered into the decree in order to simply get Plaintiffs off its back, yet never seriously intended to live up to it." Unwilling, however, to impose the LAF's proposed new order, despite the agency's "three years of bad faith conduct" and the fact that plaintiffs "have not received even so much as a minute of compliance" with the decree, the court continued the terms of the original decree for an additional two years, ordering DCFS to pay attorney fees and costs (*Bates v. Johnson* 1989, 7–9).

DCFS appealed the finding of contempt, entered on June 29, 1989, but did not request that the appellate court modify or set aside the order. Instead, the state returned to the original 1986 decree and amended its visitation rules under the emergency clause of the IAPA that allows an agency to amend its regulations without having to conform to the normal notice and comment procedures. Although the district court judge expressed his displeasure with DCFS and stated in open court on July 18 that the department must return to the original rules, he refused to enter a written order interpreting the modification rule in the original decree or to enjoin the modification. On appeal again, the state argued that it was not bound by the judge's oral statements. The Seventh Circuit agreed, declaring that "at the moment, Illinois is under no decree. It need not dance to the judge's tune. Until the judge enters an injunction, Illinois may carry out its plans. [And] because the state is not under an enforceable constraint, there is nothing before us on appeal" (*Bates v. Johnson*, 1990, 1428).

The story did not end there. Five years after the 1986 decree had been signed, the plaintiffs sought additional relief from the court, citing the report of the special master, Dr. Brandon Greene. Appointed by the court on January 29, 1990, to monitor DCFS's compliance with the consent decree, the special master's study showed, "In Cook County, only 15% of the 71% of parents with weekly visitation plans actually received weekly visitation." Moreover, "the average delay in having the first parent child visit is 35 days, with 65% of cases having no visit in the first month" (*Bates v. Suter* 1991a, 2).

The study also found that parents "remain almost completely unaware of their visitation rights and concerning any recourse they may have if visitation is denied to them" (*Bates v. Suter* 1991a, 3).

As a result of the plaintiffs' motion, the court entered an order in which DCFS agreed that the consent decree (and the court's jurisdiction to enforce it) would remain in effect until DCFS had been in compliance with the decree for four years (*Bates v. Suter* 1991b, 2). After Johnson's resignation the agency rescinded its attempts to revise the officially stated weekly visitation policy and committed itself to retaining the principle of weekly visitation and following the nonemergency IAPA procedure for minor modifications it wished to make in the decree.

Together *Burgos* and *Bates* helped pave the way for *B.H.* a few years later. These cases showed that although state officials were aware of the department's violations, they seemed unconcerned about bringing the agency into compliance with the law. Citing financial difficulties and shortcomings in personnel, they contended DCFS was simply unable to satisfy the requirements of the consent decrees. Thus, despite the fact that *Bates* and *Burgos* had only sought to change relatively circumscribed areas of DCFS policy, they helped to establish a legal and political climate in which classes of abused and neglected children could demand changes in DCFS policy.

Media Attention

When DCFS was created, there was "great hope for this new agency, the product of a half a century of recommendations and agitation come to fruition at last" (Gittens 1994, 62). In time, however, hopes dimmed as the deficiencies of the agency, and indeed of the entire child welfare system, became increasingly visible to the public—in large part because of the media's spotlight on its flaws.

Among other things, the press helped mobilize public opinion to support reform by alerting the citizenry to the failings of the system. It also provided a forum for public officials to rail against the evils of child abuse (a prudent stance for politicians of all ideological perspectives) and to criticize an unpopular government agency for failing to prevent the parade of horrors that were inflicted on innocent children. The stories about child abuse also allowed politicians to distance themselves from the issue by blaming the parents as well as DCFS and thereby avoid taking responsibility for the underlying societal causes that contributed to these conditions.

Because the nature of its mission lent it a high visibility among state agencies, DCFS was usually subjected to intense scrutiny by the press. Indeed, Murphy acknowledged that his office deliberately sought out "the media to expose some of the court's more egregious cases and practices" (Murphy 1997, 24). Articles about child abuse—especially those presenting horrific details and offering easy targets to blame—sell newspapers. Not surprisingly, given DCFS's overwhelming responsibilities and its many spectacular failures, the attention by the press was largely negative and helped bring further censure on the agency. Moreover, articles citing high rates of turnover, burnout, and indifference among personnel throughout all segments of the child welfare system further contributed to the public's growing disaffection with it.

At times it seemed as if the media were simply interested in airing the department's mistakes. For example, in a highly publicized case in 1972, the press reported that a child who had been returned home from foster care was killed by his biological parents. Another scandal, on a larger scale, erupted when DCFS was forced to defend its policy of shipping 500 children to Texas foster care facilities. Unwilling or unable to offer a defense, DCFS ordered all 500 children back to Illinois, without determining whether any were receiving better care in Texas and without ascertaining whether there were adequate facilities within Illinois to receive them. Further press criticism was often sparked by DCFS's outspoken director, Jerome Miller, who was appointed to fill the post in 1973.[24] And in the late 1970s, the Illinois Humane Association and the Better Government Association both criticized DCFS, citing numerous deficiencies in communication, personnel, supervision, and record-keeping (Gittens 1994, 80–81).

A few years later the *Chicago Tribune* (September 14, 1986) reported that in the fiscal year ending June 30, 1986, eighty-two children had been killed, a 49 percent rise over the previous year and the highest number of child abuse deaths in five years. Even worse, in about a fourth of the deaths, DCFS had previously investigated a report of abuse or neglect. The story presented a detailed account of how DCFS and the private agencies working under its supervision had failed to take the steps that could have prevented the deaths. The article included a statement from Johnson defending his staff: "There is no way DCFS or any agency can protect all children in Illinois." At the same time, he announced a series of essentially meaningless criminal justice reform measures, such as categorizing repeated offenses of child abuse as Class X felonies, and "credited the *Tribune* inquires for spurring the action."

The *Tribune* article was part of a three-month series on the results of investigations into DCFS operations. Responding to the series, the State Government Administration Committee of the Illinois House of Representatives announced it would conduct hearings on child abuse deaths and DCFS's performance. Committee chair Michael Curran (D-Springfield) suggested that the published reports "may only be the tip of the iceberg" (*Chicago Tribune*, September 19, 1986). At the hearings, committee members heard testimony from a Cook County Hospital pediatrician who charged the department with "conducting faulty investigations" in the cases of children she had treated in the pediatric trauma unit. In reporting on the hearings, the *Tribune* story (September 25, 1986) noted that letters citing similar charges had been sent to the department by other hospital employees during the past two years.

In October 1986, amid a flurry of stories and editorials on DCFS, problems surfaced in almost all aspects of agency operations—from the abuse and neglect hotline and the protective service investigators to the caseworkers and foster care parents. The press characterized DCFS as an "agency stretched between expanding duties and limited resources," yet also charged that it "often demonstrat[ed] bureaucratic waste and insensitivity . . ." (*Chicago Tribune*, October 5, 1986). Arthur Hamilton, the presiding judge of the juvenile court, also publicly attacked the department. Although he was likely attempting to deflect criticism from himself and the juvenile court system, he pointed to a number of flaws within the agency. "My experience," he said, "is that oftentimes the cases are not assigned . . . there is change in their staff, reorganization in their offices, [and] files are not readily available" (*Chicago Tribune*, October 9, 1986).

The unfavorable publicity was unending, as the *Tribune* (May 22, 1988) continued to report numerous breakdowns within DCFS operations. An eight-year-old boy was raped by two twelve-year-olds while all three were in state custody; two caseworkers, who might have been implicated in the deaths of two children, were indicted for falsification of records and criminal negligence; a caseworker was arrested for child abduction for assisting a mother in kidnapping her two children from their father; and a child protection worker shot two fellow employees in a DCFS office. A month later, the press reported that the number of abuse and neglect reports was expected to rise by 30 percent by the end of 1988, over the previous year's record number of 91,715. Unable to keep up with the demands on it, DCFS had a backlog of approximately 900 investigations in Cook County alone (*Chicago Tribune* June 30, 1988).

Legal Players

The chief actors in the Illinois child welfare advocacy bar are the American Civil Liberties Union (ACLU), the OPG, the LAF, the private law firm of Robert Lehrer & Diane Redleaf, Northwestern University's Children and Family Justice Center, and Loyola University's ChildLaw Center.

Benjamin Wolf, who filed the suit against DCFS on June 29, 1988, had been practicing law for less than ten years. He graduated from Boston College Law School in 1979 and had an undergraduate degree from Washington University in St. Louis. After clerking for federal court judge James Moran for a year, he joined the Chicago law firm of Jenner & Block, specializing in litigation and employment law. In 1984 he left Jenner & Block to become the director of the Children's and Institutionalized Persons' Project of the ACLU. Wolf was ideally suited to file such an action against DCFS; his job at the ACLU was to bring suits on behalf of children and people with mental disabilities, primarily in class action litigation, to force the state to fulfill its responsibility to persons in its custody.[25]

Working as cocounsel with Wolf was Michael Brody, a general litigation partner at Schiff Hardin & Waite, specializing in business litigation, patent litigation, and construction litigation.[26] Brody received his B.A. from Wesleyan University in Connecticut and graduated from the University of Chicago Law School in 1979; he clerked in the federal district court for two years for Judge Bernard Decker and joined Schiff Hardin in 1981. He was brought into the DCFS litigation in 1987 when Wolf's office, which had been receiving complaints about DCFS for more than two years, sought help in preparing a suit against the department. Brody immersed himself in the department's operations and concluded that "it was a very sad system" (*American Lawyer*, March 1992).

Wolf and Brody filed their suit in federal court in the Northern District of Illinois; the case was assigned to Judge John Grady, a Ford appointee who took the bench in 1976. Educated at Northwestern University and Northwestern University School of Law, from which he graduated in 1954, Grady had been an associate at Sonnenschein, Berkson, Lautmann, Levinson & Morse from 1954 to 1956. He spent five years in government service as an assistant United States attorney in the Northern District of Illinois and returned to private law practice in 1961. He worked as a sole practitioner in Waukegan, Illinois, until 1976, when he began service on the federal court. Grady was chief judge of the Northern District of Illinois from 1986 to 1990, when he stepped down and became a full-time judge. In 1994 he retired from active duty to assume senior status.

The department hired Susan Getzendanner, a former federal court judge and partner at the prestigious New York–based law firm Skadden, Arps, Slate, Meagher & Flom to represent it; Skadden, Arps had served as outside counsel in previous federal class action lawsuits against DCFS.[27] Getzendanner, who had been appointed to the federal bench by President Jimmy Carter and served from 1980 to 1987, brought in associate Christina Tchen to work on the case under her supervision. Tchen ultimately became the lead attorney for DCFS and, somewhat ironically, ten years later was identified as the attorney who "almost singlehandedly saved the Illinois child welfare system . . ." (*National Law Journal*, November 20, 1998).

Tchen graduated from Radcliffe College and then Northwestern University School of Law in 1984. She clerked for a year in Grady's court and joined Skadden, Arps in 1985; she became a partner in the firm in 1992. Tchen was familiar with some of the issues affecting DCFS, having worked for three years as an analyst for the agency in the Illinois Bureau of the Budget after graduating from college.

Tchen had quickly achieved prominence in Illinois legal circles. Shortly after she began to represent the department, while still an associate at her firm, she successfully argued the state's appeal in the DCFS lawsuit before the Supreme Court. She received recognition as "Person of the Year" by the *Chicago Lawyer's Magazine* and was chosen by the *National Law Journal* as one of the forty leading attorneys under forty in 1995. The article announcing their selection depicted members of this group as "young lawyers who have set themselves apart by the quality of their work and their commitment to both their work and their communities" (*National Law Journal*, November 20, 1995).

Another important figure in the Illinois child welfare system, the Cook County public guardian, Patrick Murphy, was also involved in *B.H.* Although not appearing as counsel in the case, he was a constant presence throughout the litigation. In his official capacity as guardian *ad litem* for the abused and neglected children in the state, Murphy alternated between criticizing plaintiffs' counsels, Wolf and Brody, and vilifying DCFS.

Like most of the Illinois child welfare advocates, Murphy devoted his career to public interest law, representing the poor during most of his career (see McMurray 1995). After graduating from Northwestern University School of Law, he began to work for the state's attorney's office in 1964, quitting after a year to join the Peace Corps in Somalia. When he returned to Chicago, he joined the American Bar Association's National Legal Aid and Defender Association and helped establish public defender offices around the nation. In 1970 he became chief attorney for the Legal Aid Society's juvenile division.

In November 1978, reacting to a scandal in the public guardian's office, Governor Jim Thompson appointed Murphy acting public guardian. At the time this was only a part-time position, with responsibility limited to protecting elderly and mentally disabled state wards. The public guardian's office came under the jurisdiction of the chief judge of the Cook County Circuit Court in 1981. Murphy's title of "acting" was removed in 1981. With a staff of more than a hundred attorneys, the combined office of public guardian and guardian *ad litem* now devotes most of its resources to representing the tens of thousands of abused and neglected children who are the subjects of cases in juvenile court.

Murphy, a controversial figure in the child welfare system, is frequently in the public eye, taking a high-profile position on child welfare issues. A tireless battler for what he perceives as the best interests of the children of Cook County, he receives much media attention, most of it favorable. Attacking both liberals and conservatives, he has criticized the preference for family preservation and advocated placing more abused and neglected children in state-run orphanages. Accused by some of displaying racism himself, he charges his detractors with racism for allowing families of color to escape responsibility for the safety and well-being of their children (McMurray 1995, 122; see also *New York Times*, January 30, 1994; *Chicago Tribune*, December 8, 1997).

Murphy once described DCFS as "a grossly negligent, secretive, self-perpetuating bureaucracy" (*Chicago Tribune*, June 5, 1988). He is seen by some as one of the most ardent defenders of abused and neglected children of Cook County. The executive director of the state's largest residential facility for children said, "Patrick is the watchdog and conscience of the DCFS and all state agencies that work with kids" (McMurray 1995, 121). At the same time Murphy has been depicted by others, such as *B.H.* counsel Wolf, as "another government official who has gone from being part of the solution to being part of the problem" (McMurray 1995, 83).

There is some ambiguity about Murphy's initial role in *B.H.* According to Wolf (1996), Murphy had been asked, and had refused, to cocounsel *B.H.* in the early stages of the litigation. Murphy (1997, 121), however, noted that his office had "initially supported" *B.H.*, but later "vigorously opposed it" because, among other things, he believed it sought the wrong remedies to cure the problems of the system. Whatever the reality, it was clear that while the OPG and the ACLU both represented the abused and neglected children in the state, they were unwilling or unable to work in concert to further their mutual interests.

Finally, the governor of Illinois and members of the General Assembly were also important figures in *B.H.* By shaping DCFS policies, largely through its budgetary allocations, these public officials created the setting for the lawsuit. Indeed, at the press conference at ACLU headquarters when the suit was announced, Wolf placed the blame squarely on the governor, saying, "The collapse of the Department of Children and Family Services is the result of 10 years of cruelty of James Thompson" (*Chicago Tribune*, June 30, 1988).

In the years before *B.H.*, most Illinois public officials tried to distance themselves from the looming child welfare crisis. Anxious to avoid responsibility for the agency's failures, they were also unwilling to allocate sufficient funds to ensure that the agency fulfilled its obligations to the children in state custody. Often intermeshed with partisan state politics (as well as intraparty rivalries), the image of Illinois public officials' fiddling while DCFS burned seems very close to the mark.

Scrutinizing DCFS's performance in the year before *B.H.* was filed will help explain why attorneys Wolf and Brody became committed to the litigation strategy they ultimately decided to pursue in *B.H.*

Although Thompson had declared DCFS a priority of his administration at the end of 1986 (in the Illinois gubernatorial election year), there was a steady barrage of charges against DCFS in 1986, with state legislators demanding reform and an unrepentant department fighting back, seeking to extract increased funding. These exchanges were fully aired in the media, giving the public a front-row seat from which to observe the often vicious infighting between the politicians and the bureaucrats. Also playing a role in the child welfare drama during 1987 were community group leaders and child welfare advocates who continually criticized DCFS and called for reform as well as for an influx of additional resources.

The year began with a *Chicago Tribune* (January 6, 1987) story about an eight-page letter from unnamed DCFS officials and two children's advocates: Ronald Moorman, director of the Illinois Child Care Association, and Jim Lago, executive director of the Illinois Catholic Conference. In the letter to the newly reelected governor, they revealed the startling information that 60 percent of the 32,545 children for whom the department found evidence of abuse or neglect during the fiscal year ending June 30, 1985, had been left in their homes and had not been provided with services. Moreover, of the children who received services, the average amount spent was lower in 1985 than in 1983. The letter called for $15 million in new funds for the department.

Director Johnson, who was not one of the letter's authors, did not comment on it. A man with astute political instincts, his reaction to the letter set the tone for his role during the year: defending his department and simultaneously asking the legislature for more money. Mindful of the likely political consequences, he avoided explicit criticism of his benefactor, the governor who appointed him to office, aiming most of his ire at the state legislature.

Johnson attempted to explain away the 60 percent figure by suggesting that DCFS workers might try to solve some cases informally. "We don't have enough money to service all the cases that come into child abuse and neglect, so you have to set priorities," he said. Notwithstanding his earlier pledge to prioritize DCFS, the governor too had no comment on the letter. His assistant for human resources, Jess McDonald, later to become director of DCFS, responded by simply announcing that "no commitment had been made to expand" the department's budget (*Chicago Tribune*, January 7, 1987).

Although under attack for much of his tenure as director of DCFS, Johnson carefully maintained support in the community, especially among African Americans. In 1986, just before a legislative committee hearing on agency operations, a group of ministers and legislators, many African American, charged that there was a "conspiracy" among private agencies contracting with DCFS, such as the Illinois Catholic Conference, to force Johnson, also an African American, from office. They claimed that the conspiracy to oust Johnson was instigated by groups that were angry because they had not received enough contract money from the state. Johnson, who was credited with the highly popular "One Church/One Child" adoption program, was important to the governor as one of his few African American appointees. He was endorsed by Thompson, whose representative stated, "Gordon Johnson is doing an excellent job. The governor is very pleased with his performance" (*Chicago Tribune*, October 15, 1986). Shortly after this incident, however, it was reported in the *Tribune* (January 7, 1987) that, after Thompson's reelection in 1986, his transition team was seeking candidates to fill the job of director of the agency while retaining Johnson in the position as titular head for political reasons.

Later in 1987, at the start of the legislative session, Curran proposed legislation with a price tag of about $15 million that would have reduced each worker's caseload by about half—to thirty children—by June 30, 1992. Although department guidelines set a limit of forty cases, workers reported having as many as sixty or seventy cases at a time. Democrat Michael Madigan, the Illinois House Speaker, announced his support for the bill, but refrained from committing himself to a specified amount of new funding. Ironically, according to a later report in the *Tribune* (May 22, 1988), DCFS officials opposed the measure, arguing that it would require an additional $28 million to hire a sufficient number of caseworkers and supervisors to lower the caseload.

There was no shortage of studies and proposals for reforming DCFS: at the end of March 1987, a task force appointed by the governor completed a nine-month study and announced that DCFS would need $62 million in increased funding to do its job effectively (*Chicago Tribune*, March 31, 1987). Defending the $62 million as a "legitimate figure," an unidentified member of the task force nevertheless called it "pie in the sky," indicating that it was extremely unlikely that such an amount would be forthcoming. Although before this announcement Thompson had already sought an additional $32 million for DCFS for FY 1988, the increase was contingent on the tenuous prospect of receiving legislative approval for his $1.6 billion tax increase.

In the middle of the budget maneuvering in Springfield, huge increases in the number of cases of abuse and neglect were reported to the Illinois Central Register during FY 1987 (*Chicago Tribune*, June 9, 1987): 90,100 cases were reported, representing a more than 25 percent increase over the year before and the largest percent increase since 1981—with a larger increase in Cook County than in the rest of the state. Despite these figures, which had been released by Johnson in an effort to influence the legislature to approve the budget increases, the governor's office announced that unless the governor's billion-dollar tax increase was approved, there would be a $17.6 million cut in DCFS's budget and a reduction in its staff as well.

At the end of June, the Illinois Senate defeated Curran's caseload reduction bill, passed by the House a month before, on a 29-16 vote; thirty votes had been required for passage (*Chicago Tribune*, June 23, 1987). The session closed with the assembly also rejecting the proposed tax increases. Shortly thereafter, DCFS announced a 4 percent budget cut, accompanied by layoffs of fifty-three employees starting August 31. Forty-four vacant positions remained unfilled (*Chicago Tribune*, August 6, 1987).

At the start of 1988, a *Chicago Tribune* (February 3, 1988) story suggested that the new year would merely be a continuation of the past year. The American Federation of State, County, and Municipal Employees (AFSCME) called a press conference to demand that DCFS hire more caseworkers and assailed it for its "dangerously high caseloads." The president of the AFSCME local claimed that workers had an average caseload of sixty-two cases, with some workers responsible for as many as eighty to one hundred cases. Additionally, union leaders claimed, child abuse and neglect reports had risen to 1,300 in the month of January alone and that child deaths were also up from a year earlier.

In April a *Chicago Tribune* (April 5, 1988) story released details of a study conducted by the Chicago-based National Committee for Prevention of Child Abuse. It showed that Illinois ended the year with the nation's highest increase in child abuse and neglect reports: 91,723 reports (of which 39,006 were indicated) in the fiscal year ending June 30, 1987; this represented an increase of 30 percent over the previous year—the largest such increase in the nation. The report also noted that fifty-five Illinois children died from abuse and neglect in 1987.

In one sense 1987 had followed a familiar pattern: reports of abused and neglected children increased; the press faithfully reported DCFS's failures; children's advocates raged, citing the state's numerous shortcomings; and state officials alternately expressed sympathy with the victims, consternation with DCFS, and a determination that some action needed to be taken. Among other things, however, policymakers proved to be unwilling to impose the necessary tax increases to help bring about systemic changes. As the year progressed, it became clear to many that the system was rapidly deteriorating and the agency with primary responsibility for the care of abused and neglected Illinois children was bankrupt—both financially and administratively.

In the week before *B.H.* was filed, Wolf declared that "DCFS has ceased to function for the most part; the agency has collapsed." Similarly, Lago of the Catholic Conference of Illinois asserted: "The agency is overwhelmed" (*Chicago Tribune*, June 23, 1988).

Realizing that working through the political process was unlikely to accomplish the changes needed to transform the system, the child welfare advocates turned to the federal courts; the result was *B.H.*

4   Accountability

ASSESSING THE LIMITS OF DUTY

B.H. v. Johnson, brought as a federal class action suit, charged the Department of Children and Family Services (DCFS) with violating the due process and equal protection clauses of the Fourteenth Amendment as well as sections of P.L. 96-272, the Illinois Abused and Neglected Child Reporting Act, and the Illinois Juvenile Court Act. The "complaint paint[ed] a bleak and Dickensian picture of life under the auspices of DCFS" (*B.H. v. Johnson* 1989, 1389). This image of more than 10,000 pitiful plaintiffs, the abused and neglected children in state custody, pitted against the nameless and, often, hapless bureaucrats of DCFS, was a public relations nightmare for the agency.

In defending itself against a child welfare reform case, a state typically moves to dismiss the case under Rule 12(b)(6) of the Federal Rules of Civil Procedure, arguing that the plaintiffs had failed to state a claim on which relief could be granted. The court must then determine whether the plaintiffs have stated a cognizable legal claim. True to form, in the battle over the Illinois child welfare system, as with many attempts to achieve system-wide reform through litigation, the plaintiffs' first challenge was to survive the state's motion.[1]

Parties

The suit against DCFS named Gordon Johnson in his official capacity (director) as the defendant; the name of the case would be altered over time to reflect the successive changes in DCFS leadership.[2] Although Johnson headed the agency at the time the suit was filed, he was one of a long progression of DCFS directors, none of whom had distinguished himself in the job in a positive way. In January 1979, Governor Jim Thompson appointed Gregory Coler as director of DCFS to replace the contentious Jerome Miller, who left to become the director of the governor's office of planning. Miller had exhibited hostility toward social work professionals in outside agencies as well as toward those within DCFS and had hastened the departure of many DCFS caseworkers to private agencies (Gittens 1994). Coler, who had been an associate commissioner of New York's Department of Social Services, was reappointed in 1981; in December 1983, Thompson moved him to the Department of Public Aid, replacing him at DCFS with Johnson.

Johnson joined DCFS in 1979 as deputy director of the program operations division; he had served as the deputy commissioner of the Division for Children's Services for the New York State Department of Social Services from 1977 to 1979 and as director of Pennsylvania's Bureau of Child Welfare from 1973 to 1977.

On the other side, there were ten named plaintiffs, all identified by their initials only. They ranged in age from two to seventeen. The lead plaintiff was B.H., a seventeen-year-old boy who had "been lost in the DCFS system for over four years" and had been in "at least ten different placements" after being removed from his home. The other named plaintiffs included C.H., a fifteen-year-old boy who had been in five different placements in the preceding six months; J.E., who, at thirteen, had "been in the custody of DCFS as long as he can remember" and was being "warehoused" in a mental institution and given "strong doses of psychotropic mediation [sic]"; and C.Z., a seventeen-year-old honor student with seven different placements, who was removed from her home after she charged that her stepfather sexually abused her. As a group, the complaint alleged, these children had been neglected by their caseworkers and condemned by the system. A few had even attempted suicide in an effort to escape the tragedy of their lives. When Benjamin Wolf and Michael Brody filed their complaint, there were 15,000 children like these in DCFS custody; more than 4,000 had been away from home for two years or longer, and more than 4,300 had been in at least six placements (*B.H. v. Johnson* 1989, 1389–91)

At the press conference announcing the lawsuit, Wolf cited the three years of investigation that had prompted the decision to seek systemic reform of DCFS: "When we take on problems at an individual DCFS institution," he declared, "they move the problem." Claiming that underfunding was only one source of the department's failures, he accused Johnson of "run[ning] the agency with an eye to public relations. He has never asked for enough money even remotely to address the needs of children in his care, but he responds to page one stories." In response, while conceding that "the department is not providing basic services," Johnson—somewhat inexplicably in light of his concession—defended DCFS, calling it "one of the best agencies in the country." While ostensibly accepting responsibility for the agency's failures ("I am in charge of the department, and the buck stops here," he said), Johnson insisted that blame really belonged elsewhere because he was "not the one who appropriates money to the department or raises money in taxes. That is for the legislature to do" (*Chicago Tribune*, June 30, 1988).

Claims Made

Summarizing the complaint against DCFS, Grady stated that the abused and neglected children in DCFS custody alleged that they were:

> repeatedly subjected by DCFS to serious damage to their mental health, development and physical well-being because DCFS fails to provide them with safe and stable placements, shuffles many children among six or more temporary living arrangements, fails to provide appropriate services to prevent removal from their homes or reunify them with their families, warehouses them in violent and overcrowded shelters and psychiatric hospitals, and places them in foster homes where many of them are victims of the very same kinds of abuse and neglect which prompted them to be removed from their homes. Plaintiffs also alleged that DCFS failed to provide them with adequate medical and mental health care, education, shelter, clothing, and food (*B.H. v. Suter* 1991, 2).

Specifically, the suit indicted Johnson for assigning as many as sixty cases to each caseworker, despite evidence that they should be limited to only twenty cases at a time, and for failing to investigate reports of abuse and neglect in a timely manner. The plaintiffs charged that DCFS had virtually stopped providing services to children and their families, so the children were not being reunited with their families. Additionally, they accused the agency of placing children with any available foster parents without regard to their needs, thereby alienating foster parents who were given responsibility for children they were unable to control. The complaint also stated that Johnson closed his eyes to the cataclysmic state of affairs within the department, attempting to divert attention from its many failures by "calling for legislative initiatives, more severe criminal penalties, punishment of caseworkers or study of the issue" (*B.H. v. Johnson* 1989, 1391–92).

The plaintiffs filed suit under the Civil Rights Act of 1871, 42 U.S.C. § 1983, the post–Civil War statute that provides a federal remedy for the violation of a federal constitutional right by a state actor; more precisely, when used properly, § 1983 opens the doors of the federal courts to individuals who have been deprived of a "right, privilege or immunity secured by the Constitution and laws" of the United States by persons acting "under color" of state law.

Children in state custody, their lawyers claimed, had constitutional rights to "family privacy and autonomy, freedom of association, safe and humane conditions and treatment, freedom from bodily restraint, due process and equal protection of the law" (*B.H. v. Johnson* 1989, 1392–93). Although they cited procedural due process and equal protection violations, the thrust of their claim, that states were required to protect children in foster care from harm, stemmed from their reliance on the substantive due process doctrine.[3] As established in caselaw, the "substantive component [of the due process clause], sometimes referred to as 'substantive due process' . . . bars certain arbitrary government actions 'regardless of the fairness of the procedures used to implement them'" (*Daniels v. Williams* 1986, 337).

The complaint alleged that DCFS had not offered them "minimally adequate shelter, supervision, treatment and services." Moreover, the plaintiffs charged that DCFS had placed them in "conditions that 'shock the conscience' and put their emotional and physical well-being at serious risk" (*B.H. v. Johnson* 1989, 1393). The suit also accused DCFS of violating Titles IV-B and IV-E of P.L. 96-272 by not placing them "in the least restrictive (most family-like) setting" nor exerting "'reasonable efforts' to eliminate the necessity of removing the child from the home or to return a child home" (*B.H. v. Johnson* 1989, 1401). They asked the court for a declaratory judgment against the state and to order the state to submit a reform plan, appoint a master to oversee implementation of the plan, allow class members to sue individually for damages, and award them attorney fees and costs.

In evaluating the merit of the plaintiffs' claims against the state, Grady surveyed the status of child welfare law in the United States, focusing particularly on decisions made in the Seventh Circuit. In deciding whether to grant the defendant's motion to dismiss, he was required to ascertain the extent of the state's responsibility to the abused and neglected children within its borders as well as the degree to which the federal courts could enforce that responsibility.

Constitutional Duty

In defending themselves against child welfare suits, most state and local governments initially assert that the plaintiffs' claims are invalid because the government has no affirmative duty to safeguard the children from harm. The principles governing the state's responsibility to the plaintiffs in child welfare suits can be traced to two Supreme Court cases, *Estelle v. Gamble* (1976) and *Youngberg v. Romeo* (1982), involving prisoners and mentally disabled patients, respectively.

In *Estelle*, prisoner J.W. Gamble sued Texas prison authorities for failing to provide adequate medical care, despite his repeated complaints, for his severe back pain. The lower court dismissed his complaint; on appeal, the Fifth Circuit reversed. Reviewing the protection afforded by the Eighth Amendment's ban on cruel and unusual punishment, the Supreme Court ruled that, because prisoners have no other means to secure medical attention, the Eighth Amendment requires the state to provide care for their serious medical needs.

And, the Court ruled, a prisoner who alleges deliberate indifference to those needs has stated a sufficient constitutional claim against the state. In adopting this standard, the Court emphasized that a prisoner had to show more than negligence by prison officials, that medical malpractice by itself does not violate the Eighth Amendment. After announcing the standard, however, the Supreme Court reversed the appellate court, ruling that even if liberally interpreted, at most Gamble asserted a case of medical malpractice against the prison's medical staff. The case was remanded to determine if Gamble had stated a cause of action against the warden and the director of the Department of Corrections, as opposed to the prison medical personnel.

Estelle v. Gamble (1976) was based on the Eighth Amendment's cruel and unusual punisment clause; *Youngberg v. Romeo* (1982), which was the first Supreme Court case to consider the rights of involuntarily committed mentally disabled individuals, addressed the substantive rights conferred by the due process clause of the Fourteenth Amendment. The mother of thirty-three-year-old Nicholas Romeo, who was described as "profoundly retarded," filed suit against the Pennhurst State School and Hospital in Pennsylvania. She claimed that injuries he received while in the hospital's care—from other patients as well as a result of his own violence—violated his rights under the Eighth and Fourteenth amendments. Applying the Eighth Amendment standard, the trial judge instructed the jury that the defendants could be found liable only if they had been "deliberately indifferent" to Romeo's "serious medical needs." The jury found for the state.

Sitting *en banc,* the appellate court reversed, ruling in part that the Eighth Amendment did not apply to Romeo's situation and that it was more appropriate to apply a Fourteenth Amendment analysis. But the court did not agree on the proper standard for determining the defendant's liability.

On appeal, the Supreme Court had no trouble concurring that involuntarily committed patients have a liberty interest in safety and freedom from bodily restraint. The more troubling issue for the Court was whether the Constitution requires states to provide habilitation, that is, training, for "mentally retarded" persons such as Nicholas Romeo. Although the Court noted that a state is not ordinarily obligated to provide treatment for such individuals, it assumed some degree of responsibility for his safety and welfare when it institutionalized him. To meet that obligation, the Court held that the state had to provide Romeo with the minimal training needed to ensure his welfare. Finally, the Court ruled that the Constitution required state officials to exercise their professional judgment to avoid liability for injuries that occurred to patients.

Another line of cases that affected the state's liability for children in care under § 1983 began with *Martinez v. California* (1980), a case involving the murder of a fifteen-year-old girl by a parolee, Thomas, from a state prison. Here the Supreme Court was asked to decide if the due process clause imposed an obligation on a state to protect the victim from such violence, thereby making the state liable for her death. The Court refused to answer the question, however, affirming the lower court's dismissal of the claim on the narrower ground that the state had not deprived her of her life because the parole board's decision to parole Thomas was too far removed from the victim's death to constitute state action under the Fourteenth Amendment. Because she was killed five months after his release and because the members of the parole board had no special reason to know that she, as distinguished from any other member of the public, was in danger, the Court held that her death was "too remote a consequence of the parole officers' action to hold them responsible" (*Martinez v. California* 1980, 285).

In subsequent cases raising similar issues of state liability, a number of lower courts interpreted *Martinez* for the proposition that once the state is aware of danger to an individual and indicates a willingness to protect him or her, a special relationship is created that imposes a constitutional duty (enforceable through the due process clause) on the state to protect the individual from harm.

Although for the most part the courts declined to extend the state's liability to individuals in the absence of such a special relationship, several circuits relied on the *Martinez* exception to expand state responsibility to abused and neglected children in state custody. The Second Circuit set the national standard for imposing governmental liability for children in custody in *Doe v. New York City Department of Social Services* (1981).[4]

Two-year-old Anna Doe was placed in foster care in 1963; continually in the legal custody of New York City's welfare department, she remained in the same foster home for more than thirteen years. When she was ten, her foster father began physically and sexually abusing her. The Catholic Home Bureau, the private agency that acted for the city in supervising her placement, failed to observe the abuse despite its annual evaluations of the foster home and repeated interviews with the child. More than two years before she was removed from her foster home, however, the bureau had evidence that her foster father lied about her sexual past. Following a psychiatric evaluation, a psychiatrist had concluded she was subject to sexual abuse. Notwithstanding these warning signs, the bureau never reported any suspicions to the city agency assigned to monitor its activities.

Anna was finally taken out of the home after six years of abuse, and only because her foster mother, involved in a bitter divorce with the foster father, admitted that she had witnessed the sexual abuse.

The suit, brought by Anna's parents on their behalf as well as hers, was against the New York City Department of Social Services, the Catholic Home Bureau, and a number of individual defendants. After some of their claims were dismissed and others settled, the bureau was left as the sole defendant on appeal. Though not a government agency, the bureau was properly subject to a suit for a constitutional violation because, among other reasons, as an agency supervising a foster home, it was mandated to report all cases of suspected child abuse to state authorities (*Doe v. New York City Department of Social Services* 1983, 787).

The lawyers for the Doe family claimed that the bureau was liable because it should have uncovered evidence of her abuse and reported it to the proper authorities while removing her from the home. Following the trial, the jury returned a verdict for the defendant Catholic Home Bureau. On appeal, the Does argued that the trial judge's jury instructions were erroneous.

Citing *Estelle v. Gamble* (1976), the appellate court held that government officials could be held liable for violating Anna's constitutionally protected liberty interest by failing "to do what is required"; the court explained that "when individuals are placed in custody or under the care of the government, their governmental custodians are sometimes charged with affirmative duties, the nonfeasance of which may violate the constitution." For such conduct to rise to a constitutional violation, the court indicated, two elements must be shown: 1) the governmental inaction "must have been a substantial factor leading to the denial of a constitutionally protected liberty or property interest" and 2) "the officials in charge of the agency being sued must have displayed a mental state of 'deliberate indifference'" (*Doe v. New York City Department of Social Services* 1981, 141).

Expressing some sympathy for the trial judge's dilemma in determining if the child welfare agency's failure to act to save Anna was caused by "deliberate indifference," the Second Circuit nevertheless held that the jury instructions inappropriately distinguished negligence from indifference. The appellate court warned that unlike a prison situation, deliberate indifference should not be inferred simply from a failure to act because there might be good reason for an agency's unwillingness to intrude into a foster family's life.

Reversing the jury's verdict, the court remanded the case to the lower court, ruling that the outcome should turn on whether bureau officials displayed "deliberate indifference" to Anna's constitutional rights. Back in the lower court, a new jury found for Anna Doe, awarding her $225,000 in damages. The trial judge, however, entered a judgment notwithstanding the verdict for the defendant because he believed "the evidence was so overwhelming that no reasonable jury could have concluded the Bureau acted with deliberate indifference" (*Doe v. New York City Department of Social Services* 1983, 787). The appellate court reversed and again remanded the case to the lower court, with instructions to reinstate the verdict.

Thus the Second Circuit laid a foundation for other circuits to follow in extending the state's responsibility for children who were abused while in foster care. A few years later, in *Jensen v. Conrad* (1984), a consolidated case on appeal from two South Carolina district courts, the Fourth Circuit was also asked to expand the state's duty to protect children from harm. The cases involved the deaths of a seven-month-old baby and a three-year-old toddler; one was killed by the mother and the other by the mother's male friend.

Both complaints, filed in separate courts, had been dismissed. The facts revealed that the respective county child welfare departments, aware that the children were in danger, had taken some preliminary steps to protect them but had stopped short of placing either child in state custody. The lawyers argued that the South Carolina Child Protection Act "created a 'special rela-tionship' between the state and victims of suspected child abuse by imposing an affirmative duty on the state government . . . that gives rise to a right under the fourteenth amendment to affirmative protection by the State" (*Jensen v. Conrad* 1984, 189).

Citing *Estelle v. Gamble* (1976) and *Doe v. New York City Department of Social Services* (1981), the circuit court reviewed the state's responsibility to prison-ers as well as to children in custody. Turning to the more difficult question, the court assessed the duty a state owed to individuals who were not in cus-tody, but with whom it might have a special relationship.

The *Jensen* court first considered whether the state would be liable if a state official had been responsible for placing an individual in danger. This question had arisen in *Bowers v. DeVito* (1982, 618), a Seventh Circuit case in which a parolee killed a woman a year after his early release from a mental health facility. In *Bowers,* the appellate court upheld the lower court's dismissal of the complaint, stressing that a state has no "federal constitutional duty" to protect individuals from being "murdered by criminals or madmen." The court noted, however, that a state might be constitutionally liable if a state actor put individuals in danger and then declined to protect them.

Another Seventh Circuit case that played a role in the *Jensen* court's analy-sis, *Jackson v. City of Joliet* (1983), involved the limits of the state's duty to res-cue. The case arose when a Joliet police officer failed to rescue the occupants of a burning vehicle, merely summoning the fire department for assistance and directing traffic away from it. The district court dismissed the claim against the city. On appeal, the Seventh Circuit affirmed because the officer did not create the danger to the passengers in the car; he merely failed to help. As in

Bowers v. DeVito (1982), said the court, negligent action by a government employee—even an action in which death results—is not within the ambit of the Fourteenth Amendment.

The Fourth Circuit revisited its ruling in *Fox v. Custis* (1983), a case with facts similar to those in *Martinez v. California* (1980). In *Fox*, a prisoner who committed a series of violent crimes after his release from the state penitentiary was not returned to prison despite his parole officers' knowledge of his criminal acts. Although it upheld the lower court's dismissal of the complaint, the Fourth Circuit noted that a right to protection might "arise out of special custodial or other relationships." Unfortunately for the plaintiffs in *Fox*, the appellate court limited special relationships to situations involving state prisoners or mental patients. Without defining the kind of relationship that would be considered "special," the court indicated that on the facts presented in this case, no such relationship existed.

After reviewing the holdings in these cases and reiterating the familiar theme that the state has no constitutional obligation to protect most individuals from the criminal activity of others, the *Jensen* court nevertheless stated that a claim for protection was not necessarily limited to individuals in state custody. Although, as in *Fox*, the court did not specify the factors that create a special relationship and give rise to a right of affirmative protection, it suggested that such relationships were not only limited to prisoners or patients in mental hospitals. They might also develop, the court indicated, in situations where either the victim or the assailant is in custody, where the state explicitly states a desire to offer protection to an individual or group of individuals, or where the state knows about a victim's special circumstances (*Jensen v. Conrad* 1984, 194 n.11).

The issue of whether custody was a requisite for a special relationship also played a key role in *Estate of Bailey v. County of York* (1985). In this case, the court assessed the state's liability in the death of Aleta Bailey, who was fatally beaten by her mother and her mother's paramour. Five-year-old Aleta was removed from her mother's home after being abused by the man with whom her mother lived. The county child welfare agency placed her in a relative's home, warning the mother that she would not be returned to her unless the man moved out of the house. Despite his obvious presence there, however, Aleta was returned home the next night. A month later, she died of injuries inflicted by them. The man was convicted of first-degree murder, her mother of third-degree murder.

Aleta's father filed suit, claiming that the state had a responsibility to protect her from harm. Distinguishing the facts here from those in *Doe v. New York City Department of Social Services* (1981), where Anna Doe had been in the state's custody while she was abused, the district court dismissed the case, reasoning that the state was not liable because Aleta was not in custody, nor was her death caused by persons under the state's supervision or control.

Citing *Jensen v. Conrad* (1984), the Third Circuit reinstated the complaint, thereby diminishing the import of custody as a requisite to liability. Reiterating the steps the agency had taken to save Aleta from harm, beginning with its initial assumption of temporary custody, the appellate court ruled that the state's knowledge of the danger she was in gave rise to a special relationship such that it had an obligation to protect her from that harm, despite the fact that she was not in state custody (*Estate of Bailey v. County of York* 1985, 510–11). The court remanded the case to the lower court to determine the merits of the claim.

Thus by the mid-1980s the circuits had extended the state's umbrella of protection, first offered in *Estelle v. Gamble* (1976) and *Youngberg v. Romeo* (1982), to children in custody, agreeing, for the most part, that states should be constitutionally liable for harm inflicted on children in state care. A conflict soon arose among the circuits, however, when some courts extended the state's protection even further, finding that a "special relationship" existed between the state and children who were not in custody at the time of their injuries or deaths. The vehicle for testing the limits of the state's responsibility for abused and neglected children was the Seventh Circuit case of *DeShaney v. Winnebago County Department of Social Services* (1987).

The dreadful story of Joshua DeShaney, a four-year-old boy living at home under the supervision of the county child welfare agency, began when the boy's parents were divorced in January 1980 just after his first birthday. His father, Randy, was awarded custody and subsequently moved from Wyoming to Wisconsin. Soon remarried, the father quickly divorced again in 1982. During the second divorce proceedings, his wife's lawyer told the police that "Randy had hit the boy, causing marks and is a prime case for child abuse" (*DeShaney v. Winnebago County Department of Social Services* 1987, 299). Winnebago County's social services department (DSS) investigated the charge, but took no action.

In January 1983, Joshua was admitted to a hospital with multiple bruises and abrasions. DSS obtained an emergency order, placing him in the hospital's temporary custody; an ad hoc child protective team, comprising a lawyer, psychologist, pediatrician, police officer, several DSS employees, the county's civil attorney, and hospital officials, was assembled to discuss the case. Based on their discussion, the county attorney determined there was insufficient evidence on which to act. On the team's recommendation, Randy signed an agreement with DSS to enroll Joshua in Head Start and to seek counseling. The juvenile court dismissed the case and returned Joshua to his father's custody.

Shortly thereafter, Joshua was back in the hospital. His DSS caseworker, after talking to the hospital's social worker, again concluded there was insufficient evidence of abuse. For about six months thereafter, the caseworker made almost monthly visits to Joshua's home, dutifully recording evidence of his injuries in her notes. The notes also revealed her skepticism about Randy's version of the cause of Joshua's bruises and scars: "I continue to have a great deal of concern over the welfare of Joshua . . . my primary concern with this family continues to remain the innumerable accidents that Joshua has suffered, which I seriously question as simply a child being accident-prone" (First 1989, 526 n.4).

Hospital records indicate that during 1983 Joshua was seen for bumps, a scratched cornea, a scraped chin, a bloody nose, bruised shoulders, and a swollen ear. Each time the hospital notified DSS, but no action was taken.

On March 8, 1984, two weeks shy of his fifth birthday, Joshua was so severely beaten by his father that he fell into a coma. The day before this tragic episode, his caseworker had been at the home and was told Joshua had inexplicably fainted a few days earlier; she did not ask to see him.

Joshua's mother, Melody, was summoned from Wyoming and on her arrival, his caseworker said to her, "I just knew the phone would ring someday and Joshua would be dead" (*DeShaney v. Winnebago County Department of Social Services* 1987, 300). The hospital confirmed that his injuries, including the destruction of half his brain, had resulted from a series of assaults over the preceding several months. As a result of his father's brutality, Joshua was left permanently brain-damaged and profoundly retarded and will require institutionalization for the rest of his life.

Randy was convicted of child abuse and sentenced to two to four years in prison; he was paroled after serving less than two years of his sentence (Oren 1990; Reidinger 1988).

The federal damage action brought by Joshua and Melody in the Eastern District of Wisconsin alleged that the state's failure to protect Joshua from his father's violence deprived him of his Fourteenth Amendment right to liberty— his right to bodily integrity—without due process of law.[5] In an unpublished opinion, dated June 20, 1986, the lower court granted summary judgment to the state.

Unanimously upholding the lower court on appeal, the Seventh Circuit rejected Joshua's claim for two reasons (*DeShaney v. Winnebago County Department of Social Services* 1987). First, it held that the state's failure to protect Joshua from his father's violence did not deprive him of a constitutional right because neither the state nor the local government has a constitutional obligation to protect a citizen from violence caused by a private individual. Second, although agreeing that the state was clearly negligent in failing to protect him, the court held that the state could only be held liable if its officials caused Joshua's injuries. At most, however, the actions of DSS only slightly increased the probability that he would be harmed. Therefore, because it shared no responsibility in the beatings, the state had not deprived Joshua of his liberty.

The court distinguished Joshua's claim from one raised by children in an earlier Seventh Circuit case, *White v. Rochford* (1979). There, police officers, after arresting their uncle for drag racing, refused to transport the three children to safety (or even to a telephone), leaving them stranded on a busy highway on a cold night. The court held that because the complaint alleged that the police had placed the children in danger, it properly stated a constitutional claim, which must be based on an act of gross negligence or reckless disregard for the person's safety, and should not have been dismissed by the lower court.

Joshua's case was different, said the circuit court. Unlike the police officer in *White*, the DSS caseworkers had played no role in harming Joshua. A Wyoming court, not DSS, gave custody to Randy, and there was no evidence that the agency had acted recklessly in restoring Joshua to Randy's custody after his initial hospital stay. Indeed, to buttress its view that the county had not acted recklessly in returning Joshua to Randy at that time, the court noted that Randy might have filed suit against it if the county had acted to terminate his parental rights. Additionally, said the court, this case is distinct from *Doe v. New York City Department of Social Services* (1981) where Anna Doe had been in the state's custody and placed with foster parents whom agency officials knew or believed might abuse her. DSS bore no responsibility for Joshua's abuse because, unlike Anna, Joshua was in his father's custody, not the state's.

In sum, the appellate court ruled, there was no action or inaction for which the state could be held constitutionally liable. In reaching this conclusion, the court expressly declined to follow the holding in *Estate of Bailey v. County of York* (1985) and the statement in *Jensen v. Conrad* (1984), suggesting that special relationships may exist outside the custodial situation.

In a final paragraph, the court warned about the policy implications of a suit such as Joshua's for state child welfare agencies and the federal courts and for the relationship between the two.

> The concept of special relationship, when extended as far as the Third Circuit extended it in *Estate of Bailey* [*v. County of York* (1985)], makes it more costly for a state to provide protective services to an individual in need, since by doing so it may be buying itself a lawsuit should its efforts fail. Moreover, the idea that by once assuming custody of a child a state becomes obligated by federal law to act with some minimum competence in overseeing the child's

welfare would inject the federal courts into an area in which they have little knowledge or experience: that of child welfare. Balancing the rights of parents with those of their children is a task as difficult as it is delicate, and we doubt that it will be performed better under the eyes of federal courts administering constitutional law than by the state judicial and administrative authorities (*DeShaney v. Winnebago County Department of Social Services* 1987, 304).

A few months after the Seventh Circuit dismissed Joshua's claim, a similar case involving a child who died in his mother's custody was decided by the Eighth Circuit. In *Harpole v. Arkansas Department of Human Services* (1987), the grandmother of two-and-a-half-year-old Gary Demay, who died in his sleep after his mother forgot to turn on his apnea monitor, sued state and county officials. She claimed that despite their knowledge that three of her daughter's children had died as infants while in her care—two of Sudden Infant Death Syndrome and one of apnea—they allowed Gary to remain with his mother.

The determinative fact for the appellate court was that, unlike Anna Doe, little Gary was in his mother's custody, and therefore the state had no affirmative duty to protect him. In dismissing the claim, the court firmly rejected imposing responsibility for the welfare of children on the government, broadly stating, "The State of Arkansas does not have a duty to provide around-the-clock services to every sick child, nor must it monitor family relationships closely enough to prevent children from being injured by the negligence of their parents" (*Harpole v. Arkansas Department of Human Services* 1987, 926). The *Harpole* court approvingly cited *DeShaney v. Winnebago County Department of Social Services* (1987) and specifically rejected the views expressed in *Estate of Bailey v. County of York* (1985) and *Jensen v. Conrad* (1984) that the state's awareness of danger to an individual, particularly a child, creates a special relationship that requires it to provide sufficient protection to ensure the child's safety.

Less than a week after *Harpole* was decided, the Eleventh Circuit ruled on the question of the state's duty to protect children in custody from harm in *Taylor v. Ledbetter* (1987). Kathy Jo Taylor, like Anna Doe, had been placed in foster care when she was two and had been so brutalized by her foster mother that she remained in a coma. Her guardian *ad litem* charged that the county and state officials, who placed her in the home and failed to supervise it properly, displayed deliberate indifference to her rights. The lower court granted the defendant's motion to dismiss; an appellate panel affirmed; and the Eleventh Circuit reconsidered *en banc* to determine, among other issues, whether *Estelle v. Gamble* (1976) applied to a case involving an abused child.

In one of the clearest expositions of the substantive due process doctrine, the circuit analyzed the liberty interest involved here, defining it as the "right to be free from the infliction of unnecessary pain . . . and the fundamental right to physical safety" (*Taylor v. Ledbetter* 1987, 794) and analogizing it to the right found in *Youngberg v. Romeo* (1982).

Because this involved an appeal of the lower court's dismissal of the case, the only issue at hand was the sufficiency of the plaintiff's claim. In considering the state's duty to the child, the Eleventh Circuit adopted the Second Circuit's reasoning in *Doe v. New York City Department of Social Services* (1981). Although it acknowledged that the relationship between prison officials and inmates differed from the one between a state agency and foster parents, it asked whether "a foster child involuntarily placed in a foster home in a situation [is] so similar to that of a prisoner involuntarily placed in an institution that similar rules of law should apply" (*Taylor v. Ledbetter* 1987, 796). Finding the similarity sufficient, it answered its question affirmatively, ruling that a state may be liable if it can be shown that its officials were deliberately indifferent to the child's well-being. Furthermore, the court noted, a number of other circuits imposed affirmative obligations on states to protect citizens with whom they have special relationships; and although the courts have been reluctant to define special relationships precisely, they have agreed that, among other things, they exist in a custodial situation.

The Illinois Cases

Despite the Seventh Circuit's refusal to extend the reach of the due process clause to children who were injured while in their parent's custody in *DeShaney v. Winnebago County Department of Social Services* (1987), there was caselaw within the circuit that indicated that the state could be held responsible for injuries to children who were injured while residing in state institutions.

In *Spence v. Staras* (1974), the mother of mentally disabled Jerome Spence sued the state after he died while a patient in a state hospital. She claimed that the hospital was liable because it should have protected him, knowing that he had been a frequent victim of beatings by fellow patients. In reversing the lower court's dismissal of the complaint, the Seventh Circuit stressed that the state's liability stemmed from its failure to live up to its responsibility to protect him from the known dangers posed by the other patients.

Rubacha v. Coler (1985) was a similar case, involving developmentally disabled Maria Rubacha who was beaten by other children in a DCFS-operated shelter. Although the complaint cited one incident (unlike *Spence*, there was no pattern of abuse), the district court judge denied the state's motion to dismiss. Her claim was sufficient, the court held, because she had alleged that the shelter officials knew of the danger to her and were indifferent to her safety.

It was hardly surprising that the circuit court would find the state liable for injuries to children who were committed to state institutions; it was uncertain, however, that it would also hold the state accountable for harms that befell children in foster care. This issue was addressed in a 1987 case involving Brenda Doe's suit against DCFS and Cook County officials after her daughter, Michelle, was sexually abused while in DCFS custody.

DCFS had assumed custody of Michelle and her brother after removing them from home because of their mother's alcohol abuse. The children were temporarily placed in their aunt's home despite their mother's warnings of violence and substance abuse in the household. At the children's temporary custody hearing, Doe again expressed her concerns and agreed not to contest the custody if DCFS would place her children in a proper foster home. Brenda's fears were realized when Michelle was repeatedly sexually abused in the aunt's home.

After most of the claims were dismissed, the only one remaining was against the DCFS official known as the guardianship administrator. In refusing to dismiss the claim against him, Judge Brian Duff of the Northern District of Illinois pointed out that when the agency placed Michelle in the foster home, it became responsible for supervising her care there. Adopting the Second Circuit's reasoning in *Doe v. New York City Department of Social Services* (1981), he ruled that when child welfare agencies display deliberate indifference to known risks to a child, they may be held accountable for injuries that arise. Like Anna Doe, he noted, Michelle was in the state's custody when she was harmed. And unlike Joshua DeShaney, who the court found would have been hurt regardless of the state's role, Michelle had been taken away from home and placed in harm's way by DCFS (*Doe v. Bobbitt* 1987). Duff approvingly quoted from *Archie v. City of Racine* (1988, 1222–23), another Seventh Circuit decision assessing governmental liability under § 1983, in which the court stated, "If the government hurls a person into a snake pit, it may not disclaim responsibility for his safety."

Although Brenda Doe later dismissed her complaint against the guardian, she subsequently amended it to add other DCFS employees. The lower court rejected the defendants' motion for summary judgment on the grounds of qualified immunity (*Doe v. Bobbitt* 1988). On interlocutory appeal, the Seventh Circuit reversed, ruling that because there was no controlling Supreme Court or Seventh Circuit decision on the issue at the time, there was no clearly established constitutional right, and therefore the defendants were immune from suit. Nor was there clearly established caselaw from another circuit, said the appellate court, because *Doe v. New York City Department of Social Services* (1981) was not clearly on point (*Doe v. Bobbitt* 1989).

A similar case, *Doe v. Lambert* (1988), was brought to court after DCFS, with the approval of the Cook County juvenile court, had placed two children with foster parents who subsequently moved to North Carolina. One of the children, a little girl, died after being tortured by the foster parents, who were tried and eventually convicted of murder. Her brother filed a federal lawsuit against DCFS, claiming the agency had deprived both children of their Fourteenth Amendment rights.

After rejecting most of the state's defenses, the court deliberated whether to dismiss the claim on the basis of *DeShaney v. Winnebago County Department of Social Services* (1987). The court was ultimately persuaded that the facts in the case were more similar to the facts in *Doe v. New York City Department of Social Services* (1981) than in *DeShaney*. In New York, the court pointed out, as in Illinois, the injured child was in the state's custody and it could not deny liability for her death at the hands of her foster parents—even though the injury occurred outside the state.

The Supreme Court Decides

Thus by the late 1980s most circuits were in accord that states were constitutionally obliged to protect children in custody, at least from harm caused by others. And on the thornier question of children injured by their parents, the circuits were split, with at least two holding that the state's constitutional duty to abused children does not rest solely on the existence of a custodial relationship. These courts believed that states may be constitutionally liable when special relationships exist in situations where states know children are in danger and undertake to protect them—even from their own parents.

Granting certiorari in *DeShaney v. Winnebago County Department of Social Services* (1987), the Supreme Court explained that, because of its impact on state and local governments, the intercircuit conflict regarding the state's obligation to protect citizens from harm required resolution. The narrower question presented by the case was the importance of custody in determining the parameters of the state's constitutional obligation to safeguard a child from abuse. At issue was the Court's willingness to broaden the reach of substantive due process by imposing federal liability on the state for taking some, ultimately unsuccessful, affirmative steps to shield a child not in custody from harm.[6]

Speaking for a six-to-three Court, Chief Justice William Rehnquist recited the familiar refrain that the Constitution bars states from depriving individuals of life, liberty, or property, but does not command them to preserve these interests from harm. And with no affirmative duty to act, he said, the state cannot be held liable for its inaction.

After easily disposing of the issue of the state's affirmative obligation to protect members of the general public, the Court next assessed the argument that a "special relationship" existed between Joshua and the state, arising from its knowledge of his father's abuse and its stated intent to protect him from it.

Conceding that states have affirmative duties to citizens in limited situations, Rehnquist explained that the duty does not derive from the state's awareness of danger, nor from offers of assistance to the citizens. Rather, he declared: "In the substantive due process analysis, it is the State's affirmative act of restraining the individual's freedom to act on his own behalf—through incarceration, institutionalization, or other similar restraint of personal liberty—which is the 'deprivation of liberty' triggering the protections of the Due Process Clause, not its failure to act to protect his liberty interests against harms inflicted by other means" (*DeShaney v. Winnebago County Department of Social Services* 1989, 200).

Therefore, said the Court, *Estelle v. Gamble* (1976) and *Youngberg v. Romeo* (1982) do not help Joshua's case. Unlike the plaintiffs in those cases, Joshua was injured not while in the state's custody, but while in his father's. Echoing the lower court, the high court absolved the state from any responsibility for Joshua's injuries. Although state officials may have been aware of the danger he was in, they had played no role in creating it. Moreover, by initially placing Joshua in temporary custody during his first hospital stay while it investigated the abuse charge, DSS had not promised to safeguard him forever; returning him to his father made him no worse off than if he had not been removed from home at all.

The Court was somewhat vague as to when a special relationship that *would* trigger a state's constitutional responsibility to protect a child arises. In a key footnote, Rehnquist explained that *if* the state had, "by the affirmative exercise of its power removed Joshua from free society and placed him in a foster home operated by its agents, we *might* have a situation sufficiently analogous to incarceration or institutionalization to give rise to an affirmative duty to protect" (*DeShaney v. Winnebago County Department of Social Services* 1989, 201 n.9; emphasis added).

Citing *Doe v. New York City Department of Social Services* (1981) and *Taylor v. Ledbetter* (1987), Rehnquist acknowledged that some lower courts had relied on *Estelle v. Gamble* (1976) and *Youngberg v. Romeo* (1982) to hold states liable for injuries to children in foster care. But because it was not faced with a foster care situation in this case, the Court declined to speak "on the validity of this analogy" (*DeShaney v. Winnebago County Department of Social Services* 1989, 201 n. 9).

Possibly, said Rehnquist, the state's efforts to protect Joshua might have created liability under state tort law, but the due process clause does not convert every state tort claim into a federal constitutional violation. Expressing sympathy for Joshua, Rehnquist reiterated that the state was not responsible for hurting him; his father was. And while the people of Wisconsin may want to hold the state liable through its tort law system, the Court was not inclined to do so through an expansive interpretation of the due process clause.

By suggesting that the outcome of the case might have been different had Joshua been in foster care, the Court appeared to accept implicitly the prevailing view among the lower federal courts that children in state custody have a constitutional right to be safe. Therefore, although the Court's ruling was a severe disappointment to child welfare advocates, its constrained interpretation of state accountability had little effect on suits brought to enforce the constitutional rights of children in the child welfare system, most of whom were in foster care (Skoler 1991; Kearse 1996; Ryan 1993).[7]

Statutory Duty

Passage of P.L. 96-272 in 1980 had raised hopes for reforming the nation's child welfare systems. During the 1980s, however, evidence mounted that, despite P.L. 96-272, child welfare agencies were systematically failing large numbers of children by allowing them to languish in foster care rather than returning them home or preparing them for adoption. Lawsuits filed by child welfare advocates across the nation charged states with failing to comply with the federal mandate to protect the abused and neglected children in their care.

Before proceeding to the merits of their claims in these suits, however, the courts were required to rule on the state's initial argument that the plaintiffs were not entitled to judicial relief because Congress had conferred enforcement authority for P.L. 96-272 solely on the Department of Health and Human Services (HHS). Citing a number of Supreme Court cases, the plaintiffs countered that there was ample precedent for judicial enforcement of statutes that do not specify causes of action—either through a judicially implied right of action or through a lawsuit based on § 1983 (see Mezey 1983).

The question was not merely academic; it had enormous implications for the future vitality of P.L. 96-272 as well as § 1983. The hurdle that plaintiffs had to overcome was that, by itself § 1983 does not confer substantive rights; it merely serves as an entree into federal court for individuals whose federal rights have been abridged by agents of the state. Although § 1983 was originally applied to constitutional violations only, in 1980 the Supreme Court affirmed that it provides access to the federal courts for violation of statutory rights as well (*Maine v. Thiboutot* 1980). A year later, however, in *Middlesex County Sewerage Authority v. National Sea Clammers Association* (1981, 19), the

Supreme Court narrowed the scope of § 1983, ruling it does not provide a remedy if the federal law at issue does not create enforceable rights within it or if Congress forecloses a § 1983 remedy in the law. The Court noted that a comprehensive remedy in a statute, such as the withholding of federal funds by a governmental agency, could serve as evidence of congressional intent to foreclose a § 1983 remedy.[8]

In the same year, in *Pennhurst State School and Hospital v. Halderman* (1981), the Court clarified how to interpret the existence of an enforceable right in a statute enacted under congressional spending authority. Spending clause legislation, explained the Court, is in effect a contract between a state and the federal government in which the state accepts funds in exchange for agreeing to provide certain rights or guarantees to the beneficiaries of the act. Following principles of contract law, the Court requires plaintiffs to show that the language of the statute is sufficiently "clear" and "unambiguous" that the state understands the terms of the "contract"; that is, the state knows what is required of it under the act. To this end, a spending clause statute must speak in mandatory language in creating the conditions to which the state must conform in exchange for federal funding; a statute that merely expresses congressional encouragement of desired behavior is not enforceable under § 1983.

Another pathway for a plaintiff to enforce a federal statute that does not expressly allow it is to ask the court to imply the remedy. Under guidelines developed by the Supreme Court in *Cort v. Ash* (1975), a federal court may imply a remedy in a statute that does not contain one: 1) if the plaintiff is a member of the class for whose "especial benefit" the statute was enacted; 2) if there is evidence of legislative intent, either explicit or implicit, to create such a remedy; 3) if the remedy is consistent with the statutory scheme; and 4) if the cause of action is not one traditionally relegated to state law. In the years following *Cort*, however, because of the Court's reluctance to infringe on state autonomy, it has become increasingly unwilling to allow the federal courts to imply private causes of action in federal statutes (Smith 1992).

Thus the crucial inquiry for the courts in interpreting statutes without specified rights of action, such as P.L. 96-272, was whether Congress had intended to allow individuals to seek judicial enforcement. An extensive body of P.L. 96-272 caselaw began to develop in the lower federal courts during the 1980s, most cases revolving around the sixteen "state plan requirements" of Title IV-E. The initial question for the courts was whether plaintiffs had a right to ask the courts for relief when child welfare agencies did not conform to the requirements of the act.

The leading case, a Massachusetts class action, served as a model for the other circuits in later P.L. 96-272 suits. Although it was complicated by the changes in federal law (Title IV-E replacing Title IV-A), the ruling in *Lynch v. King* (1982) set the standard for determining the existence of a private right of action in P.L. 96-272.

The case was initially brought by James Lynch and Danielle Blackwell and their mother and grandmother against the Massachusetts agency that administered the family foster home care program and child welfare services generally. In addition to due process claims, the plaintiffs charged the state with violating various sections of the Social Security Act, including Titles IV-B and IV-E. After the district court certified the class of children and their natural and foster families, the plaintiffs asked for a preliminary injunction requiring the state to adhere to the case plan and review provisions of Title IV-E.

Ruling on the state's motion to dismiss, in a memorandum and order dated June 9, 1981, Judge Robert Keaton of the District Court of Massachusetts discussed the use of § 1983 to enforce provisions of the Social Security Act. Keaton noted that although *Rosado v. Wyman* (1970) held that individuals may enforce sections of the Social Security Act in federal court through a § 1983 cause of action, *Pennhurst State School and Hospital v. Halderman* (1981) subsequently narrowed its application to federal statutes in which the plaintiff's interest in the state's compliance is a "right" within the meaning of § 1983.

Because the Social Security Act requires states that participate in the foster care program to provide services to persons such as plaintiffs, Keaton found that "a long line of precedent supports plaintiffs' right, as the beneficiaries of these services, to secure state compliance with the Social Security Act" (*Lynch v. King* 1981, 15; see also *Lynch v. King* 1982). Additionally, in a subsequent opinion on the plaintiffs' motion for preliminary relief, Keaton noted that "Congress . . . created requirements it thought essential to protect the welfare of foster children. The Commonwealth voluntarily undertook to fulfill those requirements as a condition of receiving federal money" (*Lynch v. King* 1982, 339).

In determining whether Congress had intended to foreclose a § 1983 remedy in the Social Security Act, the court again turned to *Rosado v. Wyman* (1970) for guidance. Rejecting the state's argument that the statutory remedy of withholding funds was exclusive, the court believed it unlikely that Congress had intended to preclude judicial review of state welfare provisions, thereby shutting the doors of the federal courts to the individuals who benefited from the statute's welfare aims.

After concluding that the statute confers enforceable rights on these plaintiffs, the judge set forth the scope of their rights in the preliminary injunction. To receive federal funds under Title IV-E, the state must provide a case plan for each child within sixty days after the child is taken into care and must review the plan at least once every six months to ensure that it remains appropriate to the child's needs.

Additionally, because a large number of caseworkers had testified that their caseload prevents them from providing adequate plans or reviews in a timely manner, much less allowing them to deliver the appropriate services to families to permit children to return home, Keaton ordered the state to assign a caseworker within twenty-four hours of a child's being taken into care and to restrict workloads to an average of twenty cases for each caseworker.

The case displayed some procedural oddities. The complaint, which had been filed before P.L. 96-272 was enacted, charged the state with violating Title IV-A of the Social Security Act. Because the foster care provisions of IV-A were replaced by Title IV-E on October 1, 1982, the court determined that if the state had not complied with the case plan and review requirements of IV-A, it would certainly not be in compliance with the more stringent and detailed IV-E. Ironically, therefore, the court fashioned relief under IV-E for violations of IV-A.

Although the court did not determine whether IV-A required the state to provide the services in the plans, it held that since IV-E—which does require the delivery of services—would not be effective until October 1, 1983, the state's failure to provide services to children and their families had not been a violation thus far. The court stated, however, that once Title IV-E was in effect, the state would be required to provide reunification services to receive federal funding under the statute (*Lynch v. King* 1982).

On appeal the First Circuit discussed the enforceability of Title IV-E in a § 1983 action, particularly whether Congress had intended the statutory remedy of withholding federal funds to be exclusive. Citing numerous cases in which the Supreme Court had allowed private individuals to use § 1983 to enforce similar provisions of the Social Security Act, the circuit court required the state to make a "strong showing" that a § 1983 remedy was not available to enforce P.L. 96-272 (*Lynch v. Dukakis* 1983, 511). Unpersuaded by the state's efforts to make this showing, and finding that the district court judge had not abused his discretion in issuing the injunction, the appellate court affirmed the lower court.

Despite the First Circuit's rather expansive ruling on the right to judicial enforcement of P.L. 96-272 in *Lynch*, two subsequent Sixth Circuit cases raised questions about the extent to which the courts would allow individual plaintiffs to assert rights under P.L. 96-272.

In *Lesher v. Lavrich* (1984), Alice and Charles Lesher sued state and county officials after the county welfare department obtained emergency custody of their two daughters and removed them from home. The children, Alice's daughters from a previous marriage, were declared abused and dependent. In addition to constitutional claims, the Leshers' suit asserted that the child welfare agency violated P.L. 96-272 by not providing services to the family before removing the children.

The district court dismissed the claim, ruling that the provision of P.L. 96-272 requiring preventive services "is merely a funding statute enacted to encourage State child welfare services and does not confer upon individuals a federal right to preventive services or reunification plans when there is a child abuse problem within the family unit"(*Lesher v. Lavrich* 1984, 81).

On appeal, the Sixth Circuit upheld the lower court, but disagreed with its blanket denial of a right to sue to enforce P.L. 96-272. The appellate court acknowledged that the First Circuit had allowed the class of foster children to sue under § 1983 to force the state to comply with certain conditions for receiving federal funds. Unlike the plaintiffs in *Lynch,* the appellate court held, the Leshers had not asked for an injunction ordering the state to revise its procedures; rather they sought to collect money damages and to reverse the state court's determination of child abuse. "Whatever rights [P.L. 96-272] might confer on parents," concluded the court, the rights sought by these plaintiffs were not contemplated within it (*Lesher v. Lavrich* 1986, 197).

Similarly, in *Scrivner v. Andrews* (1987), the Sixth Circuit also considered the claim that P.L. 96-272 required the state to provide meaningful visitation to parents of children in foster care. Leslie Scrivner and her daughter Ashley sued the three social workers employed by the Kentucky Cabinet for Human Services who had placed eight-month Ashley in a foster home. Although not questioning the placement, Leslie challenged the visitation schedule, and, citing § 1983, she maintained that she and her daughter were deprived of "their joint federal right to 'meaningful visitation'" under P.L. 96-272 (*Scrivner v. Andrews,* 1987, 262).

In an unreported opinion, the Kentucky lower court dismissed the complaint. The question, said the circuit court on appeal, was whether P.L. 96-272 created a federal right to visitation similar to the right to a case plan and review system established in *Lynch v. Dukakis* (1983). Concluding that the act contains no such right, thereby invalidating the § 1983 claim, the appellate court affirmed the lower court's judgment.

Meanwhile, reflecting the dissemination of child welfare litigation to other circuits, another case was percolating in the Fourth Circuit. Shortly after *Lynch v. Dukakis* (1983) was decided, attorneys at the Maryland Legal Aid Bureau and the Children's Defense Fund filed a federal lawsuit on behalf of a class of approximately 2,800 foster care children who were, or would be, in the custody of the Baltimore City Department of Social Services. They claimed that the city's violation of the Constitution and P.L. 96-272 led to the children's physical and sexual abuse and medical neglect. In addition to injunctive relief, some of the named plaintiffs sought money damages.

Rapidly dismissing the city's argument that plaintiffs were totally barred from enforcing P.L. 96-272 in a § 1983 suit, Judge Joseph Howard determined that the plaintiffs met the criteria for a preliminary injunction and ordered the agency to submit a plan in which it outlined its procedures. The plan must, he said, specify that the agency would review a foster home following a report of maltreatment; monitor each child in foster care on a monthly basis— weekly, following a report of injury; ensure that children receive adequate medical care; and refer all complaints of maltreated foster children to the juvenile court and the child's attorney within five days (*L.J. v. Massinga* 1987).

In reviewing the preliminary injunction, the Fourth Circuit initially considered whether the plaintiffs had a right to sue to enforce the Social Security Act under § 1983. Pointing out that foster care children had been entitled to protection under Title IV-A since 1961, the court noted that the state's statutory duty to ensure that every "child in foster care receives 'proper care'" was clarified and expanded in Titles IV-B and IV-E.

Explaining the parameters of the state's duty under the act, the appellate court first emphasized that each state must have a plan that provides for a responsible agency to maintain standards in foster homes. The court next pointed to the state's obligation to create a case plan and review system for each child in care as a condition of receiving federal funds. Finally, it noted that each state plan must specify that an agency report unsuitable conditions in foster homes to appropriate courts or law enforcement authorities. "Taken together," the court concluded, "we think that these statutory provisions spell out a standard of conduct, and as a corollary rights in plaintiffs. . . . It is true that the statutes are largely statutes relating to appropriations, but . . . they are privately enforceable under 42 U.S.C. § 1983" (*L.J. v. Massinga* 1988a, 123). After the appellate court upheld the preliminary injunction, the parties entered into settlement negotiations and reached an agreement that was submitted to the district court two and a half months before the trial was scheduled to begin. According to the court, "The consent decree that embodies the settlement retains substantially those measures ordered by the court as preliminary injunctive relief" (*L.J. v. Massinga* 1988b, 511).

Children in foster care also attempted to bring a § 1983 action in federal court to enforce P.L. 96-272 in the Fifth Circuit. In 1986 lawyers for the New York Civil Liberties Union and the New Orleans Legal Assistance Corporation filed a § 1983 suit on behalf of children in foster care against Governor Edwin

Edwards and other Louisiana state officials for money damages and injunctive relief. Fifteen children were named as plaintiffs, their lawyers seeking to certify a class of 6,000. The children charged that the state's failure to implement the case plan and review procedure, to supervise the foster homes, and to adhere to the "reasonable efforts" provision violated P.L. 96-272.

The district court denied their motion for class certification (*Del A. v. Roemer* 1990), but in an attempt to avoid court-ordered system-wide relief, the state agreed to extend the remedies resulting from the lawsuit to all children in foster care and those at risk of being placed in foster care (*Del A. v. Roemer* 1991).

The defendants countered with a defense of qualified immunity. But because the qualified immunity doctrine is designed to shield government officials from liability in the performance of discretionary acts, that defense is only available to officials who have "not violate[d] clearly established statutory or constitutional rights of which a reasonable person would have known" (*Harlow v. Fitzgerald* 1982, 818). Citing the prevailing caselaw, Judge Morey Sear of the District Court for the Eastern District of Louisiana held that the children had enforceable rights under P.L. 96-272 to a case plan and review procedure and "reasonable efforts" as well as a constitutional right to safety while in foster care (*Del A. v. Edwards* 1988a).

The defendants appealed, claiming that they were entitled to immunity from damages because P.L. 96-272 did not create enforceable rights and, if it did, they had not been clearly established at the time of the suit. A Fifth Circuit panel upheld the lower court, holding that many of the requirements of the act were "obviously clearly established in a particularized sense" so that "any reasonable person would know, for example, when to develop a plan, when to review the plan, when to hold a hearing, what elements to include in the case plans, and that an information system must be developed" (*Del A. v. Edwards* 1988b, 1153–54).

The panel's decision was later vacated following a rehearing *en banc* (*Del A. v. Edwards* 1988c). The state withdrew its appeal after the plaintiffs voluntarily dismissed their claim for damages (*Del. A. v. Edwards* 1989). The case proceeded very slowly; trial began in 1989, was adjourned for more than a year to allow settlement talks to proceed, and finally resumed in 1990.

By 1988, when *B.H.* was filed, therefore, most courts that had considered the question believed that children in care were entitled to bring § 1983 actions against state and local governments when child welfare agencies failed to comply with the case plan and review requirements of P.L. 96-272. Although the Sixth Circuit had not squarely addressed this issue, it implied that it was inclined to follow the majority view in such cases.

Thus, after more than a decade of child welfare litigation, when Wolf and Brody initiated their suit against DCFS, a consensus had emerged among the circuits that states were bound by the due process clause of the Fourteenth Amendment to protect children in custody. Most courts concurred that child welfare agencies receiving federal funds were, at a minimum, required to adhere to the case plan and review provisions of P.L. 96-272, and that children in care, the beneficiaries of the act, could sue agencies for failing to do so.

By firmly establishing the federal court's involvement in child welfare policymaking, these decisions paved the way for Grady's ruling in *B.H.*

5 Adjudication

DEVISING A BLUEPRINT FOR SYSTEMIC REFORM

The adjudication process in systemic reform cases is typically characterized by the court's attempts to persuade the parties, with varying degrees of insistence, to reach a negotiated settlement with which they can both live. Before engaging in settlement talks, however, most defendants attempt to avoid legal liability by moving to dismiss the plaintiffs' claims. The court's preliminary ruling on the state's motion to dismiss is often the most crucial factor in determining the outcome of the case.

Preliminary Rulings

The *B.H.* plaintiffs scored their first major victory when, on February 22, 1989, pursuant to Rule 23 of the Federal Rules of Civil Procedure, Grady certified a class of plaintiffs "consisting of all persons who are or will be in the custody of the Illinois Department of Children and Family Services and who have been or will be placed somewhere other than with their parents" (*B.H. v. Johnson* 1989, 1389). Then on May 30, 1989, almost a year after the suit was filed, the court ruled on the state's motion to dismiss. Carefully adhering to existing caselaw, Grady grounded his decision in constitutional and statutory principles that included consideration of the role of the federal courts in the state policymaking process.

In fulfilling its adjudicatory function in child welfare reform litigation, a court must determine whether the state has a constitutional obligation to the plaintiffs. After noting that the Fourteenth Amendment ordinarily does not impose a duty on states to protect citizens, Grady observed that there were exceptions to this general rule. He began his analysis by considering the effect of *Estelle v. Gamble* (1976) and *Youngberg v. Romeo* (1982) on the reach of the substantive due process doctrine.[1] In these cases, he pointed out, the high court relied on a more expansive reading of the substantive due process clause to require the state to guarantee the safety of involuntarily committed individuals. Citing the Seventh Circuit decision in *Spence v. Staras* (1974) and the rulings in two Northern District of Illinois cases, *Rubacha v. Coler* (1985) and *Doe v. Lambert* (1988), Grady rejected the state's blanket disavowal of responsibility for protecting its citizens. Finally, he extrapolated from the Supreme Court's opinion in *DeShaney v. Winnebago County Department of Social Services* (1989) and *White v. Rochford* (1979) to conclude that the substantive due process clause imposes a duty on states to keep children in custody safe from physical and emotional harm. Grady also drew on *Mendez v. Rutherford* (1986), another case in the Northern District of Illinois, to support this conclusion. In *Mendez,* a three-year-old girl, claiming that she was emotionally traumatized, brought a § 1983 action against the city of Chicago because police officers arrested and beat her father in front of her. Denying the state's motion to dismiss, Judge Marvin Aspen also cited *White v. Rochford* (1979) to indicate that due process protection applies to a plaintiff's physical and mental well-being.

Reminding the court that the issue of substantive due process clause protection for children in custody had been left open by the high court in *DeShaney,* the state argued that its liability for children in foster care had not been determined and that any responsibility it might have for these children devolved onto private individuals—foster parents and private agency workers. To the court, however, it was not really an open question. Grady firmly held "that a child has a § 1983 action against the state for injuries suffered while in foster care where the state is deliberately indifferent to the likelihood that a foster home is unsafe, yet places a child there or allows the child to remain there" (*B.H. v. Johnson* 1989, 1396). Grady cited *Taylor v. Ledbetter* (1987) and *Doe v. New York City Department of Social Services* (1981) for support as well as the two lower court opinions in his own district, *Doe v. Bobbitt* (1987) and *Doe v. Lambert* (1988). In cases such as these, he said, involving injuries to children in foster care, the courts allowed the children to claim that they were deprived of their substantive due process rights.

Concluding, Grady upheld the plaintiffs' right to be in court, saying that they "have stated a substantive due process claim to be free from unreasonable and unnecessary intrusions upon their physical and emotional well-being, while directly or indirectly [in foster care or other nonstate institutions] in state custody, and to be provided by the state with adequate food, shelter, clothing, and medical care and minimally adequate training to secure these basic constitutional rights" (*B.H. v. Johnson* 1989, 1396).

The plaintiffs also asserted that their right to family autonomy and privacy required the state to provide for family reunification, parental and sibling visits, placement in the least restrictive environment, and an adequate number of caseworkers. The court rejected their claims, interpreting these Fourteenth Amendment guarantees as a right to be left alone rather than as an entitlement. Citing *Black v. Beame* (1976), Grady held the state has no obligation "to make efforts to reunify families that have been separated by legitimate state intervention" (*B.H. v. Johnson* 1989, 1397).

After ruling that the plaintiffs' allegations satisfied the requirements of a § 1983 suit against a state official, the court turned to the state's final parry against an expansive substantive due process interpretation.[2] The state argued that principles of federalism required federal courts to allow states exclusive jurisdiction over the allocation of resources. The court responded, however, by affirming that it must adjudicate cases in which the plaintiffs allege their constitutional rights have been denied, adding that "concern with the availability of resources is rarely part of the constitutional decisionmaking process where a recognized constitutional right is violated" (*B.H. v. Johnson* 1989, 1398).[3]

In appraising the plaintiffs' statutory claims (after rejecting their equal protection and procedural due process arguments), the court considered whether § 1983 provided a remedy for a violation of P.L. 96-272. Citing *Maine v. Thibotout* (1980), *Pennhurst State School & Hospital v. Halderman* (1981), and *Middlesex County Sewerage Authority v. National Sea Clammers Association* (1981), Grady noted that the plaintiffs' first task was to establish that Titles IV-B and IV-E contained enforceable rights that Congress intended to create as a condition of receiving federal funds.

The plaintiffs contended that by authorizing federal funding to states to provide services to abused and neglected children and their families, Title IV-B imposed duties on the states and rights in the plaintiffs. Grady disagreed, believing instead that "Congress intended Title IV-B to be an expression of goals and guiding principles rather than an enactment that creates enforceable federal rights" (*B.H. v. Johnson* 1989, 1401).

Grady also remained skeptical that Congress had intended to create enforceable rights to the "least restrictive setting" and "reasonable efforts" provisions of Title IV-E. Plaintiffs could not rely on *Joseph and Josephine A. v. New Mexico Department of Human Services* (1982), *Lynch v. Dukakis* (1983), and *L.J. v. Massinga* (1988a), he said, because those cases had only recognized a right for children to enforce Title IV-E's case plan and review system. Moreover, he held, the statute did not confer a right on siblings to be placed together; nor, he said, citing *Scrivner v. Andrews* (1987), did it confer a right to meaningful visitation between parent and child. Grady agreed, however, that P.L. 96-272 imposed an affirmative obligation on states and a corollary right in plaintiffs to maintain individualized case plans and conduct periodic reviews of the children in their care.

Even if children in care have a right to case plans and reviews, argued the state, Congress precluded judicial enforcement of these rights by authorizing the Department of Health and Human Services (HHS) to cut federal funds if a state plan does not comply with the act or if a state substantially fails to comply with its plan. The issue for the court to resolve, of course, was whether this administrative remedy was intended to be exclusive; the burden is on the state to prove Congress intended to preclude private enforcement of the law.

The state cited several cases in which the Supreme Court held that statutory enforcement provisions evidenced congressional intent against private judicial enforcement under § 1983. The court reviewed the statutes in those cases and concluded that, unlike them, P.L. 96-272 "does not contain a comprehensive system of procedures and guarantees" that indicates Congress intended those as exclusive remedies (*B.H. v. Johnson* 1989, 1403). Moreover, the judge said, every other circuit that considered this issue concluded that plaintiffs such as these may enforce the case plan and review provisions of P.L. 96-272 through § 1983. The court also quickly disposed of the defendant's attempts to rely on *Scrivner v. Andrews* (1987) and *Harpole v. Arkansas Department of Human Services* (1987). In the first case, the plaintiff tried to enforce a right of meaningful visitation, not the case plan and review requirement; in the second case, the action was dismissed because the child was not in state custody at the time of his death.

Finally, Grady addressed the existence of an implied right of action in P.L. 96-272. Citing *Cort v. Ash* (1975), he noted that, as in the § 1983 analysis, the central question was whether Congress intended to create a private remedy within the statute. Because he found that these plaintiffs have a right to sue under § 1983 to enforce the case plan and review provision, he held that they also have an implied cause of action under the statute.

By refusing to dismiss the case, the court held the Department of Children and Family Services (DCFS) at least partially accountable for the safety and well-being of the thousands of Illinois children in foster care. And in concluding that the state has a constitutional and statutory duty to the abused and neglected children in its custody, Grady committed himself to long-standing oversight of the Illinois child welfare system. In doing so, the court moved into virtually uncharted territory that would ultimately involve it in one of the nation's most far-reaching attempts to reform a child welfare agency.

Conditions of Settlement

A negotiated settlement ending in a consent decree offers advantages to all parties in a lawsuit (see Harriman and Straussman 1983; Anderson 1986; Stein 1987; Welling and Jones 1988). The respondents in this study believed that the parties agreed to settle *B.H.* because each side finally saw the wisdom of ending the protracted litigation.

Regardless of the merits of the case, a settlement allows each side to avoid "legal fees, the expenses of discovery, the expenses of waiting, and the uncertainty of putting the matter to a court" (Easterbrook 1987, 19). Additionally, litigants often find a decree preferable because they believe they are in a better position than a judge to determine what their needs are and how to satisfy them (Anderson 1983). Thus the willingness to enter into settlement negotiations often signifies an understanding between the parties, usually tacit, that a consent decree will embody a more satisfactory outcome than either could achieve at trial. And a settlement agreement, negotiated in good faith, may also facilitate the reform effort by creating an atmosphere of reduced conflict and adversarialness between the parties.

For the plaintiffs, one incentive to settle stems from the hope that the defendant might commit itself to more than the minimal constitutional requirements (Welling and Jones 1988; Harriman and Straussman 1983). An agency has even more reason to settle such a case, however; at a minimum, a settlement avoids an embarrassing trial in which the agency's flaws are examined in microscopic detail. A settlement may also help an agency preserve control over its day-to-day operations and is likely to reflect a more realistic understanding of the agency's concerns. Given these considerations, it is not surprising that almost two decades ago, Lloyd Anderson (1983, 582) predicted that "consent decrees promise to become one of the hallmarks of public law litigation."

Following the practice among judges, Grady (1996a) encouraged the parties to enter into negotiations, believing that they would be able to settle their differences and reach agreement without having to go to trial, a trial that he thought would be lengthy and complex. Looking back some time later, he indicated that he saw "no substantial disagreement [between the parties] over plaintiffs' entitlement to the general kind of relief they sought. What separated the parties was a variety of disagreements over the best ways to provide the necessary services" (*B.H. v. Ryder* 1994a, 1286). A respondent on the DCFS side agreed, saying that the consent decrees entered into by DCFS merely codified "the best practice policy in each area"; there was "no dispute about what had to be done."

Nevertheless, despite this understanding between the two sides and the numerous advantages of settling a structural reform lawsuit, when *B.H.* was filed, according to Getzendanner, "the agency resisted the idea of settling" (*American Lawyer*, March 1992). For although a settlement may be the best alternative from a policy perspective, an agency's willingness to enter into a negotiated agreement is sometimes hampered by the leadership's fear that a settlement might create an image of being too accommodating to the plaintiffs and surrendering too easily to their demands. Initially at least, according to most respondents, the *B.H.* settlement was held hostage to such political considerations.

The changeover of DCFS directors was a key factor in the eventual settlement. Anticipating Jim Thompson's departure from the governor's office, Gordon Johnson, like a number of state agency directors, resigned in July 1990—a few months before the gubernatorial election in November—to become the executive director of the Hull House Association. When asked about the settlement talks between DCFS and the plaintiffs' attorneys, a number of respondents confirmed that Johnson was primarily responsible for the state's initial refusal to settle and that a realistic chance of settlement arose only after he left office. As one of the attorneys involved in the case put it, "Johnson's DCFS was not interested in settling." One respondent stated even more forcefully: "Gordon Johnson insisted on litigating." The respondent speculated that "settling means admitting you were wrong and maybe Johnson who was there for so long, did not want that." Whatever his reason, on his resignation, "the state's attitude [toward settlement] changed drastically" (*American Lawyer,* March 1992).

Johnson was replaced by Jess McDonald, Thompson's special assistant for human services, who had worked for Thompson since 1983. McDonald served as acting director of DCFS from July 21, 1990, to January 1, 1991, the last months of Thompson's fourteen-year tenure in office. He had begun his career with DCFS as a caseworker in 1970 and served as executive deputy director from July 1975 to July 1976.

McDonald, realizing the benefits of a negotiated agreement, did not share his predecessor's opposition to consent decrees. While serving as Thompson's liaison before becoming head of DCFS, McDonald had announced that the governor sought "a global solution" for the litigation against DCFS. Not surprisingly, during McDonald's brief stint as director, according to a number of respondents, he took the lead in trying to settle the lawsuits, including *B.H.,* that were pending against the agency.

The advantages of settlement are heightened when both sides are fully engaged in fashioning the remedy for the charges made against the agency. DCFS was involved in selecting the expert witnesses, and, as all respondents agreed, agency officials and their attorneys actively participated in the negotiations. The views of the department were, as one respondent put it, "well-considered." According to Laurene Heybach (1996) of the Legal Assistance Foundation of Chicago (LAF), agency officials played "significant roles" in crafting the *B.H.* agreement; others described the agency as "totally" and "absolutely" involved in the process. Summarizing these views, a respondent noted that *B.H.* was "a product of the parties'" efforts, with "both sides tr[ying] to be realistic in their demands."

The talks continued under Thompson's successor, fellow Republican Jim Edgar, who seemed more inclined to settle than to engage in protracted negotiations (Schuerman, Rzepnicki, and Littell 1994). Shortly after the parties reached an agreement, Edgar signed it.

From the day Wolf and Brody filed *B.H.* on June 29, 1988, to December 20, 1991 (when the decree was approved), a number of significant developments in child welfare law were occurring throughout the nation: class action litigation for systemic reform of child welfare agencies was becoming more commonplace; more and more federal judges were recognizing that states owed duties to children in foster care and were exhorting government agencies to enact the necessary reforms. Obviously the increasing emphasis on litigation as an impetus for reform of child welfare agencies augmented the role of the federal courts in child welfare policymaking.

Aristotle P.

B.H. was the first of four child welfare cases decided in the Northern District of Illinois within one year. In the months that followed Grady's ruling on the state's motion to dismiss, three other Illinois lower federal courts determined that the state was obligated to keep children in custody safe from harm. As one respondent put it, "The agency [DCFS] was getting hammered in court." Courts outside Illinois reached similar conclusions about the state's responsibility to abused and neglected children.

A few months after *B.H.* was filed, on September 15, 1988, the Cook County Public Guardian (OPG) sued DCFS in federal court on behalf of the plaintiff, Aristotle P., and a class of children who were wards of the court under the guardianship of DCFS. Ranging in age from one to eighteen, the children had been separated from their siblings when they were placed in care and were unable to visit them regularly. Charging the agency with violating P.L. 96-272 as well as several federal constitutional provisions, the OPG sought to compel DCFS to allow children in foster care to have reasonable opportunities to visit their siblings.

Ruling on the state's motion to dismiss on September 6, 1989, Judge Ann Williams held that children in state custody have a constitutionally protected right to associate with their siblings and a substantive due process right to safety and well-being. However, although she agreed that certain parts of P.L. 96-272—like the case plan and review provision—were judicially enforceable in a § 1983 action, she ruled that the specific rights claimed by the plaintiffs, "such as the right to be placed 'in the least restrictive, most family like setting' and the right to have DCFS make 'reasonable efforts to reunify families,' are amorphous and not subject to precise definition." Additionally, she pointed out the "right to meaningful sibling visitation" was nowhere to be found in the statute (*Aristotle P. v. Johnson* 1989, 1012). Accordingly, Williams dismissed the plaintiffs' statutory claim. Despite Williams's ruling in its favor, the state entered into settlement talks with the plaintiffs; several years later, settlement was reached.[4]

Artist M.

On December 14, 1988, Patrick Murphy's office, the OPG, filed another class action suit against DCFS on behalf of the plaintiff Artist M. and children in Cook County "who are or will be in the custody [of DCFS] or in a home under DCFS supervision . . . and who are now or will be without a DCFS caseworker for a significant period of time" (*Artist M. v. Johnson* 1989, 691).[5] The OPG charged that DCFS's failure to assign a caseworker for as long as four to six weeks after a temporary custody or protective order and/or to reassign the case to a replacement worker when necessary violated the "reasonable efforts" provision of P.L. 96-272.

On November 21, 1989, Judge Milton Shadur ruled on the state's motion to dismiss. Relying on the principles first articulated by the Supreme Court in *Cort v. Ash* (1975), he pointed out that an "implied right" analysis requires the plaintiffs to show that Congress intended to create a private remedy. Shadur noted that "other courts have found support in the AAA's [P.L. 96-272] language and internal structure for the implication of some rights of action" (*Artist M. v. Johnson* 1989, 694). Both *Joseph and Josephine A. v. New Mexico Department of Human Services* (1982) and *B.H. v. Johnson* (1989), he pointed out, permitted children in custody to sue to enforce the case plan and review provisions of P.L. 96-272. Because he believed "there is nothing to distinguish among the several statutory requirements—to suggest that one is less mandatory than the others," Shadur found that the plaintiffs had an implied right of action to enforce the reasonable efforts provision of P.L. 96-272 (*Artist M. v. Johnson* 1989, 695).

Turning to the plaintiffs' contention that § 1983 also provided a federal remedy for a violation of P.L. 96-272, Shadur relied on the Supreme Court's analysis in *Middlesex County Sewerage Authority v. National Sea Clammers Association* (1981) and the more recent *Wright v. City of Roanoke Redevelopment Housing Authority* (1986). Unlike a plaintiff's burden of proving the existence of an implied right of action, he said, a § 1983 action is presumed valid unless there is evidence of contrary congressional intent and an absence of enforceable rights in the statute. Shadur again looked to earlier P.L. 96-272 decisions, namely, *Lynch v. Dukakis* (1983), *L.J. v. Massinga* (1988), and *B.H. v. Johnson* (1989), in which the plaintiffs were allowed to enforce the case plan and review provisions of the act under § 1983. Because he had concluded that the statutory mandates were indistinguishable, he held that the courts could enforce the "reasonable efforts" provision of P.L. 96-272 under § 1983 as well. He dismissed the state's argument that the statute was not "clear and unambiguous" enough, as required by *Pennhurst State School and Hospital v. Halderman* (1981), to make it aware that it had entered into a contract with the federal government to provide "reasonable efforts." A state that "accepted federal funds under it [P.L. 96-272] had to know it was obliged both to provide case plan and case review services *and* to provide services aimed at preventing removal and facilitating reunification" (*Artist M. v. Johnson* 1989, 696).

Having satisfied himself that P.L. 96-272 contained enforceable rights, Shadur next determined whether Congress intended to preclude a § 1983 remedy. He was not persuaded by the state's claim that HHS's ability to withhold federal funds, as well as the state plan provisions for a postdeprivation or dispositional hearing constituted sufficient evidence of a "comprehensive remedial scheme" to prevent private enforcement. Citing *Rosado v. Wyman* (1969), in which the Supreme Court rejected the view that HHS enforcement of the Social Security Act precluded the plaintiffs' seeking federal relief, he concluded that the defendant had not met its burden of showing congressional intent to foreclose a § 1983 cause of action.

However, because the plaintiffs had not alleged facts to indicate that the defendant was "deliberately indifferent" to their constitutional rights, a necessary element in proving a due process violation, Shadur dismissed their substantive due process claim.[6]

On March 2, 1990, following a hearing on the merits, Shadur granted a preliminary injunction requiring DCFS to assign a caseworker within three working days of the time the child's case is first heard in juvenile court and to assign a replacement within three working days if the original caseworker absents himself or herself from the case (*Artist M. v. Johnson* 1990, 984).

The Seventh Circuit affirmed the injunction against DCFS on October 29, 1990.[7] After a lengthy review of the language of Titles IV-B and IV-E, the court agreed that plaintiffs could enforce the "reasonable efforts" provision of P.L. 96-272 in federal court—either as an express right under § 1983 or an implied right in the statute itself. Rejecting the defendant's argument that the "reasonable efforts" clause is too vague and amorphous to be judicially enforced, but agreeing that DCFS has wide latitude in implementing P.L. 96-272, the appellate court stated that it has the capacity to judge whether the efforts are "reasonable."

The court dismissed the state's efforts to portray the injunction as "an invitation for this and future plaintiffs to use the AAA [P.L. 96-272] as a tool for federal court interference with all state decisionmaking with respect to its vast child welfare system." Instead, the court characterized the injunction as "merely fulfill[ing] the minimal requirements" of the act that the state curtail "unnecessary foster care placement and family disruption" (*Artist M. v. Johnson* 1990, 984). In his dissent, Judge Daniel Manion echoed DCFS's warning. By allowing each child to "challenge the reasonable efforts of the DCFS," he said, "we can anticipate an avalanche of lawsuits seeking to obtain specific social services and mandatory injunctions governing every imaginable detail over the operation of the DCFS" (*Artist M. v. Johnson* 1990, 996).

The state's petition to the U.S. Supreme Court for a writ of certiorari, filed on March 20, 1991, was granted on May 13, 1991.[8]

Norman

On February 27, 1989, the LAF filed a class action suit against DCFS on behalf of "impoverished parents and legal guardians who have lost . . . or cannot regain custody of their children from [DCFS] because they are homeless or unable to provide food or shelter for their children" (*Norman v. Johnson* 1990, 1184). The LAF lawyers claimed that DCFS violated P.L. 96-272 by failing to make "reasonable efforts" to reunite such indigent families with their children.

Many considered the *Norman* case to be the most successful action against DCFS; the story of the *Norman* plaintiffs is perhaps the most heart-wrenching of all the cases involving the department. Although almost all DCFS plaintiffs evoke some degree of sympathy, surely the most moving was James Norman, a widower with three children. Norman, who had a heart condition, quit his job to care for his terminally ill wife. Because he was unable to pay the bills, their electrical service was turned off. When a DCFS caseworker visited the home, although she found it untidy, with spoiled food in the refrigerator (the result of no electricity), the children looked fine. However, because the caseworker filled out the risk assessment form incorrectly, the children were summarily removed from their home and placed in the custody of their great grandparents, living ten miles away; this was done without discussion with their father.

Norman's situation became even more untenable with a crippling heart condition, no job, no car, and no access to public transportation to allow him to see his children. DCFS provided little or no relief for these conditions, thus diminishing further his prospects of regaining custody of his children. After finally being granted disability benefits for his heart condition, he secured housing and sought to get his children back. Twelve days before the juvenile court hearing to consider his petition, James Norman died of a heart attack.

In his ruling on May 18, 1990, Judge William Hart found, as Shadur had, that the "reasonable efforts" clause of P.L. 96-272 was federally enforceable in a § 1983 action. "Courts are accustomed," he said, "to applying reasonableness standards and state actors and others are accustomed to being required to comply with such standards" (*Norman v. Johnson* 1990, 1187). Before the circuit court ruled on the state's appeal, the parties reached a settlement agreement that was approved by the court on March 28, 1991. As part of the agreement, DCFS withdrew its appeal (*Norman v. Suter* 1991).

K.H.

In 1990 the Seventh Circuit addressed the question left open in *DeShaney v. Winnebago County Department of Social Services* (1989). The OPG filed suit against DCFS on behalf of K.H., a child removed from her parents and placed in DCFS custody at seventeen months. Transferred nine times over four years, she was subjected to repeated physical and sexual abuse in her foster care placements. Citing *Youngberg v. Romeo* (1981), Judge George Marovich refused to dismiss Count 1 of her complaint, which alleged a deprivation of her constitutional rights.

"The complaint paints an ugly picture of official neglect of human misery," began the opinion by Judge Richard Posner (*K.H. v. Morgan* 1990, 848). More to the point, he said, it suggests a violation of the state's constitutional duty. Although *DeShaney v. Winnebago County Department of Social Services* (1989) absolved the state from the requirement of protecting all children from parental abuse, it was still obligated to protect children in state custody from harm. Distinguishing *DeShaney*, the court stressed that the state's obligation arose from its act of rescuing the child from her parents' abuse and placing her in state custody. By doing so, the state accepted at least some responsibility for her well-being and must share the blame for the emotional trauma that resulted from her foster care placement.

Outside Illinois, other circuits reached similar conclusions about the state's responsibility to children in custody. In the Sixth Circuit, for example, a father of three children who were sexually abused in foster care sued the Kentucky Cabinet for Human Resources. The district court dismissed the case; the circuit court reversed and remanded. Distinguishing the Supreme Court's ruling in *DeShaney* and citing *Taylor v. Ledbetter* (1987), the court held that "due process extends the right to be free from the infliction of unnecessary harm to children in state-regulated foster homes" (*Meador v. Cabinet for Human Resources* 1990, 476).

Even more significant, the rulings on the defendants' motions to dismiss, holding that states are constitutionally obligated (and, in some cases, statutorily bound as well) to protect children in care were followed by court orders and consent decrees mandating system-wide reform. In some locales, as in Alabama (in *R.C. v. Hornsby*), the parties negotiated a settlement without a trial, but in others, as in Washington, D.C. (in *LaShawn A. v. Kelly*), the defendants insisted on going to trial. Whether the parties reached a settlement agreement or not, these cases provided steadily mounting evidence that litigation was a valuable tool for reform of child welfare systems. It is likely as well that these developments in related child welfare cases, unfolding during the *B.H.* negotiations, helped persuade DCFS of the wisdom of settling rather than risking a judgment following trial. An overview of the Alabama and the Washington, D.C., cases at this juncture will help place the *B.H.* litigation in the context of the national child welfare reform movement.

R.C.

On November 15, 1988, attorneys from the Civil Liberties Union of Alabama, the Washington-based Mental Health Law Project, and the Southern Poverty Law Center filed suit against the Alabama Department of Human Resources (DHR) on behalf of R.C., an emotionally disturbed eight-year-old from Jefferson County, Alabama. They claimed that the department had systematically failed to provide proper care and services to R.C. and his family, violating his constitutional right to family integrity and protection and his rights under P.L. 96-272 and the 1973 Rehabilitation Act. Like other emotionally disturbed children in foster care, they charged, R.C. had been "inappropriately separated from his parents, moved needlessly from place to place, maintained in inappropriate placements, and deprived of services that would enable him to return home. [And] as a result, his emotional condition has deteriorated" (*R.C. v. Hornsby* 1988, 1).

Judge Joel Dubina denied the state's motion to dismiss and/or for summary judgment in an opinion dated April 19, 1989, and shortly thereafter certified a class of at least 1,500 Alabama children in state custody suffering from emotional and behavioral problems. After numerous motions from both sides, on June 5, 1991, the parties submitted a consent decree that was subsequently approved by the court on December 18, 1991 (only two days before the *B.H.* decree was approved).

Underscoring the wisdom of a negotiated settlement for both sides, Dubina said: "The parties' agreement to entry of this decree is the outcome of negotiations and bargaining. Both the plaintiffs and the defendant have made concessions that they believed were unnecessary. . . . Likewise, both plaintiffs and the defendant have obtained concessions they might not have obtained from this Court" (*R.C. v. Hornsby* 1991, 1).

The decree required DHR to develop an acceptable implementation plan by October 1, 1992, and to achieve statewide compliance by October 1, 1999. The agency committed itself to establishing a "system of care" for class members and their families that aimed, among other things, to protect children from abuse and neglect; to provide services according to an "individualized service plan" and to promote permanency for each child in care; and that would allow children to live with their families whenever possible or, at least, to be near their homes. The parties also agreed to appoint a monitor to oversee compliance with the decree.[9]

LaShawn A.

On June 20, 1989, attorneys in the New York Civil Liberties Union Children's Rights Project and the Washington office of the American Civil Liberties Union (ACLU) filed a class action suit against the District of Columbia's Department of Human Services (DHS) on behalf of seven named plaintiffs, including LaShawn A. The plaintiffs represented a class of approximately 2,200 children in foster care under DHS supervision as well as children reported to be abused or neglected but not yet in DHS care.

The plaintiffs charged that the District's child welfare system was "characterized by ineptness and indifference, inordinate caseloads and insufficient funds" (*LaShawn A. v. Kelly* 1993, 1320) in violation of the due process clause of the Fifth Amendment, P.L. 96-272, the Child Abuse Prevention and Treatment Act (CAPTA), and several D.C. statutes. Specifically, they accused DHS, arguably one of the worst foster care systems in the nation, of failing to investigate reports of abuse and neglect in a timely manner; place children in appropriate foster care facilities; provide services for children and their families; develop case plans and monitor children in care; and achieve permanency.

Lawyers for the children presented evidence that, in 1989, District children spent an average of fifty-eight months in foster care, more than twice the national average of twenty-six months in 1985; only sixty-nine children were placed in adoptive homes in 1990. DHS caseloads ranged from 60 to 200 children for each caseworker, and, as of October 1990, almost half of the 275 staff positions remained unfilled (*Washington Post*, February 7, 1991).

On April 18, 1991, following a three-week bench trial in which numerous experts testified and thousands of pages of documents were introduced, Judge Thomas Hogan issued an opinion that began by describing the plaintiffs as "a lost generation of children whose tragic plight is being repeated every day" (*LaShawn A. v. Dixon* 1991, 960).

Hogan, a Reagan appointee, made detailed findings of fact and determined there was abundant evidence of the District's failure to meet its obligations under P.L. 96-272. Attempting to avoid the possibility that the District could evade its responsibility under the act by foregoing federal funding, Hogan also ruled against DHS on constitutional grounds; he easily distinguished *DeShaney v. Winnebago County Department of Social Services* (1989) because the children were in the District's custody.

With Hogan's ruling, *LaShawn A.* was the first case in the nation in which a federal court found a child welfare agency liable for violating the constitutional rights of the children in its custody (*Washington Post,* April 19, 1991). The court's displeasure with the defendant was revealed in the final paragraph of the opinion. "The Court views the evidence in this case as nothing less than outrageous. The District's dereliction of its responsibilities to the children in its custody is a travesty. Although these children have committed no wrong, they in effect have been punished as though they had" (*LaShawn A. v. Dixon* 1991, 998).

Shortly after the opinion was announced, the parties entered into settlement talks, with Hogan imposing a two-month deadline for proposals. The parties were able to agree on the following changes: installing a computerized system of tracking the children, increasing the number of caseworkers, and improving efforts to recruit adoptive parents. They differed over the question of who should take charge. The plaintiffs' attorneys wanted to bring in a receiver; DHS resisted, claiming it could produce the necessary reforms without outside interference (*Washington Post,* July 3, 1991). Hogan approved the agreed remedial order in August 1991.

One month later, somewhat inexplicably, the District appealed Hogan's finding of liability, denying, however, that the appeal would affect the reform effort. The head of the corporation counsel's appellate division stated: "We're going to come up with programs to show the doubters that we mean business in terms of delivering services to kids, no matter what happens to the lawsuit" (*Washington Post,* October 1, 1991).

In contrast to *R.C.,* where the settlement agreement was accepted by the parties as a reasonable blueprint for reform, the *LaShawn A.* decree was constantly under attack from District politicians. Their refusal to abandon their legal challenges to the court order, despite their denials, likely undermined the reform effort.[10]

DCFS officials in Illinois, who were undoubtedly aware of the developments in Alabama and the District of Columbia, thus had a clear picture of the advantages of reaching a negotiated settlement with the plaintiffs' attorneys and the disadvantages of engaging in protracted litigation against them.

Experts

Despite the inducements, the *B.H.* settlement did not come easily. The adjudication stage of the litigation was characterized by extensive discovery and protracted interaction among the judge, DCFS officials and their attorneys, the plaintiffs' attorneys, and a multitude of children's advocates and child welfare experts. In an effort to shape the settlement agreement and expedite negotiations, the court suggested that the parties postpone further discovery and attempt to reach a settlement. On August 31, 1990, the court entered an agreed order appointing a panel of experts whose "duties were to assist the Court and the parties in developing recommendations, where necessary, to ensure that the Department of Children and Family Services ('DCFS') meets its statutory and constitutional obligations as to children in the custody of DCFS who are placed someplace other than with their parents. . . ." Giving them a broad mandate, he directed them to "make whatever factual inquiry they may determine necessary in order to fulfill this charge, including inquiry as to the nature of such obligations, the ability of the existing DCFS system to meet those obligations, and the efficacy of proposed recommendations" (*B.H. v. Johnson* 1990a, 2–3). In addition to the experts, Judge John Grady asked the parties to agree on the name of a manager who would meet with the panels and report their progress to the parties on a weekly basis and to the court on a monthly basis.

The order outlined the procedure by which the experts would meet their obligations, including the minimum number of meetings (two) to convene, who was permitted to be present at such meetings, and the personnel and records to which the experts would have access. The appointees were instructed to submit preliminary written reports to the parties and the manager by October 31, 1990, and then meet with them to discuss the final report that would be presented to the court. Grady made it clear that the panels' reports were advisory and that the parties were free to negotiate a settlement "at any time following receipt of the preliminary report" (*B.H. v. Johnson* 1990a, 5). In an effort to bring closure to the settlement negotiations within a reasonable period of time, Grady (1996a) also established a "firm trial date."

Grady (1996a), relying on the authority of Federal Rule of Civil Procedure 706, considered it worthwhile to bring in experts to aid in the settlement process; he said he learned about this approach from a Connecticut district court judge while attending a judicial conference.[11] He thought the practice of bringing in experts to aid in settlement was a good one because the testimony developed in this process would be helpful to the court in establishing the parameters of the court's actions—whether the parties settled or not.

The panels were headed by experts in children's health, education, and welfare from around the nation—mostly from Illinois, but also from Washington, D.C., New York, and Colorado. Specifically, their substantive areas of expertise included education, adoption and permanency planning, health, mental health, developmental disabilities, and substance abuse. They were drawn from organizations such as the American Humane Association, Hephzibah Children's Association, La Rabida Children's Hospital and Research Center, the Center for the Study of Social Policy, Loyola University, and the University of Illinois at Champaign-Urbana.

In an order dated October 26, 1990 (*B.H. v. Johnson* 1990b, 1–2), Grady identified the thirteen experts and listed the following areas of their expertise:

- "child protective services (including investigation, follow-up services and in-home services);
- services for developmentally disabled children;
- mental health services for children;
- health care for children;
- substance abuse services for children;
- education (including special education);
- placement services for children 12 and under (including foster care, residential care, independent living, visitation and permanency planning);
- placement services for children 13 and over (including foster care, residential care, independent living, visitation and permanency planning);
- adoption; and
- case management, monitoring and quality assurance (including case plan and administrative case review system, service appeals and monitoring)."

Each of the experts headed a panel composed of individuals mutually agreeable to both sides; the panels met with the experts to identify the key issues, assisted in fact-finding, and responded to drafts of the reports and recommendations.

Grady also appointed attorney Joseph Monahan of the law firm Monahan & Cohen as a comanager of the Rule 706 Expert Panel (as it was officially titled), with Donald Hallberg, President of Lutheran Social Services, as the other comanager. They were given the responsibility of receiving the reports and submitting a final report that distilled the views of the experts.

To aid the process, DCFS created workgroups consisting of caseworkers, supervisors, and managers to formulate their own judgments about the changes needed in the system. The experts interviewed children and foster parents in the foster homes and DCFS facilities. They were given complete access to DCFS data, offices, and personnel, including the workgroups, thus short-circuiting the discovery process. "The result," said Monahan (1997), "as hoped for, was that the discovery process moved much quicker." The expert panel conducted hearings and focus groups, interviewed numerous parties, and reviewed DCFS documents. Again, according to Monahan (1997): "The panel, in some instances, presented papers and data to us [the managers], which we used to prepare a report that was provided to both parties and the court on October 31, 1991. The report summarized and organized the data collected into one document so that the parties and the court would have a compilation of the materials that had been collected over the many weeks prior to the October 31, 1991 deadline."

Although most respondents felt the experts played a useful role in the settlement process, some disagreed, one saying they took too many resources out of the agency's budget. One respondent answered neutrally: "The reports were o.k., but nothing new." Another respondent, however, a member of one of the panels, caustically stated that the panels were "a sham." He elaborated by saying they were too large and did not have enough knowledge of the system. Their "recommendations" were, he said, "meaningless." One other pronounced the panels "pretty useless."

The Consent Decree

Ultimately the settlement negotiations yielded results. On December 20, 1991, without determining liability, Grady approved a sixty-nine page consent decree that was, he said, "the result of compromise and settlement" (*B.H. v. Suter* 1991, 5). As one respondent noted, the decree "was based in large part" on the recommendations of the Rule 706 experts. It listed DCFS responsibilities ranging from protective services and intake assessment to case plans, permanency goals, and adoption services.

The essence of the decree was contained in sections four and five, the so-called Bill of Rights. In these two sections DCFS affirmed its commitment to the children in its care and pledged itself to system-wide reform.

Section four noted that the purpose of the decree was to "assure that DCFS provides children with at least minimally adequate care," defined as a "standard of care" in which children would be "free from foreseeable and preventable physical harm." DCFS pledged that the children in care "shall be free from unreasonable and unnecessary intrusions by DCFS upon their emotional and psychological well being." Finally, more broadly, DCFS promised that "children shall receive at least minimally adequate training, education and services to enable them to secure their physical safety, freedom from emotional harm, and minimally adequate food, clothing, shelter, health and mental health care" (*B.H. v. Suter* 1991, 9). To carry out these pledges, the department promised to develop a system that "provides that children would be timely and stably placed in safe and appropriate living arrangements"; for those unable to be reunited with their parents, DCFS would "promptly identify and take the steps within its power to achieve permanency . . . in the least restrictive setting possible." The newly established system would also ensure "prompt identification of the medical, mental health, and developmental needs of the children" and "timely access to adequate . . . services" to meet these needs. It would also ensure that children in DCFS custody "receive a public education of a kind and quality comparable to other children not in DCFS custody" and "such services and training as necessary to permit them to function in the least restrictive and most homelike setting possible" (*B.H. v. Suter* 1991, 10).

Ironically, the decree also contained a "reasonable efforts" provision very similar to the provision in P.L. 96-272. Here DCFS pledged that in its new system "reasonable efforts . . . shall be made to prevent removal of children from their homes and stably to reunite children with their parents, where appropriate and consistent with the best interests of the child."

The insertion of "reasonable efforts" language into the decree came about largely as a result of propitious timing. On November 16, 1990, following the Seventh Circuit's ruling in *Artist M. v. Johnson* (1990) that the "reasonable efforts" clause of P.L. 96-272 was judicially enforceable, the plaintiffs asked the court to reconsider its original dismissal of their claim. The court responded by allowing the plaintiffs to file an amended complaint charging DCFS with failure to use "reasonable efforts" to keep families together. At the time the *B.H.* consent decree was approved by the court in December 1991, the Supreme Court had not yet ruled on the state's appeal in *Artist M.* The parties therefore included a "reasonable efforts" provision in the consent decree and specified that an adverse ruling by the Supreme Court in *Artist M.* on the judicial enforceability of "reasonable efforts" would not be grounds for modifying the decree.

The decree contained a series of staggered deadlines for compliance. It specified that by January 1, 1992, DCFS must ensure that each child in care would have a case plan within thirty days after entering into temporary custody. The agency agreed that by July 1, 1992, it would provide parents with a handbook outlining procedures for temporary custody, guardianship, and termination of parental rights, and that by July 1, 1993, it would distribute a handbook detailing parents' rights and obligations as well as their relationship with DCFS.

The department was required to change its procedures in protective services and initial assessments by July 1, 1993, and in comprehensive assessments by July 1, 1994. The centerpiece of the consent decree, however, was the case staffing and management section, highlighting DCFS's commitment to reduce the caseworker-to-child ratio. By July 1, 1993, each DCFS child protective services investigator would be limited to investigating twelve new abuse and neglect cases during nine months of the year and fifteen new cases in the other three months. Follow-up caseworkers also had limits placed on them. At the time the decree was entered into, DCFS caseworkers were routinely assigned fifty to seventy-five children each (even higher in Cook County). The decree mandated that by July 1, 1993, caseworkers providing services to intact families would be limited to twenty-five families for each caseworker; by July 1, 1994, each caseworker's maximum caseload for intact families would be twenty families. Similarly, by July 1, 1993, caseworkers responsible for children in substitute care would be limited to thirty child cases each; by July 1, 1994, each caseworker responsible for services to children in placement would have a maximum caseload of twenty-five child cases. The decree also specified maximum caseloads for supervisory personnel.

The sixty-nine pages were full of detailed rules, regulations, and guidelines covering a vast range of services and procedures, including emergency placements, clerical staff, psychiatric hospitalizations, overnight stays in DCFS offices, recruitment and licensing of foster parents, and computerized informational and data management systems. DCFS also committed itself to improving the delivery of health care, education, and adoption services and establishing a quality assurance unit "to evaluate the services and care provided by private agencies, foster parents and caretakers, case managers and DCFS staff to children and their families" (*B.H. v. Suter* 1991, 54).

The decree established that the court would appoint a monitor, at the state's expense, to ensure compliance with the decree and report to the court. The agency was also required to submit an implementation plan to the plaintiffs' attorneys and the monitor; the plan would include a description of the actions DCFS would undertake to fulfill the provisions of the decree and a timetable for completing the work. It was also mandated to produce an annual plan showing its accomplishments in complying with the decree. Throughout, the court indicated its intent to let the parties and the monitor attempt to reconcile their differences among themselves, turning to the court only when they were unable to resolve their conflict.

According to the terms of the decree, DCFS agreed to virtually all the plaintiffs' demands and promised comprehensive reform in all aspects of its performance. Despite the widespread belief that DCFS had merely capitulated to the plaintiffs in settling the lawsuit, however, as one respondent noted, "DCFS was happy with *B.H.*"

There were a number of possible explanations for DCFS satisfaction. In addition to the usual advantages of settlement, the agency benefited from the decree's preclusive effect on subsequent litigation; it could argue that new actions dealt with issues already litigated in *B.H.* and should be dismissed as moot.[12] And although it allowed a "reasonable efforts" clause to be inserted into the decree, no lawsuits would be brought on the basis of the agency's failure to expend "reasonable efforts." Finally, and perhaps most important, *B.H.* was a victory for the agency because the legislature would now be compelled to appropriate the dollars that DCFS had contended all along were necessary to allow it to do its job.

6 Implementation

UNDERTAKING SYSTEMIC CHANGE

 Charles Golbert, an assistant public guardian of Cook County, saying it "was easy to get a decree, hard to implement it," described the implementation phase of public law litigation as the "hardest [phase] by far" (Golbert 1996). The implementation phase of *B.H.*, characterized by varying levels of (dis)harmony among staff members at the Department of Children and Family Services (DCFS), the court, the monitor, the plaintiffs' attorneys, and state political leaders, was no exception, as all sides tried to cope with the immensity of the tasks before them. The challenge of implementing *B.H.* was heightened by the fact that the consent decree was aimed at "reform[ing] virtually the entire breadth of the child welfare system" and was "unprecedented nationwide in the magnitude and complexity of the reforms it contemplate[d]" (*B.H. v. McDonald* 1995a, 1–2).

DCFS's ability to comply with the decree during the implementation phase was hampered by its rapidly growing responsibilities. While the lawsuit and the resulting consent decree committed the agency to improving the child welfare system, they did little to stem the rising tide of child abuse and neglect and the poverty, substance abuse, homelessness, and urban decay that accompanied it. Thus, adding to the dilemma of attaining meaningful reform within DCFS, the demands on agency resources were steadily escalating, placing enormous pressure on it at a time when it was under a mandate to transform itself utterly.

The appendix tables demonstrate the range of problems plaguing the agency during the implementation period, stretching the agency's resources and ability to cope almost to the breaking point. As appendix table 1 shows, the Illinois Central Register was recording more than 300,000 calls a year by FY 1992 (Illinois Department of Children and Family Services 1998a). Such increases were accompanied by a concomitant rise in the number of children reported as abused or neglected (see appendix table 2) as well as the number of "indicated" cases (see appendix table 3). As illustrated in appendix table 4, the child welfare caseload rose from 43,000 (in FY 1992) to more than 60,000 within a short period of time (Illinois Department of Children and Family Services 1995, 3-1; Illinois Department of Children and Family Services 1998d). As a consequence of the increased number of abuse and neglect cases, the number of children placed in substitute care, shown in appendix table 5, almost doubled, from 29,000 in FY 1992 to more than 50,000 a few years later (Illinois Department of Children and Family Services 1995, 4-1; Illinois Department of Children and Family Service 1998c). Between December 1991, when the decree was signed, and March 1994, the number of children in DCFS custody had risen by 86 percent (*B.H. v. Ryder* 1994a, 1291).

A study released by the Child Welfare League in 1997 offered further evidence of DCFS's expanded burden. In 1995 Illinois's substitute care population of 17.1 children per 1,000 in the population was the highest in the nation—and almost three times the median number of 6.3 children per 1,000 in the population (Petit and Curtis 1997, 73). Part of the explanation for the agency's surging caseload is the length of time Illinois children spend in substitute care. The multistate child welfare study shows that the median length of time for Illinois children was 32.7 months, exceeding that for children in the other states in the survey. The median length of time in care for children in Cook County was almost five years (58.4 months), more than four times longer than for children outside Cook County (Wulczyn, Harden and Goerge, 1997, 23).[1]

The overload of the child welfare system was also manifested in the increased demand on the juvenile courts. During much of the implementation phase, its docket was large and growing. In 1993 the *Chicago Tribune* (December 21, 1993) had reported that the six juvenile court judges in Cook County each had an average of 3,800 cases. By 1995 each juvenile court judge in the Cook County Child Protection Division still had responsibility for an average of 3,500 to 4,000 cases (Mezey 1995; see Merry and others 1997).

Thus, from the late 1980s to the mid-1990s, a time when the agency was expected to comply with the consent decree and achieve top-to-bottom reform, the system was inundated with cases: more children were entering, they were staying longer, and fewer were leaving (see *B.H. v. Ryder* 1994b).

Agency Culture

Implementing a major public policy change requires altering the behavior and norms of large-scale institutions (see Nakamura and Smallwood 1980; Pressman and Wildavsky 1984). Moreover, there are special difficulties when courts are given the responsibility of superintending the changes to effect compliance with a decree (Levine and Perkins 1997). The problems are compounded because the agency's efforts at implementation frequently necessitate an influx of resources controlled by others, most often state legislators and the governor—both relatively immune from judicial influence (see Note 1980).

Structural reform litigation, whether resolved by settlement or trial, succeeds largely to the extent that it alters the conduct of the personnel within the institution (Wood 1990). A decade ago Lowry (1988, 293) noted that for litigation to succeed, it must "result in fundamental changes in procedures and policies, changes that can reach down to the worker level." To this end, said Kentucky District Court Judge Richard Fitzgerald, a decree should optimally be used "as a creative document for strategic planning, which changes the culture of practice . . ." (*National Law Journal,* June 27, 1994). A child welfare litigator in San Francisco similarly believed that transforming a child welfare system requires a "sea change" in the culture of the agency responsible for the care of the children. And in Illinois, Gaylord Gieseke (1996), senior projects director for Voices for Illinois Children, felt that DCFS reform depended on the litigants' ability to effect a "cultural change" within the agency.

Changing a bureaucracy is an enormous task, made more arduous by the staff's ability to subvert, or at least to delay, reform efforts—often without openly refusing to implement new policies (Schuerman 1997). Wood (1990, 53–57) offers three possible scenarios of agency responses following litigation aimed at reform: "obstructionism," "technical [but largely illusory] compliance," and "if you can't beat them, join them." However, even if agency personnel decide to "join them," external forces such as state legislators, governors, and other public officials can torpedo such a decision by withholding financial or logistic support (Note 1980). In assessing the likelihood of successful reform of human services agencies, therefore, Levine and Perkins (1997, 359) suggest that it is not surprising that "change efforts fail but that successful change takes place at all."

The obstacles to securing bureaucratic reform loom even larger when litigation is the catalyst for the change. Because it is in the nature of bureaucracies to "resist change" (Stein 1987, 158), judicial attempts at reforming public institutions are often viewed suspiciously by the personnel working within them. Courts must be sensitive to the fact that the high administrative officials who agreed to the terms of the settlement likely did not consult the street-level workers before signing the agreement. Consequently, the greatest threat to successful implementation of a court-ordered remedy, suggests Timothy Wilton (1982, 190–91) in his study of a desegregation suit against the Ann Arbor School District, is not open defiance but rather "quiet resistance at the bottom of bureaucracies . . . [from] people harboring deep-seated resentment and hostility that cannot be changed by contempt proceedings but which nonetheless will quite effectively sabotage a court's remedial program."

Successful reform of a public institution therefore necessitates more than signatures on a consent decree. It requires a commitment to reform at the top and a willingness to effect change by agency personnel, as well as external support from political leaders. According to many respondents, successful implementation of the *B.H.* decree was compromised at the outset by failings in all areas.

As a number of respondents noted, successful implementation of the *B.H.* consent decree required DCFS's top leadership to create an environment for reform within the department and to set an example for line workers. The respondents were divided in the extent to which they believed that administrators changed agency norms during the implementation period. Although most believed that the agency's leadership was generally committed to reform, they felt that, with the exception of Jess McDonald, they lacked the ability to change the culture of the bureaucracy.

An important barrier to creating change within the agency was the revolving door of DCFS directors. There was a consensus among respondents that McDonald genuinely tried to set a new standard for agency performance, but he was not in charge during most of the implementation phase. After serving as director during the final months of Jim Thompson's tenure as governor, when he began the process of negotiating settlements in the lawsuits pending against DCFS, McDonald was forced to resign to fulfill Jim Edgar's campaign pledge to replace the Thompson appointees with his own. Leaving DCFS for a new position as executive director of the Illinois Association of Community Mental Health Agencies, McDonald was replaced by Sue Suter, former head of the Department of Public Aid and the defeated Republican candidate for state comptroller in the 1990 election.

After serving in the office only a year and a half, Suter abruptly resigned as director in August 1992—ostensibly to protest the looming personnel cuts—and was replaced by her executive deputy director and former general counsel, Sterling Ryder. Ryder, who was named acting director of DCFS in August 1992, was in the director's office for only twenty months. He resigned in May 1994, claiming that Edgar undermined his authority by appointing attorney Anne Burke as special counsel for Cook County operations of DCFS, a position reporting directly to the governor.

The reason for Burke's appointment was unclear. The chair of the Illinois Democratic party accused Edgar of using Burke, married to Democratic Chicago Ward Alderman Edward Burke, to deflect criticism away from him during the 1994 election (*Chicago Tribune,* May 19, 1994). Whatever his reason, Edgar abolished the position of special counsel a few months later.

Two weeks after Ryder left the office, Edgar brought McDonald, then serving as head of the state's Department of Mental Health, back as director of DCFS. Although the children's advocates welcomed the appointment, McDonald soon came under fire from the Republican senate president who delayed his confirmation vote for more than a year as a way, he said, of showing displeasure with DCFS.

During the post-decree stage, almost everyone involved in the litigation was engrossed in measuring the degree to which the agency complied with the decree, particularly in how well it was meeting its objective of reducing the caseworker-to-child ratio. The agency's ability to comply with the order to reduce the caseload ratios was jeopardized, however, by the turmoil over DCFS budgetary appropriations in the state legislature and the consequences of this for agency operations during the implementation phase.

In anticipation of the *B.H.* decree, the agency had received a 21 percent spending increase in 1991, which allowed it to hire 163 new staff members, according to Ed McManus, a DCFS spokesperson. The budget increase, McManus indicated, allowed the agency to satisfy all the first-year requirements of the decree by July 1, 1992 (*Chicago Daily Law Bulletin*, August 6, 1992).

A year later, in his April 1992 budget message, Edgar proposed an 8.6 percent increase (about $40 million) in appropriations for DCFS (Schuerman, Rzepnicki, and Littell 1994, 222). After opposition arose from Speaker Michael Madigan, leader of the Democratic-controlled House, the two sides eventually compromised. Ultimately DCFS was left with only a 4.6 percent increase for programs, $20 million less than the amount Edgar had proposed. No new funds were allocated for operations, a budget category that in large part covered salaries for agency personnel (*Chicago Tribune*, August 9, 1992). Thus, when DCFS was expected to reduce the caseload ratio—at a time when the number of children in the system was rising—it was forced to eliminate more than 300 staff positions.

The layoffs, amounting to about 10 percent of the 3,200 workers, fell primarily on management, supervisors, and support staff, creating near-chaotic conditions within the department as senior workers bumped the more junior level workers from their positions (Schuerman, Rzepnicki, and Littell 1994, 224). Not surprisingly, the budget cuts also had a debilitating effect on agency morale, with more than 400 DCFS workers demonstrating in front of the State of Illinois building to protest the projected layoffs. Caught between the demands of the decree and the realities of the budget, DCFS temporarily halted all hiring. Eventually, to meet its obligations under the decree, it began a compressed hiring process involving hundreds of employees over the next two years. This process raised apprehensions about the qualifications and training of the newly hired workers. Reflecting the concerns of many, the executive director of the Illinois Child Care Association said, "The question I have is simply about the department's ability to bring all of these people on, train them, and get the supervisory and monitoring structures in place" (*Chicago Tribune*, March 15, 1993).

Meanwhile, as a result of the layoffs, relations between the parties had deteriorated, further jeopardizing the implementation process. The American Civil Liberties Union (ACLU) refused to grant DCFS an extension in which to prepare its implementation plan, and Wolf threatened to return to court to force the agency to implement the necessary reforms, saying, "We're extremely skeptical that there'll be any compliance during the next many months" (*Chicago Daily Law Bulletin*, August 12, 1992).

In July 1993, plaintiffs charged DCFS with failing to hire the additional caseworkers necessary to achieve the initial caseload reduction.[2] Rather than seeking a sanction against the agency, however, the plaintiffs reached a new agreement with DCFS in which the agency agreed to fulfill its hiring obligations by September 1, 1993, and to begin hiring new workers to meet the final July 1994 deadline.

An independent audit conducted in 1993 by William Holland, the auditor general of Illinois, also showed that the norms of behavior in the agency had not changed greatly. In addition to a $2.8 million discrepancy in the department's accounts for FY 1992, Holland found that DCFS caseworkers were not making the requisite monthly visits to all children in care, were not including current case plans in a significant percentage of children's files, were taking longer than the sixty-day limit to complete abuse and neglect investigations for all children, and were not conducting criminal background checks on all prospective foster parents (*Chicago Tribune*, May 21, 1993).

Another source of contention over the agency's compliance with the decree was the care of children in emergency shelters operated by DCFS. The decree stated that "no child will stay overnight in an office or hotel in lieu of an appropriate placement," but two years later children were still being left in offices overnight, or longer, without adequate supervision. In two court appearances, on June 29, 1993, and September 9, 1993, agency officials again promised to halt this practice. Although by the end of the year DCFS was paying more attention to the issue of the "sleepovers," the plaintiffs' attorneys continued to express concern about the agency's reliance on office space to house the children.

DCFS maintained that it had corrected the problem by staffing the center with physicians, counselors, and workers to monitor the children and provide activities for them. According to Executive Deputy Director Cleo Terry, these measures satisfied the agency's promise not to shelter children in DCFS offices. Wolf, however, acknowledged that while "they have made some significant improvements in child care there, partly because of pressures from our litigation . . . a nice office is still an office" (*Chicago Tribune*, December 3, 1993).

The continuing changeover of DCFS directors, in addition to the uncertainty over job security created by the 1992 budget cuts and the added pressure from the Wallace crisis that increased the apprehension among the staff about family reunification policy, interfered with the bureaucracy's ability to perform its tasks. Some respondents felt that these were factors hindering DCFS's ability to comply with the consent decree. However, despite DCFS's expanded duties and the tumultuous conditions in which the agency was often forced to operate, few respondents were willing to express much sympathy for it.

Most respondents agreed that DCFS had not made much progress in complying with the consent decree during the implementation phase of the litigation. While respondents on DCFS's side painted a brighter picture of the agency's efforts, an ACLU report, appearing in June 1994, charged—without mincing words—that DCFS was "massively out of compliance with both the letter and spirit of the consent decree" (*Chicago Tribune*, June 28, 1994).

The respondents were more divided on the degree to which they considered the department was committed to changing the norms under which it operated and exerting its best efforts to comply with the decree. Many attributed DCFS's problems in complying with the decree to its inability to change the culture of the bureaucracy; a number felt that events outside the department were in large part responsible for its plight. Although most believed that DCFS was "in significant noncompliance" with the decree, some thought the agency should be credited for making a good-faith attempt at compliance. A significant number, however, were less charitable, faulting the agency for its failures to plan for the increased number of children in the system, to ask for more resources from the state, and to carry out the much-needed reform plan.

Legal Developments

As DCFS struggled to implement *B.H.* in the early 1990s, significant legal developments threatened to sap the agency's ability to devote itself to reform. Other plaintiffs representing classes of abused and neglected Illinois children sued DCFS, citing a variety of deficiencies in its programs and practices. Most resulted in consent decrees, and, although none were as extensive as *B.H.*, they all required major expenditures of time and money to implement. Additionally, the *Artist M.* case, which the state refused to settle and litigated all the way to the U.S. Supreme Court, forced DCFS personnel and legal staff— as well as numerous Illinois child welfare advocates—to devote a great deal of energy to the ensuing legal battles. Although its outcome did not directly affect DCFS compliance with the *B.H.* decree, *Artist M.* had widespread implications for national child welfare law as well as for the federal court's role in determining child welfare policy.

Constitutional Cases

Rulings such as *B.H.* expanded the boundaries of the state's responsibility to abused and neglected children by affirming its constitutional duty to children in custody. Never challenged in the Supreme Court, the ruling in *B.H.* was echoed by other federal courts and soon became the prevailing view of the circuits. These decisions made it clear that the Supreme Court's stance in limiting the state's responsibility to abused children, by narrowly interpreting the substantive due process doctrine in *DeShaney v. Winnebago County Department of Social Services* (1989), was a relatively minor setback for most attorneys representing children in foster care.

In a case involving a child who died from inadequate medical treatment while in substitute care, Judge Susan Webber Wright of the Eastern District of Arkansas explained why *DeShaney* posed no barrier to widening the scope of the state's protection to children in custody: "The Supreme Court has never recognized a constitutional duty of care or protection beyond the cases of incarcerated prisoners and involuntarily committed mental patients. Lower courts, however, have not treated this as an exhaustive list, and *DeShaney* clearly left open the possibility that the Due Process Clause may impose an affirmative duty to provide care and protection to children placed in foster homes by the state" (*Norfleet v. Arkansas Department of Human Services* 1992, 1199).

Citing the extensive caselaw in other circuits, Wright, whose ruling was affirmed by the Eighth Circuit a year later in *Norfleet v. Arkansas Department of Human Services* (1993), held that a child placed in a foster home by the state has a clearly established right to protection. She also refused to dismiss the case against the defendants on the grounds of qualified immunity.

The Tenth Circuit also firmly established the state's constitutional obligation to children in custody. In refusing to grant immunity to state officials in a suit against the state child welfare agency, the court declared "that if the persons responsible place children in a foster home or institution they know or suspect to be dangerous to the children they incur liability if the harm occurs" (*Yvonne L. v. New Mexico Department of Human Services* 1992, 893).[3]

P.L. 96-272 Cases

In contrast to their willingness to impose constitutional obligations on the state, the courts remained divided on how much protection P.L. 96-272 offered to children in substitute care. In particular, they were split over whether the "reasonable efforts" clause was judicially enforceable.

According to several respondents, after Shadur ruled on the issue of liability in *Artist M. v. Johnson* (1989), he sought advice from both sides in determining an appropriate remedy. He rejected the plaintiffs' demand that DCFS be required to assign a caseworker within twenty-four hours after the temporary custody hearing. Instead, he allowed the agency a three-day window in which to assign a caseworker, an order with which DCFS officials themselves believed they could comply. As the appellate court later emphasized, "The district court sought out and discovered a method of enforcing the 'reasonable efforts' requirement that is tailored to DCFS practices" (*Artist M. v. Johnson* 1990, 988). The department nevertheless opposed Shadur's order on a number of grounds and appealed the decision to the circuit court, in part because it feared that if the ruling were left unchallenged, it would open a floodgate of litigation brought to vindicate differing interpretations of the "reasonable efforts" requirement (Tchen 1995).

On appeal, the circuit court affirmed Shadur's ruling, principally relying on the Supreme Court's opinion in *Wilder v. Virginia Hospital Association* (1990), in which the high court held that the Boren amendment to the Medicaid Act— requiring states to reimburse health care providers treating medicaid patients at "reasonable and adequate" rates—was enforceable under § 1983.

As in most cases involving a § 1983 remedy, the appellate court was primarily concerned with whether the statute created a right in these plaintiffs. Citing *Wilder,* the court said that the questions to be answered in such cases are whether the provision was "intended to benefit the plaintiff"; whether it "imposes a binding obligation on the state"; and whether "the right is not so amorphous that courts are unable to adequately enforce it" (*Artist M. v. Johnson* 1990, 986).

Borrowing from the Supreme Court's analysis in *Wilder,* the circuit court held that, despite DCFS's ability to select the specific services offered, "The judiciary is nevertheless capable of determining whether the state is exerting 'reasonable efforts' to provide those services" (*Artist M. v. Johnson* 1990, 987). Moreover, finding no evidence that Congress intended to foreclose a § 1983 remedy, the appellate court concluded that the plaintiffs were entitled to seek federal court relief for violation of the "reasonable efforts" provision of P.L. 96-272. Similarly, applying the four-part test in *Cort v. Ash* (1975), the court held that the statute created an implied private right of action in these plaintiffs.

While *Artist M.* settled the issue of judicial enforceability of the "reasonable efforts" clause within the Seventh Circuit, there were still differing views on how to interpret "reasonable efforts" outside the circuit. In an appeal from a case arising out of the Eastern District of Pennsylvania, the Third Circuit was asked to decide whether the "reasonable efforts" provision of P.L. 96-272 entitled the families of children in foster care to weekly visits lasting four hours. Although the court agreed with plaintiffs that they were entitled to enforcement of the "reasonable efforts" provision, it refused to concede that they had a right to "a specified time and frequency of visitation" (*Winston v. Children and Youth Services* 1991, 1389). And in a surprising turn of events following lengthy judicial proceedings, the court in the Eastern District of Louisiana rejected the prevailing view that P.L. 96-272 contained at least some enforceable rights and flatly denied that P.L. 96-272 was judicially enforceable in a § 1983 cause of action (*Del A. v. Roemer* 1991).

Given the importance of this issue for the federal court's role in child welfare policymaking, it is not surprising that the Supreme Court would agree to resolve the conflicting interpretation of P.L. 96-272 among the circuits; it chose to do so by granting certiorari in *Artist M.*, placing DCFS in the limelight of national child welfare policymaking.

Viewing this as a clash over judicial constraints on state autonomy, the U.S. Solicitor General, attorneys general from thirty-eight states and the District of Columbia, as well as the National Governors Association, the National League of Cities, the National Association of Counties, and the National Conference of State Legislators filed amici curiae briefs on behalf of Illinois, arguing that the Court should reverse.

On the plaintiffs' side, thirteen Illinois state and local bar associations, numerous child welfare and child advocacy groups, eleven national child welfare organizations, the American Bar Association, the National Association of Counsel for Children, the ACLU, the Youth Law Center, and the National Council of Juvenile and Family Court Judges filed briefs urging the Court to affirm.

In a seven-to-two opinion, the high court reversed the courts below, holding that Congress had not intended to allow individual plaintiffs to sue a state for failing to comply with the "reasonable efforts" provision. Focusing on the "reasonable efforts" clause, Chief Justice William Rehnquist acknowledged that it speaks in mandatory language, but he disputed the plaintiffs' interpretation of the mandate. He agreed that the statute "does place a requirement on the States, but that requirement only goes so far as to ensure that the State have a plan approved by the Secretary [of HHS] which contains the 16 listed features" (*Suter v. Artist M.* 1992, 358). The Court denied that the phrase "the plan shall be in effect in all political subdivisions of the State" dictated that the plan be "in effect"; rather it meant, said the Court, that the plan must apply throughout the entire state. Moreover, Rehnquist pointed out, unlike the Boren Amendment and its accompanying regulations detailing the method for determining reasonable reimbursement rates, P.L. 96-272 did not indicate how to measure the reasonableness of the state's prevention and reunification efforts. The act, he said, clearly left it to the state to determine the meaning of "reasonable efforts" in each case.

The Court also quickly disposed of the appellate court's finding that P.L. 96-272 created an implied private right of action in the plaintiffs. Without evidence of congressional intent to allow a federal cause of action in P.L. 96-272, said the Court, there was no entitlement to an implied right of action.

Although the children were unable to sue child welfare agencies, Rehnquist reflected, they were not totally without a remedy against a negligent agency. He reminded the plaintiffs that the Department of Health and Human Services (HHS) was empowered to withhold federal funds from any state that did not have a "reasonable efforts" provision in its state plan or from a state that failed to comply with its plan.

The Court was not asked to consider whether the state had a constitutional duty to children in foster care—the question left open in *DeShaney*—and did not express an opinion on that issue.

Artist M. created consternation within the child welfare community because the Court's narrow reading of P.L. 96-272 threatened to deprive children's advocates of one of their most potent weapons against state agencies. The opinion was roundly criticized by most observers, who, in addition to their concern about its effect on the continued vitality of P.L. 96-272, were also apprehensive that it would deter litigation against other state social service agencies, particularly public aid offices. They feared that, despite long-standing precedent, the lower courts would interpret *Artist M.* to preclude judicial relief for plaintiffs suing states for violating federal mandates imposed by the Social Security Act or other spending clause statutes (Smith 1992; Frye 1993).

Child welfare advocates lobbied Congress in an effort to repair the damage caused by *Artist M.* Their proposal, known as the "Suter Fix," after DCFS director Sue Suter, sought to reverse the Court's ruling on judicial enforcement of the "reasonable efforts" clause of P.L. 96-272 as well as to respond to the broader issue of standing to sue states to enforce state plan provisions in federal funding statutes.

In 1993, while deliberating on the Family Preservation and Support Bill (enacted as part of the Omnibus Budget Reconciliation Act of 1993), Congress considered proposals to contain *Artist M.* A House bill that would have explicitly retained an individual's right to sue a state for failing to comply with state plan requirements was dropped in conference. In any event, the bill would not have disturbed the Court's ruling on the "reasonable efforts" clause; it would merely have required HHS to conduct a study of the way in which the states were implementing the "reasonable efforts" requirement of the act.[4] Then in 1994 Congress finally clarified the applicable legal standard, stating that *Artist M.* should not be interpreted to overrule earlier Supreme Court rulings on judicial enforcement of state plan requirements. It let stand, however, the Court's prohibition against suits brought to enforce the "reasonable efforts" clause of P.L. 96-272, thereby enhancing the state's dominion over child welfare policy by limiting judicial oversight.

Implementing *LaShawn A.*

An important development in child welfare law was also taking place in the District of Columbia in the 1990s, the dates roughly paralleling the implementation phase of *B.H.* The story of the *LaShawn A.* case represents a microcosm of the problems that arise during implementation of a systemic reform order, though it is unclear whether the problems in D.C. were exacerbated by the fact that the case resulted in a finding of liability against the city's Department of Human Services (DHS) rather than a consent decree, as occurred in the majority of child welfare reform cases.

Although *Artist M.* had placed the federal court's ruling against DHS in jeopardy, as it turned out the threat from *Artist M.* was only a minor obstacle to implementing Judge Thomas Hogan's 1991 remedial order to reform the D.C. child welfare agency. The events in D.C. during the 1990s illustrate the predicament in which federal courts are often placed when they are required to supervise the reform of a child welfare system.

Despite its stated commitment to reform and its acquiescence in the remedial order, the District went back into federal court, arguing that *Artist M.* had precluded the federal statutory cause of action in *LaShawn A.* Judge Abner Mikva, speaking for the District of Columbia Circuit Court, essentially sidestepped *Artist M.* by holding that the lower court decision was sustainable under the District's own "equally . . . comprehensive" child welfare statutes and regulations (*LaShawn A. v. Kelly* 1993, 1324). He remanded the case to allow the district court to revise the original remedial order, delete any references to federal statutory violations, and fashion a new order based entirely on D.C. law.

On January 27, 1994, the lower court issued a second remedial order reflecting the appellate court's ruling. Throughout this time, however, beginning with the 1991 order, the parties proceeded with efforts at remediation, with the D.C.–based Center for the Study of Social Policy appointed as monitor during the implementation process.

At the outset of the litigation, the plaintiffs had asked Hogan to designate a receiver over the agency; they continued to press for this remedy in the midst of the legal maneuvering between the parties. Unwilling to take this drastic step, Hogan agreed to appoint limited receiverships in the several areas in which DHS was out of compliance with the decree. Finally, in May 1995, after the plaintiffs had filed their third motion for contempt against DHS, Hogan became convinced that the defendants "either cannot or will not make the fundamental changes necessary to improve the plight of abused and neglected children" (*LaShawn A. v. Kelly* 1995, 299).[5] Finding the agency in contempt, he ordered DHS placed in full receivership and asked the parties and the monitor to prepare an order detailing the duties and the authority of the receiver. Hogan seemed particularly affronted by the fact that D.C.'s mayor had attempted to "abolish private rights of action to enforce local statutory responsibilities to care for and protect abused and neglected children" (*LaShawn A. v. Kelly* 1995, 314).

Hogan's action was significant because this resolution of *LaShawn A.* represented the first time a judge placed a child welfare agency in receivership (*Washington Post,* May 23, 1995). It has not happened since.

In October 1995 a different three-judge panel of the D.C. Circuit held that, when the case had initially been remanded, the district court should have ascertained whether *Artist M.* had stripped it of its pendant jurisdiction to enforce the institution-wide decree against the District on the basis of local law (*LaShawn A. v. Barry* 1995).[6] The appellate court again remanded to allow the lower court to determine if it had proper jurisdiction over the case. During this time, while continuing to challenge the court's jurisdiction, the District insisted it was still committed to reform. Gradually, the conflict between the parties moved out of court and began to revolve around the actions of the receiver.

Hogan appointed the controversial Jerome Miller, a former director of DCFS and head of the Massachusetts juvenile court system, as receiver over DHS in May 1995.[7] Miller was given widespread control over the $53 million agency and soon began to express public criticism of it. Reporting on his first 120 days on the job, he called the DHS bureaucracy "unresponsive to children" (*Washington Post,* January 24, 1996).

DHS personnel fought back, attacking Miller's management style and charging Miller with reducing the morale of the agency and causing divisiveness among agency staff members (*Washington Post,* April 7, 1996). Miller's attempts to privatize child welfare services created further turmoil among agency workers and drew union opposition as well. Relationships between Miller and agency personnel soon reached a state of nearly open hostility.

Forced to assume a more pro-active role in the implementation process, Hogan ordered the Center forthe Study of Social Policy to recommence its work as monitor. The center reported "grave concern" over Miller's oversight of the agency, citing a 500 percent increase in the number of cases that had not received timely administrative reviews, an "'intolerable' backlog of neglect investigations," continuing "staff shortages," low morale, and "unacceptably high" caseloads for many workers (*Washington Post,* May 8, 1997).

A month later, amid continuing clashes, Miller announced his resignation, leaving after twenty months in office. Wilfred Hamm, director of the Children's Bureau at HHS and the District's former head of adoption services, was named acting receiver by Hogan. Hamm was replaced by Ernestine Jones in October 1997. The agency remains under receivership.

The D.C. experience demonstrates that implementing a child welfare reform decree depends on a number of factors, possibly most important, cooperation from the political branches of government. It also suggests that the mere presence of a receiver is not a panacea for producing change and may even be detrimental to engendering a culture of reform within an agency.

Most knowledgeable persons interviewed for this study characterized the D.C. child welfare agency as a "disaster" and a "mess" and noted that if it were appropriate to appoint a receiver anywhere, it would be in the District of Columbia. However, respondents were generally hesitant about the wisdom of appointing receivers in institutional reform litigation. They believed receivers should be employed as a last resort, in cases of "gross mismanagement only," according to Julie Biehl (1996), a former assistant public guardian who now directs the Clinical Evaluation and Services Initiative of the Cook County Juvenile Court. Michael Dsida (1996), another former assistant public guardian—who had argued the *Artist M.* case in the Supreme Court—characterized a receivership as "an extraordinary remedy." Summing up the views of several respondents, Charlotte Wenzel (1996), associate director of the Citizens Committee on the Juvenile Court, asked rhetorically: "How are they [receivers] going to know any more about solving the problems of the agency?" None of the respondents felt that conditions within DCFS warranted the appointment of a receiver.

The federal court judges interviewed for this study agreed that receivers were a necessary enforcement mechanism, but believed that they must be used very sparingly. Commenting on the appointment of a receiver, Shadur (1996) called it "very drastic"; Hart (1996) said appointing a receiver was an "extreme step, an uninviting prospect"; and Judge Ruben Castillo (1996) said it should be used only as "a last ditch" effort. Similarly, Judge John Nordberg (1996) agreed the option should be available to the court but said, "It is the last thing you want to do unless there is complete defiance." And Plunkett (1996) believed that receivers should be limited to a situation in which the agency leadership is incompetent or has bad motives, which, in his view, is rarely the case.

Only one judge, Marvin Aspen (1996), reported that he had ever resorted to this remedy; he placed the Chicago Housing Authority in receivership in a case involving scattered site housing.

Whether Carter, Reagan, Bush, or Clinton appointees, these judges were clear that courts should bring in receivers only in narrow circumstances. Hogan, who probably shared these judges' views on the limits of receivership, likely believed he had exhausted alternative remedies. Reflecting on the experiences of the District, however, it seems clear that receivership by itself does not guarantee a bureaucracy's compliance with a decree.

Illinois Consent Decrees

Christina Tchen, DCFS's outside counsel from Skadden, Arps, believed that the Supreme Court's ruling in *Artist M.* would restrain the lower courts' tendencies to "micromanage" child welfare policy, using the reasonable efforts clause (Tchen 1995). Initially it appeared that by reaffirming the state's preeminent role in child welfare policymaking, *Artist M.* would curtail the federal court's involvement with the lives of abused and neglected children. By entering into a series of consent decrees with different classes of plaintiffs during the early 1990s, however, DCFS seemed to guarantee the court's steady involvement in child welfare policy.

Prior to *B.H.*, DCFS had agreed to enhance its services to Spanish-speaking families in *Burgos v. DCFS* (1977) and to facilitate weekly visits between parents and children in *Bates v. Johnson* (1986). During the final stages of negotiation over *B.H.*, in September 1991, DCFS created the Office of Litigation Management to manage the implementation of its existing and upcoming consent decrees.

By 1996 the Illinois child welfare system was operating under a multi-faceted regime of consent decrees and court orders; DCFS policy was governed by eight decrees resulting from class action suits in federal and state court. Between 1991 and 1994, the agency had entered into consent decrees relating to emergency housing provisions in *Norman v. Suter* (1991); procedural safeguards for relatives of children in substitute care in *Reid v. Suter* (1992), a decree later vacated because of changes in state law; procedures for holding dispositional hearings in *Dana W. v. Ryder* (1993); policies toward pregnant and parenting teenagers in *Hill v. Erickson* (1994); and policies toward sibling placements and visits in *Aristotle P. v. Ryder* (1994). Of these eight cases, the Legal Assistance Foundation of Chicago (LAF) represented the plaintiffs in four, the Office of the Public Guardian (OPG) in two, the ACLU in one, and the Northwestern University Legal Clinic in one.

Although the decrees were uneven in the degree to which they demanded alterations in DCFS policy, all affected some area of DCFS operations. They also served as models of DCFS compliance, allowing the *B.H.* attorneys and other child welfare advocates to compare their results with those achieved by attorneys in other cases.

Norman

The heart of the *Norman* decree, signed by DCFS and the LAF in 1991, consisted of a pledge by DCFS not to separate a child from a parent because of the "living circumstances of the family, or lack of provision for the child's subsistence needs" unless the child was in imminent danger and the agency made "reasonable efforts" to keep the family united. "Reasonable efforts" included "assistance in locating and securing housing, temporary shelter, cash assistance, in-kind services . . . or advocacy with public and community agencies providing such services" (*Norman v. Suter* 1991, 7–8). Absent imminent danger, DCFS also promised not to remove a child from a parent living in substandard housing nor to remove a child whose parent failed to protect him or her from domestic violence. In essence the agency was promising not to remove children from parents who were not guilty of abuse or neglect, but were trapped by circumstances beyond their control.

Furthermore, DCFS agreed to notify class members about the decree and to establish a "*Norman*" fund from which it would provide a stipend of up to $800 per family per calendar year for housing assistance such as rent, security deposits, utility connections, or furniture.[8] DCFS also pledged to cooperate with the Department of Public Aid to seek federal approval to continue a family's welfare benefits for a limited time after the children were placed in DCFS temporary custody or to allow a family to receive public aid benefits before the children were home in order to facilitate their return home. Finally, DCFS agreed to establish a housing advocacy program and to train its caseworkers to request housing assistance from community agencies and to work with the Chicago Housing Authority and other public housing authorities to secure housing for *Norman* families.

Jeanine Smith, district director of the Jewish Children's Bureau and holder of an advanced degree in social work, was jointly nominated by the parties to serve as monitor—at the state's expense—for a four year term beginning July 1, 1991. She was charged by the court with gathering information to assess DCFS compliance with the decree in several areas and to issue semiannual reports beginning January 1, 1992, and ending July 1, 1995. In assessing whether DCFS was meeting the requirements of the decree, Smith had to determine whether caseworkers disbursed the requisite cash assistance to *Norman* families and made reasonable efforts to provide services that obviated the need to remove their children or hastened their reunification after they were removed.[9]

After Smith submitted her sixth monitoring report in May 1995, the plaintiffs moved to extend her monitoring activities for another two years, arguing that the state was out of compliance with several parts of the decree.[10] DCFS objected, claiming that it was in substantial compliance and that monitoring was no longer necessary. Although Smith had reported that *Norman* saved the state more than $11 million during the last six months of 1994 (*Norman v. McDonald* 1995, 17), the agency argued that the cost of the monitor, approximately $100,000 a year, was money that could be used in better ways. Appendix table 6 shows the expenditures resulting from the *Norman* litigation and the number of families served by the decree.

Although there were disputes over how well DCFS was serving the *Norman* population, Smith's report indicated that in the second half of 1994 almost half a million *Norman* dollars ($475,785) had been spent, representing an increase of $125,000 over the first six months of 1994 (*Norman v. McDonald* 1995, 2). Her report showed that since FY 1992, the Illinois General Assembly had appropriated a total of $1.8 million to implement the *Norman* decree (*Norman v. McDonald* 1995, 9).

Hart gave Smith a ringing endorsement, declaring that she "has served an important and crucial function in the implementation of the Consent Order that appears to have been more than worth its cost" (*Norman v. McDonald* 1996, 1225). While not giving Smith all the credit for the cost savings, Hart concluded that the benefits to the state from compliance with *Norman*, which he believed was enhanced by her work as monitor, clearly outweighed the monitoring expenses.

Dana W.

In March 1993 DCFS signed another decree in which it agreed to modify its procedure for dispositional hearings. The case arose because the agency was not meeting the criterion of holding a dispositional hearing within eighteen months of a child's placement in substitute care, as required for the receipt of federal funding. Represented by Patrick Murphy's office, the Office of the Public Guardian (OPG), the plaintiffs filed suit in 1990, charging DCFS with failing to hold dispositional hearings in a timely fashion.

The parties entered into talks, joined by representatives of the Cook County board and the chief judge of the Cook County Circuit Court. In the final decree, set to expire in three years, the board and the court agreed to provide two new full-time courtrooms (or calendars)—with six additional ones later—and to hire eight new court administrators. Under the new procedure, all incoming abuse and neglect cases would be placed on the active calendar and, for existing cases on the Guardianship Calendar, permanency planning hearings would be held in conjunction with DCFS internal reviews. As part of the agreement, DCFS committed to paying the county $1.5 million over three years (*Dana W. v. Ryder* 1993).

The lawyers for both sides continued to battle over implementation of the decree after the agreement was signed. Eventually, the parties returned to court, jointly moving to modify the consent decree and citing structural changes in the juvenile court system as well as revisions in state law. In February 1995 Shadur approved a modified decree.

Hill

The next consent decree, this one arising out of a state court proceeding, resulted from a suit against DCFS and the Illinois Department of Mental Health and Developmental Disabilities. Represented by the LAF, the plaintiffs, a class of pregnant and parenting minor wards of DCFS, charged the agency with failing to provide them with adequate services. The parties entered into settlement negotiations, during which DCFS agreed to develop three new programs and to hire Denise Kane, a social worker with child welfare experience who had been associate director of the Citizens Committee on the Juvenile Court, a court watchdog group, to oversee implementation of the programs.

A final decree, approved by the court in January 1994, committed DCFS to establishing new procedures and practices for the members of the class. The agency also promised to create the position of teen parent coordinator and staff it for at least six years; the coordinator would be assisted by a consultant, who would be retained for at least two years. After two years, the consultant would assess DCFS's treatment of the class and, depending on the findings, DCFS would be permitted to abolish the consultancy position (*Hill v. Erickson* 1994).

Charlotte Wenzel was appointed as Teen Consultant (Wenzel 1996); she had taken over the position on the citizens committee when Kane left the organization to become the inspector general of DCFS. Wenzel presented her first report to the court in October 1996 and remains in that position today, reporting to the court and DCFS on the status of DCFS compliance with the decree.

According to Wenzel, because of *Hill,* teenage mothers are not moved from one placement to another without approval from their caseworkers, their foster parents, and a clinician. Overall, she believed *Hill* was a "pretty neat consent decree" and thought that DCFS was "trying very hard" to comply with it.

Aristotle P.

In March 1994—after a long spell of argument and negotiation—DCFS and the OPG finally reached an accord in *Aristotle P.,* the case involving sibling placements and visits. In the decree, originally set to expire in March 1997, DCFS committed itself to new procedures that would place siblings together under normal circumstances; if forced to separate them, it would facilitate visits among them at least twice a month (*Aristotle P. v. Ryder* 1994). Shortly before the decree expired, in an effort to avoid another legal battle over the department's compliance with the decree, the parties jointly moved the court to extend the implementation period until March 1999 (*Aristotle P. v. McDonald* 1997).

Thus, while it was expected to develop the new procedures and practices required by *B.H.*, DCFS was preoccupied with reform efforts by child welfare litigants on several fronts. The continuous attempts by children's advocates to bring DCFS into compliance with federal and state laws and the demands placed on the agency by the resulting consent decrees created severe pressures on the agency and added to the challenge of fulfilling its obligations under *B.H.*

Judicial Oversight

Despite the suspicions voiced by Horowitz (1977) and others, most observers agree that the federal courts do not seek out opportunities to thrust themselves into disputes over the governance of public institutions. Wishing to conserve limited judicial resources and to avoid long trials, most judges typically encourage the parties to enter into settlement negotiations, in part to obviate concerns over the court's capacity to determine proper relief. Although the court must ultimately approve the resulting settlement, once the parties have reached agreement, most judges endeavor to limit their intrusion into the agency's decisionmaking. Despite their intentions, however, resolution of systemic reform litigation by consent decree frequently involves a greater degree of judicial involvement in agency affairs than the courts initially anticipated (Cooper 1988; Effron 1988). During the implementation phase, courts can become drawn into disputes between the parties who "find themselves quickly back in court, pressing for interpretation, enforcement, modification or relief from the very decree that originally promised to end it all" (Effron 1988, 1807). Aware of the limits on their ability to compel results in agency policy, many judges also try to resist being drawn into such disputes between the parties.

In their study of the consent decree involving access to education for Pennsylvania's mentally disabled children, Janet Rosenberg and William Phillips (1982) described the efforts of Judge Edward Becker of the Eastern District of Pennsylvania to achieve a negotiated settlement among the parties by presiding over hearings in open court for about three years (see also Conrad 1989). In contrast, Judge John Grady maintained a relatively low profile during the settlement talks, limiting himself to encouraging the parties to settle, attempting to structure the negotiations with input from child welfare experts, and ultimately placing his imprimatur on the agreement reached by the parties. The resulting decree was the product of extensive negotiations among the parties, based to a large extent on the recommendations of the child welfare experts Grady brought into the process.

During the implementation phase, Grady held periodic status hearings and sought to make it clear to everyone that he would not tolerate the state's failure to comply with the deadlines imposed in the decree. Yet throughout, he also demonstrated awareness of the complexities involved in DCFS's task of administering a child welfare agency. When asked whether agencies such as DCFS are able to comply with court orders and consent decrees, Grady (1996a) replied "yes," noting, however, that "a lot of the problems [DCFS] has are difficult human problems." He said he was, as a matter of due process, unwilling to compromise on the issue of the state's obligation to keep children in substitute care safe.

At the same time he recognized that DCFS was forced to deal with an expanding caseload, increasingly complex cases, and an upsurge in the number of children with emotional as well as physical problems (Grady 1996a). Moreover, Grady was aware that factors outside the department, such as the availability of placements and foster care parents, affected the department's ability to comply with the decree. In a ruling on an ancillary matter in 1994, Grady demonstrated his realization of the immensity of the tasks facing DCFS: "Challenges associated with the overlapping problems of poverty, growing unemployment, homelessness, crises of various kinds in the public school system, teenage pregnancy, violence and drug abuse infiltrate almost every aspect of the task assigned to DCFS. This is not to say that DCFS is excused from exerting its best efforts to comply with the decree, but it is background necessary to an understanding of the compliance questions" (*B.H. v. Ryder* 1994a, 1291).

Successful implementation of a consent decree depends on a number of factors, not least of which probably are "the personalities of the judge and [the] master" (Kirp and Babcock 1981, 330). Judges vary in the degree to which they intervene during the implementation phase, with some participating more directly in the ongoing administration of an agency and others more inclined to let developments occur and receive periodic progress reports from the parties at status hearings, intervening only when necessary to resolve contested matters.

Although many judges may encourage the parties to resolve their own disputes during the implementation process, there are times when the parties are unable to settle their disagreements and must return to court. When they do, a "judge may prefer to nudge along, rather than coerce, the process of compliance in hopes of keeping alive the spirit of consent" (Anderson 1986, 727). Although conscientious about performing his judicial function, Grady seemed to view his role primarily as encouraging the parties to agree on the direction and goals of the state's child welfare policy, subject to his approval, and to "nudge" them into compliance with those goals. One respondent described him as "rely[ing] to a great extent on the parties to work things out." Yet he often expressed dismay at the slow progress of agency reform and at the endless conflicts that surfaced between the two opposing sides. He complained of being "frustrated at the lack of specific suggestions and comments. Everybody has got a complaint," he said, "about what is going on in this or that or another area. But the really helpful people, of whom there are very few, are the ones who come up with solutions" (*Chicago Tribune*, December 3, 1993).[11]

While the court's posture during the implementation process depends in part on the temperament of the presiding judge, there are also structural reasons why some judges may play less active roles in resolving disputes over the implementation of systemic reform cases. Had *B.H.* gone to trial—and a long trial was anticipated—Grady would have been forced to assimilate a great deal of detailed information about the operation of the child welfare system. Aware that he lacked expertise in child welfare policy, Grady compensated by trying to educate himself about the child welfare system and, more important, by enlisting the aid of experts to assist the court. Yet, as he himself commented (Grady 1996a), he would have been "better educated" about the child welfare system had the case gone to trial. And, as one respondent noted, a trial that produced evidence of the agency's long-standing failures might have made Grady "angry" and more inclined to be firmer with DCFS during the implementation stage.

Judges have an array of enforcement mechanisms available to compel an agency's compliance with a decree; their powers include imposing sanctions or fines and can even extend to imprisoning top agency personnel or state officials. In cases of prison reform, judges have sometimes resorted to ordering prisons closed until the violation is cured (Welling and Jones 1988). Conscious of the constraints of federalism, however, most federal judges are wary of taking steps that raise concerns about excessive federal court interference in state policymaking. Thus, reluctant to evoke disquieting images of judicial activism, judges are inclined to tread carefully in exercising the authority of their robes.

In evaluating Grady's performance in *B.H.*, most respondents believed him to be fair and open-minded; he was seen as a neutral referee in this complex litigation. He was given high marks for having "a good grasp of the issues," although clearly not an expert in child welfare policy himself (nor was he expected to be). One respondent spoke approvingly of the fact that "he was willing to get his hands dirty," meaning he was amenable to learning about the child welfare system and how DCFS operated. The prevailing view was that he did not expect to decide every issue himself, but rather that he "was interested in having the sides work out the issues that divided them" and "reach a consensus." He "listened to both sides," one respondent explained.

Grady seemed to have a clear sense of the direction in which he wanted the litigation to proceed and was generally willing to allow the parties a good deal of leeway in determining how to get there. He held numerous hearings to oversee the agency's compliance with the decree but largely refrained from imposing his own view on the parties, confining himself, for the most part, to approving agreements made between them. As one respondent commented, he was "concerned about the limitations of the judge's role," yet also endeavored to allow the litigation to be used "as a forum for improvement."

Opinions on Grady's effectiveness varied greatly, depending, to some extent, on which side of the litigation the respondent was on. One respondent on DCFS's side said he was "great." To some, however, he appeared too hesitant to exert his authority over the defendants. Two respondents expressed disappointment in his style, wanting him to play a more forceful role in the litigation; one disapprovingly stated that Grady "was not an activist" and the other was critical that "he [Grady] did not hold DCFS's feet to the fire." Another of the child welfare advocates stated that he would have preferred "a more interventionist judge" who would have "required the department to follow through on the monitor's recommendations."

Although, not surprisingly, Grady did not please everyone involved in the *B.H.* litigation, his actions during both the adjudication and implementation phases, as demonstrated in his published opinions and as described by respondents, were not those of an interventionist judge. In contrast to the image of activist judges presented by some critics of public law litigation, Grady refrained from imposing his convictions on the litigants and, aware of his limitations, was willing to seek counsel from all parties involved in the litigation, as well as from a vast array of experts in the child welfare field. Yet he was also firm in his dedication to overseeing the implementation process of the decree and having DCFS move as quickly as possible toward meeting its demands.

The Monitor

The *B.H.* consent decree specified that an "independent and impartial" monitor was to be appointed to "evaluate and report upon implementation and compliance," with funds provided by the defendant (*B.H. v. Suter* 1991, 56).

Under the authority of Rule 53 of the Federal Rules of Civil Procedure, federal judges may appoint such officials as masters, monitors, or receivers, the last having the most independent power and being the least common. Horowitz (1983, 1272) argues that Rule 53 had a limited purpose, originally intended to allow district court judges to appoint masters for fact-finding purposes prior to judgment and only under rather exceptional circumstances. Whatever the intent, however, with the growing reliance on institutional reform litigation, masters and monitors now perform an increasingly important role in assisting the court during the implementation stage.

Rule 53 appointees serve in a variety of functions at several stages of the litigation, with varying degrees of access to litigants, experts, and the court (Horowitz 1983; see also Kirp and Babcock 1981).[12] Most often appointed for their expertise, masters and monitors help the court in formulating a remedy or, more typically, assist in monitoring compliance with the decree during the implementation stage (see Special Project 1978). Both are ultimately responsible to the court, but generally masters are permitted greater supervisory powers over the daily work of the institution and may be delegated decisionmaking authority by the court; monitors are typically confined to gathering information on compliance with the decree and reporting to the court (Cooper 1988; Chilton 1991; see also Special Project 1978).

Chilton's (1991, 107) inquiry into the Georgia Prison System characterized the litigation there as a "lawsuit that worked to achieve the desired change." The institution, he said, was "transformed" by the efforts of a special master, a special monitor, and an independent monitor, all charged with oversight of the implementation process.

Similarly, in his examination of the institutional reform litigation of the Maine mental health system, Murray Levine (1986, 277) depicted the suit filed there as "relatively successful," in part attributing its achievements to the work of the two special masters. He cited particularly the activism of the first master and his relationship to the judge (see also Aronow 1980).

All the respondents in this study agreed that successful implementation of a consent decree in a systemic reform action frequently depends on the presence of an aggressive master or monitor, acting, as one noted, "as the eyes and ears of the court." When asked to assess the importance of a monitor, Diane Geraghty (1998), chair of the Citizens Committee on the Juvenile Court, noted that when courts have to manage large systems following institutional reform litigation, monitors "make eminent sense." Clark Peters (1998) of the Chapin Hall Center for Children agreed that monitors play an "absolutely useful role" in institutional reform litigation; Gaylord Gieseke (1996) called a monitor "crucial." More forcefully, Robert Lehrer (1997), former deputy director of the LAF, stated, "Without a monitor, [a plaintiff] might as well stay home." And Jeanine Smith (1996), the *Norman* monitor, stated that absent a monitor there is no "accountability" in a consent decree. Others were more cautious, contending that the usefulness of monitors depends on the role they play and the expertise they bring to the task. When asked what characterized a good monitor, Peggy Slater (1998), the director of Policy Initiatives of the Permanency Project of the Cook County Juvenile Court, said that she believed it would be someone "who knows the turf." Peters (1998), however, felt that it was even more important for a monitor to understand how institutions operated than to be an expert in the policy area. Also less concerned with expertise, one of the district court judges believed a competent monitor could promote compromise among the parties following a decree. Golbert (1998) summarized these views by stating that monitors in institutional reform litigation must perform three essential functions: mediating between the parties, measuring compliance, and proposing solutions for the problems confronting the agency.

Most respondents on the DCFS side were unenthusiastic about monitors, commenting that they intruded into the work of the agency and added an unnecessary burden to its budget. They conceded, however, that certain kinds of monitors could exert a positive influence on the implementation process. Mary Sue Morsch (1996), head of DCFS's Office of Litigation Management, believed that monitors with the expertise to recommend policy options can be useful; Ginger Ostro (1996), formerly in that office, noted that monitors that have a "programmatic" focus can be effective. Joseph Loftus (1998), executive deputy director of DCFS, believed a good monitor was one who saw "what needed to be done." Jess McDonald (1996) similarly commented that a monitor's usefulness depends on the role he or she wants to play. From his perspective, a monitor who acted like an "honest broker," engaged in fact-finding, and helped "shed new light on problems" was the most desirable.

Thus there was a consensus among the respondents that effective court-appointed monitors can play an important role in institutional reform litigation, in "ensur[ing] compliance with the decree during the implementation process" (Monahan 1996). However, although most agreed a monitor can affect an agency's compliance with a consent decree, there was less agreement on what the monitor should do to encourage such compliance.

The implementation stage of the *B.H.* litigation was characterized by a constant round of meetings, memos, and reports, largely revolving around the work of the monitor, former Illinois Circuit Court Judge Joseph Schneider, who assumed the position of monitor on March 18, 1992. Schneider (1996), a retired judge with a Master's Degree in Social Work and experience in child welfare policy, had been the presiding officer of the County Division of the Circuit Court from 1982 until his retirement in 1992.

In explaining his duties, Schneider (1996) pointed out that the consent decree provided that the monitor and his staff would have access to all the parties as well as to data from DCFS. When asked how he viewed his role as monitor, Schneider stated that it "was to see whether or not DCFS had complied with the provisions set forth in the consent decree." Continuing, he said, "And when there was noncompliance, I viewed my role as a facilitator who kept the parties talking about the issues." Schneider added that he believed that "DCFS worked very hard at complying."

In his role as monitor, Schneider carefully documented the agency's lack of compliance with the decree, a continual source of annoyance to DCFS. In a report to Grady on February 1, 1994, Schneider noted that the department promised reform in ninety-three areas and was failing or would fail to carry out its promises in forty-two of the areas; compliance was especially poor in Cook County, he added (*Chicago Tribune,* February 2, 1994). He concluded: "There remains a big gap between the promise of *B.H.* and the performance of the Department; or put another way the conclusion of the Monitor at this juncture is that there is serious noncompliance with the *B.H.* Consent Decree on the part of DCFS" (*B.H. v. Ryder* 1994b, 159).

Ryder responded angrily to the report, publicly attacking it for "either overlook[ing] or minimiz[ing] major improvements and reforms that have been implemented by DCFS, leaving the erroneous impression that progress is not being made" (*Chicago Tribune,* February 2, 1994).

Respondents were divided in their assessments of Schneider's success as monitor. Most agreed that because of the comprehensive nature of the decree and the immensity of the reform effort, his task was extraordinarily difficult. In assessing his accomplishments, one respondent commented that Schneider exerted a great deal of positive energy in attempting to bring DCFS into compliance with the consent decree; another said that "he worked really hard and cared a lot." Some felt he had done a good job in keeping attention focused on DCFS's lack of progress in complying with the consent decree, painstakingly pointing out the many areas where the agency was in noncompliance. Few, however, believed that his performance had brought about significant reforms within DCFS. Although many tried to blunt their criticism, conceding that Schneider had made a good faith effort, most respondents questioned his effectiveness as a monitor.

It is not surprising that some of the DCFS respondents were displeased with Schneider's work as monitor; many, after all, believed he was merely interested in documenting the agency's failure to achieve compliance. Some at DCFS also expressed concern about the cost of the monitoring activity, indicating they thought the money could have been better spent in other ways.

Ironically, many non-DCFS respondents also criticized Schneider's performance, saying he did not achieve the goals envisioned for him. He was variously described as "ineffectual," "not tough enough," and "too bureaucratic." One respondent pointed out that Schneider "did not come up with ideas" and was not good at mediating between the two sides; another suggested he should have been "more pro active." In contrast to the view offered by those on DCFS's side, most felt that he was not strict enough with the defendants and that he was insufficiently "aggressive" in keeping the pressure on DCFS. One respondent summed up the opinions of several by saying, "I don't know what went wrong but . . . it should have been better." Another was more generous, pointing out that Schneider's deficiencies were understandable, given the "magnitude of the decree."

Some respondents spontaneously compared Schneider with Smith, expressing great enthusiasm about her efforts as monitor; indeed the respondents were uniformly impressed with Smith's work. One respondent, who acknowledged that monitoring *B.H.* was a much more difficult task, nevertheless stated that the *Norman* monitor was more effective and had a "good understanding of what a consent decree requires." Another characterized Smith and her staff as "fantastic." One called her "very useful," adding that he believed there was a consensus that the "*B.H.* monitor was not useful." Another compared her to Schneider, saying she paid "better attention to detail." Thus, although some respondents traced the disparity in the accomplishments of the two monitors to differing personalities and skills, all agreed that differences in their level of achievement was in some part attributable to the type of decree they were assigned to monitor.

Given the sweeping nature of the decree, it was unlikely that the monitor would be able to satisfy everyone's expectations. In the end, there was no consensus among the respondents about how effectively the monitor and his staff had performed their tasks and what they might have done differently to improve DCFS's compliance with the decree within the specified time limits. When Schneider stepped down from his position as monitor on January 1, 1996, there was also no agreement on his replacement. Unlike Hart in his commendation of Smith's efforts as monitor, Grady did not publicly praise Schneider's work; indeed, a number of respondents believed that Grady was disappointed with the monitor's performance in overseeing the implementation process. For whatever reason, Grady never suggested appointing another monitor to replace Schneider.

7 Response

REACTING TO THE LITIGATION

 The final phase of the institutional reform litigation process, the response phase, is unique. While the other stages are divisible into relatively discrete time periods, the response phase envelops the preceding ones and is analytically, rather than chronologically, distinct, encompassing virtually the entire litigation process.

In *B.H.* the response phase was characterized by reactions from state political leaders; children's advocates, particularly the child welfare bar; the media; and the child welfare authorities, notably the Department of Children and Family Services (DCFS) and juvenile court officials. These individuals were instrumental in determining the future of the abused and neglected children within the state, and their responses also provided a measure of the impact of the lawsuit on the child welfare system.

Public law litigation raises questions about the relationship of the federal courts to state institutions, questions focusing on the issue of increased resources for the targeted agency to enable it to meet the performance standards demanded of it. Institutional reform invariably comes with an expensive price tag. It was estimated, for example, that reforming penal institutions under court orders had cost states billions of dollars (Taggart 1989, 243).

In his criticism of institutional reform litigation, Horowitz (1977) implied that officials in charge of state agencies regard litigation as a vehicle for securing resources from the state legislature, with the courts often unwitting accomplices in this scheme (see also Harriman and Straussman 1983). Later Horowitz (1983, 1294–95) stated even more directly that defendants "are sometimes happy to be sued and happier still to lose," suggesting that losing an institutional reform lawsuit serves the agency's interests as well as the plaintiff's by forcing the state to increase the agency's budgetary allocations to satisfy the terms of the court order or decree.

Similarly, in discussing the suit against the Kansas City, Missouri, school system, Seventh Circuit judge Frank Easterbrook (1991, 108) indicated that the school board viewed the district court's order to make capital improvements in the schools and its direction to the state to raise taxes to fund the improvements as a golden opportunity to avoid having to rely on the voters to increase spending for the schools. "This is frequent in litigation against local governments," he noted, "and decrees of this kind simultaneously provide benefits for the plaintiffs and liberate public officials from constraints on their own power."

Agreeing that some defendants are not displeased about such outcomes, Levine (1986, 307) viewed the matter differently. He believed that defendant agencies quite naturally (and properly) look on a judicial decree as a means of augmenting their budgets. He saw nothing wrong with the court's playing such a role; on the contrary, in his study of the class action litigation in Maine, he emphasized that "serv[ing] as the functional equivalent of a powerful political constituency in the competition for the allocation of resources [was] precisely the role envisioned for the courts in *U.S. v. Carolene Products* (1938)."

Political Leaders

Writing in 1991, before the *B.H.* decree was finalized, Lee Preston, chair of the Illinois House Committee on Children and Family Law—and later a juvenile court judge—predicted that the consent decree would necessitate greater appropriations for DCFS. He criticized his colleagues for refusing to fund child welfare services at appropriate levels, saying: "As our children's quality of life has worsened in recent years, our elected officials seem less willing to spend the dollars necessary to remedy the problem. It is easy to make speeches about children's issues, but when it comes to allocating public dollars, we find that many office holders have other priorities. Children don't vote, and few children's lobbying groups have enough influence to change legislators' minds" (Preston 1991, 580).

As a result of *B.H.*, the court became "a powerful political constituency" that forced state officials to "change [their] minds" about reordering their budgetary priorities and support child welfare services more generously. Not surprisingly, most state leaders were not pleased about this turn of events.

The impact of the litigation was almost immediate. On assuming office as governor, Jim Edgar announced a cut of more than one billion dollars from the state budget, but spared DCFS these reductions, instead allocating a 12 percent increase to the agency, in part because of the pending federal litigation (Schuerman, Rzepnicki, and Littell 1994, 219). The next year, while cutting funds from other agencies, Edgar proposed to increase DCFS's budget for FY 1993 to implement the decree. Indeed, for the next several years, DCFS continued to receive preferential treatment during the budget process.

The sharp increase in the state's appropriations for DCFS, shown in appendix table 7, represents one of the most dramatic illustrations of the effects of *B.H.* The child welfare agency, as Jess McDonald noted some years later, had "probably the fastest growing budget in state government" (*Chicago Lawyer*, February 1997). Appendix table 7, illustrating DCFS appropriations from FY 1980 to 1999, shows that there has been a spectacular growth in state expenditures for child welfare over the past ten years, with the budget increasing by more than 200 percent in just over five years and appropriations topping one billion dollars by FY 1995.

There seems little doubt that *B.H.* was responsible for this growth; the three largest annual percentage increases occurred between July 1, 1992, and June 30, 1995, encompassing the implementation phase of the litigation. Moreover, the narrative accompanying each year's budget report explicitly stated that the funding increases were due to *B.H.* In the fiscal 1993 budget, for example, the section entitled "Programs—Budget Highlights" noted that the "DCFS budget includes an additional $47.5 million, from the unreserved fiscal year 1992 appropriation of $18.1 million, for full implementation of the *B.H. v. Suter* consent decree in order to continue reforms of the child welfare system" (Illinois Bureau of the Budget FY 1993, Ch. 3-19).

The next year the budget report explained that "the department is committed to improving the child welfare system and implementing the reforms in the *B.H.* consent decree. . . . Since fiscal year 1991, the amount of General Revenue funds allocated to the department has increased 88 percent." As an indication of the significance of the decree in the state's fiscal planning, it continued, "At the recommended fiscal year 1994 general funds level of $691 million, the agency will hire approximately 400 new employees, the majority of whom will provide direct services to address new caseload ratios specified in the *B.H.* consent decree" (Illinois Bureau of the Budget FY 1994, Ch. 3-19).

Because state legislators often resent what they regard as unwarranted interference with their constitutional duty to determine how to spend state funds, *B.H.* became a source of irritation for many legislators. Although the Illinois General Assembly was forced to allocate this massive infusion of funds for child welfare services, it did not do so willingly. In addition to expressing their resentment over the increased DCFS appropriations, some state officials also indicated that they thought the court had diminished the state's role in public policymaking.

One of the district court judges interviewed for this study pointed out that because of their life tenure federal judges are able to provide agencies with "political cover" that can deflect away from the department and toward the court some of the legislature's wrath at having to fund costly improvements in agency services. Not surprisingly, therefore, legislators increasingly expressed resentment against the court for its role in the litigation, not acknowledging that the court had merely approved the settlement negotiated by the parties. Although according to Sterling Ryder (1996), "settling *B.H.* was an effort to retain state executive branch control over child welfare spending and programs," the decree became an easy target for state legislators who charged that the federal court unduly intruded into the state's child welfare system.

Notwithstanding the "cover" provided by the courts, relationships between DCFS and members of the legislature deteriorated after the settlement agreement was signed, especially as the years went by and appropriations continued to increase with no discernible improvement in the child welfare system. The perception that DCFS was in constant crisis, a fact reported in a barrage of unfavorable media reports, made legislators even "grumpier," one respondent noted. Some respondents also suggested that the resentment against DCFS was a manifestation of some of the suburban and downstate legislators' hostility to Cook County and to the largely poor and minority population served by DCFS there.

Although the politicians could not deny the need for child welfare reform, they were unwilling to assume responsibility for improving the state's poor performance in delivering child welfare services. Instead, they directed their anger at the agency, attacking it for acquiescing to the demands of the American Civil Liberties Union (ACLU) in the settlement agreement. Echoing Horowitz's and Easterbrook's conspiracy theory, some state legislators publicly accused McDonald of promoting *B.H.* to secure funding increases from the general assembly (*Chicago Tribune,* November 1, 1995). The legislative voices became even more strident after the Republicans assumed control of the general assembly following the 1994 election. Republican state senator Peter Fitzgerald, elected to the U.S. Senate in 1998, reported that he heard a "rumor" that DCFS had "actually solicited" the suit to force the state to increase its appropriations (*Chicago Daily Law Bulletin,* August 12, 1996).

The Republican takeover of the Illinois legislature in 1994 exacerbated legislative hostility toward DCFS, and especially toward Jess McDonald. Despite McDonald's close association with Governor Jim Edgar, the Republican leadership seemed to direct most of its ire at McDonald. Many characterized the settlement agreement as a "deal" between the ACLU and McDonald—overlooking the sequence of events in the settlement talks: the decree was signed months after McDonald left DCFS and a new director, another Republican appointee, was in place.

As a number of respondents pointed out, the critics were ignoring the fact that a widely publicized trial in which DCFS's flaws were fully aired, followed by a finding of liability against the agency (the almost certain outcome of a trial), would have damaged the state's image even more than a settlement—and likely would have been more costly as well. Notwithstanding this reality, the politicians attacked the consent decree, variously blaming the agency, the ACLU, and McDonald for its existence.

When asked their opinions about the legislators' charges, most respondents flatly rejected the notion of a deal between the litigants at any time, or even of any improper collaboration between the plaintiffs and the defendant. According to Christina Tchen (1995), DCFS "did not welcome the litigation—being put under a microscope." Not only was the accusation insulting to both sides, especially McDonald, a number of respondents noted, but it also implied that the lawsuit had been unfounded. Ironically, also, by accusing DCFS of instigating the lawsuit and capitulating too readily to the ACLU's demands, the Republicans were accusing Edgar, whose signature was on the decree, of complicity in McDonald's allegedly improper conduct.

The leadership also demonstrated its displeasure with the agency and the consent decree by delaying McDonald's confirmation for more than a year, forcing him to serve as acting director from June 1994 until November 1995. Justifying the senate's reluctance to confirm McDonald as director of the agency, Fitzgerald said McDonald needed to be stopped from spending so many tax dollars, adding, "We don't want any more sweetheart deals cut with the ACLU" (*Chicago Sun-Times*, June 1, 1995). James "Pate" Phillip, president of the Illinois senate, led the opposition to McDonald. Although Phillip attributed his lack of enthusiasm for McDonald to the agency's failures and its soaring budget, newspaper editorials speculated that he was motivated in part by a desire to retaliate for McDonald's criticism of Phillip's derisive comments about the work ethics of minority staff members at DCFS (see, for example, *Chicago Tribune*, June 4, 1995; *Chicago Sun-Times*, November 2, 1995). McDonald, who was increasingly impatient with his uncertain status and threatened to resign in May, was finally confirmed in November 1995 during the legislature's fall veto session.

In February 1996 the Republican leadership translated its belief in a conspiracy theory into action by introducing Senate Bill 1494. The bill, which was another manifestation of the legislature's antipathy to *B.H.*, as originally introduced would have required the approval of both chambers of the assembly by a joint resolution before the attorney general could enter into a consent decree costing more than $500,000; settlements of less than $500,000 would have required only formal notification to the two houses. Testifying before the Senate Executive Committee in favor of the bill, Fitzgerald, its sponsor, clearly had McDonald in mind when he stated, "The whole process now allows unelected bureaucrats to do an end run around our whole system of government." In other testimony in support of the bill, Senate Appropriations Committee chair Steven Rauschenberger also leveled a charge against the court. Referring to a consent decree, he said, "The judge blesses it frequently without reading it or analyzing it" (*Chicago Daily Law Bulletin*, February 29, 1996). In addition to reflecting the lawmakers' antagonism to *B.H.*, the bill was aimed at forestalling settlement in the pending ACLU suit against the Illinois Department of Mental Health (*Chicago Tribune*, February 15, 1996); that case was, however, also eventually settled.

After several months, the general assembly passed an amended version of the bill, sending it to the governor for his signature in June; Edgar signed it in August. Public Act 89-645, amending the State Finance Act, required that, effective January 1, 1997, the attorney general must *notify* the senate president and house speaker before entering into a class action settlement involving the appropriation or expenditure of $10 million or more in state funds.[1] Commenting on the law, Fitzgerald said that it furthered his goal of compelling legislative consent for all settlement agreements (*Chicago Daily Law Bulletin*, August 12, 1996).

Children's Advocates

Illinois has a well-established child welfare bar that plays an instrumental role in shaping the contours of the child welfare system. Although the attorneys share a common dedication to the goal of advancing the interests of Illinois's abused and neglected children, they often differ about the most effective strategy to solve the problems of the system. Their disagreements are both substantive and procedural. The substantive dispute is, in part, based on their disagreement over the wisdom of family preservation and the law's preference for reunifying families; procedurally, they disagree about the benefits of systemic litigation. Although Patrick Murphy believed more strongly in family preservation in his earlier years, as he stated in his book on the child welfare system entitled *Wasted*, his views on family preservation and reunification had become more negative during the 1980s. He now believes, he says, that family preservation "is a good idea in a 'proper' case, but [that] such cases are unfortunately not as common as they used to be" (Murphy 1997, 69; 1996). While others in the child welfare community might agree with this statement as written, most are more predisposed to the principle of family reunification than Murphy is.

Throughout the litigation process, the differences between the plaintiffs' attorneys and the Office of Public Guardian (OPG) were aired frequently.

Murphy publicly criticized the lawsuit virtually from its outset and continually assailed the ACLU's conduct in the case. In *Wasted*, Murphy (1997, 121) charged that *B.H.* was a "friendly lawsuit" in which the two sides, who "essentially shared the same philosophy," used the litigation to compel "the legislature to ante up."

According to Benjamin Wolf (1996), Murphy reviewed the consent decree before it was finalized and, after some discussion and modification of it, said he was substantially satisfied with it. Nevertheless, Murphy's protests against the decree were soon heard at almost every stage of the litigation process.

Apparently perturbed by his lack of involvement in *B.H.*, Murphy sought to play a more active role in the case and twice attempted to intervene in the settlement negotiations.[2] Some commentators later maintained that his "effort threatened to undo [the *B.H.*] settlement" (*Chicago Tribune*, September 17, 1996).

His first formal attempt to intervene in the settlement talks came in September 1990, when he claimed that his status as guardian *ad litem* gave him a "substantial interest" in the action and entitled him to take a seat at the negotiating table. He alleged that the plaintiffs' counsel were not adequately representing their interests, one of the criteria for granting a motion to intervene. Judge John Grady denied the motion, ruling that Murphy had not shown a "direct interest" in the case nor explained why his expertise was necessary to the negotiations; he held that Murphy's intervention at that stage of the process would be "disruptive." Murphy did not appeal Grady's ruling.

In April 1991 Murphy again moved to intervene, repeating essentially the same arguments he had presented in the first motion. When Grady denied this motion as well, Murphy appealed to the Seventh Circuit, which dismissed the action as an attempt to avoid a timely appeal of Grady's first ruling.

Murphy also tried unsuccessfully to block the court's approval of the decree at the fairness hearing. Although he convinced Grady to allow him to call witnesses and crossexamine DCFS officials during the hearing, Murphy put on a tepid performance, according to Loftus (1998), calling only one witness to the stand. Another respondent, however, more sympathetic to Murphy, suggested the public guardian was simply ignored when he tried to oppose the agreement at the hearing.

After the decree was approved, Murphy appealed Grady's order denying his motion to intervene as well as the order approving the consent decree. In a unanimous opinion by a Seventh Circuit panel, the appeals were dismissed on two grounds: first, Murphy had exceeded the thirty-day time limit for appealing the lower court ruling on his motion to intervene; and second, the court held, because he was neither a party to the case nor a proper intervenor, he lacked standing to challenge the consent decree (*B.H. v. Ryder* 1993, 199–200).

Murphy also engaged in a public relations campaign against the decree. In August 1991, when DCFS and the ACLU had been close to reaching an understanding, he was quoted as calling the proposed settlement agreement "a mealy-mouthed order" (*Chicago Tribune,* August 15, 1991). Later he claimed the consent decree was "flawed" because it failed to represent the "best interests" of the children in the system (McMurray 1995, 122). He showed his displeasure over the decree by dispatching a series of letters to Wolf, with copies to juvenile court judges and sometimes the press as well, criticizing the settlement. Wolf also forwarded copies of his responses to Murphy to the juvenile court judges and the media.

Occasionally tending toward incivility, their letters reflected their differences over the wisdom of seeking large-scale systemic reform through the courts rather than seeking more narrow relief in smaller, more manageable, lawsuits. In one letter, defending himself against Murphy's charges, Wolf wrote: "We have decided not to follow your lead in endlessly pursuing the same unsuccessful strategies" (McMurray 1995, 124).

During this time as well, friction had arisen between Murphy and some of the other Illinois child welfare advocates over the *Artist M.* case, particularly over the way his office was conducting the Supreme Court appeal. Despite the importance of the issue as a test of the judicial enforceability of P.L. 96-272, Murphy assigned Michael Dsida, a relatively inexperienced assistant public guardian, to argue the case before the high court and, according to several respondents, refused to allow him to consult with other child welfare experts or more experienced supreme court litigators.[3] Justifying his decision, Murphy maintained that the case was lost from the beginning, claiming that "the Supreme Court heard the case so they could reverse the lower court; their minds were made up" (McMurray 1995, 124; see also Wexler 1995a).

Another conflict between Murphy and the plaintiffs' attorneys was aired in December 1993 when the latter, citing the difficulty of holding hearings on compliance issues in the midst of intense media coverage, wrote a letter to Grady asking him to hold closed status hearings in addition to the hearings held in open court. After Grady agreed to hold some conferences in chambers, Murphy filed a motion in February 1994, again seeking to intervene and asking the court to hold all future hearings in public, claiming that closed hearings violated the public's right to know. Murphy later maintained the public's interest in the case arose from its contribution to DCFS revenues in tax dollars and its concern for the welfare of the children in DCFS custody

(*B.H. v. McDonald* 1995b, 296). The ACLU and the DCFS attorneys joined in opposing the motion.

In ruling on Murphy's motion, Grady described the state of events in the case thus far, indicating why he was sympathetic to the parties' desire to hold at least some closed sessions. "Since entering the decree, the court has held periodic status conferences in open court to discuss compliance questions. Members of the press and other interested persons have been present. The colloquy at these status conferences has usually been adversarial and often heated. Counsel for the plaintiffs is generally accusatory and counsel for the Department defensive. Neither side is inclined to concede anything, and this reluctance, in the court's view, is at least partly based on concern about how a concession would look in the press reports" (*B.H. v. Ryder* 1994a, 1286–87).

In light of the relevant caselaw on the public's right of access to judicial proceedings, Grady was ultimately persuaded by the parties that the in-chamber conferences should be viewed as settlement talks. He pointed out that, as in almost any case involving institutional reform, many issues between the parties remain unresolved even after a decree is signed. Although the parties formally reached a settlement agreement in the case, he believed that continuing disputes over compliance "are often resolved by the same techniques used in pretrial settlements" (*B.H. v. Ryder* 1994a, 1286–87, 1291). Acknowledging a First Amendment right of access to certain kinds of judicial proceedings, he held that it does not extend to status conferences where the purpose of the conferences would not be served by a public airing. Thus, analogizing the status hearings to settlement conferences that are traditionally closed to the press and the public, Grady denied Murphy's motion.

Murphy again appealed to the Seventh Circuit. In another unanimous opinion, announced by Alfred Goodwin, a Ninth Circuit judge sitting by designation, the panel held that Murphy had not established that he had a right to intervene nor that the plaintiff's attorneys were providing inadequate representation.[4] In ruling on the right of access to all status conferences, the appeals court believed that Grady had not abused his discretion by deciding to hold occasional sessions with the parties behind closed doors. Goodwin spoke sympathetically of the task of a district court judge in overseeing the implementation of "complex consent decrees" in which "policy questions . . . do not lend themselves to simple yes and no answers" (*B.H. v. McDonald* 1995b, 298). Noting that the conferences are intended to allow the parties to try to reach a consensus to achieve more efficient implementation of the decree, and that proceedings on the merits would still be held in open court, the appellate court affirmed Grady's ruling and upheld the exclusion of non-parties from the judge's chambers.

Modifying the Decree

Five years after the decree was entered into, although they "dispute sharply the extent of noncompliance and the Department's culpability for that non-compliance," the parties admitted "that DCFS currently is not in compliance with the Decree's provisions" (*B.H. v. McDonald* 1996b, 3). Moreover, according to a staff writer at the *Chicago Tribune* (July 25, 1996), the lawyers for both sides conceded that their efforts at reform have "not substantially improved the lives of abused and neglected children."

As the implementation phase continued, extending beyond the deadlines imposed by the decree, some of the child welfare advocates began to express more concern about outcome measures, such as securing children's safety and well-being and finding permanent homes for them, than about the procedural requirements of the decree.

The respondents who were more directly involved in the litigation believed that the decree was too narrowly focused on "process" issues, such as the caseworker-to-child ratios, and paid insufficient attention to broader "outcome" issues such as permanency or improving the quality of children's lives. Their solution was to modify the decree to refocus it on "outcome" rather than "process" measures. They planned to accomplish this, in part, by commissioning the newly established Children and Family Research Center, housed at the School of Social Work at the University of Illinois at Urbana-Champaign in downstate Illinois, to conduct research and data gathering. They also hoped the center would fill the void left by Joseph Schneider's resignation as monitor, collectively serving as a monitor. According to McDonald (1996), the Research Center, which had been under consideration for more than a year and was announced at the beginning of 1996, would have the necessary expertise to evaluate and shape the way in which DCFS met its objectives. Before the center's announced opening, McDonald had committed $200,000 of DCFS funds to support it (*Chicago Tribune*, September 14, 1995).

In a joint motion to the court, the parties stated they believed that the decree should be modified "by emphasizing the use of outcomes for children and families—are children safer? healthier? returning home or being adopted more quickly?—as the ultimate touchstone of compliance with the Decree" (*B.H. v. McDonald* 1996b, 4).

Critics of this plan to fix DCFS called it "not much more than wishful thinking" (*Chicago Tribune*, September 26, 1996). Not surprisingly, the OPG took the lead in opposing the proposed modification. This time, however, it was joined by a broad coalition of representatives from children's advocacy groups: Voices for Illinois Children, Illinois Action for Children, the Citizens Committee on the Juvenile Court, Northwestern University's Children and

Family Justice Center, and the firm of Lehrer and Redleaf, counsel for the class members in *Youakim v. McDonald* (1995).

In part, the opponents were concerned about a potential conflict of interest. The proposed head of the research center, Dr. Susan Wells, a nationally recognized expert in child welfare policy, most recently from the Research Triangle Institute in North Carolina, had been chosen after a nationwide search. She was the stepsister of DCFS deputy executive director Joseph Loftus. Acknowledging the potential for a conflict of interest, the University of Illinois had conducted an ethics review and instituted, as noted in the motion, "structural protections [that] effectively insulate the direct monitoring functions of the Center under this Decree from Dr. Wells, who will focus on the Center's other missions" (*B.H. v. McDonald* 1996b, 44). And in an attempt to deflect further criticism, they announced that they intended to delegate responsibility to Dr. John Poertner, associate dean of the School of Social Work at the University of Illinois, to direct the center's monitoring functions.

The challengers offered three main objections to the proposed modifications: first, they were troubled about the center's responsibility for developing vaguely defined outcome indicators to measure compliance with the decree and allowing DCFS six more years to achieve its goals—essentially without judicial review; second, they opposed the extension of the decree's preclusive effects on subsequent actions brought on behalf of children in DCFS custody;[5] and third, they voiced disapproval of the potential conflict of interest relating to Wells's position at the center and expressed doubt about the political and financial constraints on the center's independence, since, as part of the state university system, it would be subject to the authority of the state legislature and governor (*B.H. v. McDonald* 1996a).

In a letter to the court, DCFS Inspector General Denise Kane (*B.H v. McDonald* 1996c) questioned the sufficiency of the university's ethics review and expressed concern about the appearance of impropriety in appointing a relative of a high DCFS official to head the center. Murphy criticized both DCFS and the ACLU, charging the latter with "largely abandoning ship after discovering that turning around DCFS could not be accomplished overnight." He called the projected plan "the biggest cop-out," continuing, "The ACLU calls themselves advocates; I call them jellyfish." Of the plan, he said, "You cannot have the fox monitoring the chicken coop. All they [DCFS] have to do is please Joe Loftus's stepsister" (*Chicago Tribune*, July 25, 1996).

At the fairness hearing before Grady on October 2, 1996, Michael Brody (1996) testified that the purpose of the modification was to "get away from procedures and emphasize how people are doing their jobs." Opposed by most of the other child welfare advocates, who were represented in court by assistant public guardians Charles Golbert and Peter Schmiedel, as well as Redleaf and Lehrer, once again Brody and Wolf were in the awkward position of joining DCFS counsel Christina Tchen against the other advocates.

Grady (1996b) questioned the wisdom of locating the center outside Cook County and expressed concern that, as monitor, the center's academicians would not make on-site inspections of DCFS facilities, that they would sit in Champaign, site of the University's downstate campus, without "darkening doors in the inner city." Reinforcing Grady's skepticism, Schmiedel (1996) stressed that the children needed a "hands-on monitor" to watch over DCFS and inform the court of its activities.

On January 22, 1997, Grady rejected most of the proposed modifications. Approving a few minor revisions to the decree, he said he had no objection if the department wanted to think in terms of "outcomes" and to measure those outcomes with indicators formulated by the research center. However, he added, he saw no evidence that adopting an ill-defined outcomes approach was preferable to the present requirements of the decree, and there was no reason to modify it. "As far as the Court is concerned [he said], compliance with the Decree will continue to be measured by the extent to which the Department is substantially meeting the objectives set forth in paragraph 4 of the Decree. If there is no inconsistency between the 'outcomes' and the objectives of paragraph 4, no problem is presented" (*B.H. v. McDonald* 1997a, 5).

Because the department would not be delegating its responsibility for meeting the objectives of the decree to the research center, Grady found it unnecessary to resolve the question of a potential conflict of interest that might undermine the center's objectivity, noting that he would evaluate the "objectivity" of any evidence offered by the center at the appropriate time. Neither did he address the issue of the decree's preclusive effect on future actions against DCFS in the state and federal courts.

Paradoxically, both sides declared victory after Grady handed down his decision. Although "critics of the proposed changes cheered the judge's ruling," McDonald also stated, "We got most of what we wanted" (*Chicago Tribune*, January 25, 1997).

In April, following the submission of another motion filed jointly by the parties, Grady clarified his position, explaining that the research center could develop outcome measures for the department, but it could not take responsibility for monitoring its compliance with the decree. Instead, the parties agreed, with Grady's concurrence, to eliminate the position of independent monitor entirely. Grady ordered, "Class counsel for plaintiffs shall receive from DCFS sufficient information to permit plaintiffs to evaluate the status of DCFS's compliance with this Decree" (*B.H. v. McDonald* 1997b, 4).

Today, according to Wells (1998), the research center forms a bridge that links research, policy, and practice in child welfare. To prevent the appearance of impropriety, she serves as the overall director of the center (with a tenured full professorship in the School of Social Work), while Poertner directs the outcomes reporting function of the center, reporting to the dean of the School of Social Work rather than to her. As she explained, the center functions as an "independent third-party reporter of outcomes" and also has a responsibility to conduct research to explain the outcomes and evaluate service effectiveness.

The first report on outcomes was issued by the research center in the spring of 1998. Produced by Poertner, it was intended as the first step in the process of defining outcome measures for children in care. The center will continue to issue semiannual reports on outcomes, reporting on the safety, achievement of permanent homes, and well-being for children in substitute care.

Although it is too soon to be able to evaluate the results of the center's work, opinions among respondents thus far have ranged from calling it "largely useless" to being "optimis[tic]" about its future. And once the initial furor about Wells's relationship with Loftus had subsided, no further concerns were aired publicly about the potential conflict of interest in the center's role in the child welfare system.

The conflict over the parties' motion to modify the decree represented one of the strangest aspects of the entire decade-long litigation. While uniting some former adversaries and publicizing the dissension among the advocates, it also lent more credence to the image that the parties were not sufficiently adversarial to each other.

In an attempt to repair some of the rifts in the child welfare community, according to Wolf (1998), the children's advocates began to meet after this episode to discuss their common interests. Initiated by the plaintiffs' attorneys, and attended by representatives of Voices for Illinois Children, Illinois Action for Children, the OPG, the Legal Assistance Foundation of Chicago (LAF), Loyola University's ChildLaw Center, and Northwestern University's Children and Family Justice Center, these meetings began sometime during 1997. They started as monthly meetings, then were held quarterly, and have since dwindled, Wolf reports. Although the participants have different concerns and do not share the same views of the progress made in reaching the goals of the consent decree, the talks seemed to indicate a desire among the advocacy groups to avoid the infighting that plagued them throughout the litigation and to discuss methods of improving the child welfare system.

The Media

With the battle over child welfare reform fought on political as well as legal grounds, the media play a significant role in the litigation process. In their analysis of judicial policy implementation, Robert Nakamura and Frank Smallwood (1980, 89) depict the media as one of the links between a court decision and the general public. In fulfilling this linkage function, the media can facilitate the reform effort by generating favorable publicity for the consent decree and helping win approval for it among the public and policymakers (see Levine 1986; Mezey 1988). Although *B.H.* generated a great deal of publicity in the press, however, the treatment accorded it was often too simplistic and, at times, irresponsible.

For quite some time, the child welfare system had been a favorite target of politicians on both sides of the aisle, their condemnation usually finding its way into the news. In part, of course, attacks on DCFS simply made good press. Politicians from the left and the right had easy access to the media when they railed against the department for returning a child to a homicidal parent; for allowing nineteen children to live in a filthy, unheated, rat-infested apartment; and for failing to prevent the near starvation of a five-year-old. Even public officials who might have been sympathetic to DCFS grew frustrated at the agency's lack of progress in reforming itself. Although their censure was frequently justified, however, much of it was often politically motivated and self-serving as well. DCFS's generally inept efforts at defending itself or explaining its behavior were seized on by the press and its audience as further evidence of incompetence. All this had the unfortunate effect of breeding public cynicism over child welfare reform.

Then, during the implementation stage of the litigation, the Wallace baby was killed. The stunning news of Joseph Wallace's death was a vivid portrayal of how far DCFS and the child welfare system were from achieving meaningful reform.

The tragedy, which began the day Joseph was born, came to a head in February 1993 when Juvenile Court Judge Walter Williams heard the parties in the case recommend that he reunite Joseph with his mother again. Although most participants at the hearing knew the circumstances of Joseph's past, Williams was apparently unaware that his mother had a recurring history of mental illness. The little boy, who was removed from the home of a suburban family that wanted to adopt him, had already been returned to his mother several times, only to be removed again. Less than three months after the hearing, on April 19, 1993, three-year-old Joseph was dead, hanged with an electrical cord.[6]

Press coverage of the Wallace story, which was, not surprisingly, extensive, turned out to be a double-edged sword. Although the publicity revealed a host of systemic problems, it helped throw an already shaky child welfare system into panic and dealt it an almost fatal blow. The case epitomized the state's inability to protect children and led to the creation of a special commission to investigate the matter. It also, however, made juvenile court judges increasingly fearful of sending children home to their parents. "Everyone was paralyzed with fear," reported Nancy Sidote Salyers, presiding judge of the Child Protection Division (Gibeaut 1997, 47).

DCFS was not solely to blame for the chain of events that sent Joseph home, yet the tragedy sparked an anti-DCFS crusade by the Chicago press, fueled to some extent by its perennial critic, the public guardian (Wexler 1995a). The attacks on DCFS made its workers extremely skittish about allowing children to remain home or sending them home, thus stretching the limits of the already overextended foster care system almost beyond capacity. As one respondent noted, the media pressure in the aftermath of Joseph's death produced severe anxiety among DCFS caseworkers and juvenile court judges, who were unwilling to risk the consequences of an erroneous decision; the respondent added that Murphy's attacks on family reunification efforts also kept the pressure on the agency not to send children home. Another respondent suggested that the publicity over the little boy's death exacerbated the department's inability to comply with *B.H.* by fostering "system overload," in which too many children were taken into care and remained in care for too long. This continuing influx of children into the system without relief at the other end, a situation that the press helped aggravate, contributed to the department's difficulties in achieving compliance with the consent decree.

Although understandable, the media's continuous focus on the fatal attack—without a reasoned discussion of the principle of family preservation and the inherent, often unavoidable, dangers in all reunification decisions— was antithetical to the goals of the litigation. As Robert Schwartz, executive director of the Juvenile Law Center in Philadelphia, pointed out, "What we are doing in child welfare is risk management. . . . Every decision entails a certain amount of risk" (McMurray 1995, 121). All too often the press shirked its responsibility to explain the complexity of the issue to the public, typically oversimplifying the choices the workers faced: keep children in foster care or send them home to die.

Joseph's death also sparked another political battle aired by the media. Before the tragedy occurred, Democratic representative Tom Dart of Chicago had proposed a package of child welfare reforms. His bill passed the Democratic-controlled house but died in committee in the Republican-dominated senate. When the Republicans produced similar legislation right after the Wallace case became public, Dart and other house Democrats accused Republicans of trying to diminish the political fallout from his death (*Chicago Tribune*, May 21, 1993). The law that passed, amending the 1987 Juvenile Court Act by introducing a new "best interests" standard, resulted from a compromise among Dart, DCFS officials, and Governor Jim Edgar's office.

The media also participated in the dispute over the issue of attending the *B.H.* status conferences, weighing in heavily on the side of public access. The press was, of course, hardly neutral in this controversy, portraying the court's ruling as an unconstitutional limit on the press's ability to cover the news. Numerous editorials and columns excoriated both the ACLU and DCFS as well as the federal court. In according widespread publicity to the attacks on the consent decree and the ACLU's role in *B.H.*, the press helped cast doubt on the legitimacy of the reform process. Charges that the parties had conspired with each other appeared in editorials warning the ACLU and DCFS not to get too "cozy" with each other (*Chicago Sun-Times*, January 30, 1995). These were echoed by journalists, such as *Tribune* writer Bruce Dold, who mocked the ACLU's posture in the litigation as an "unwritten non-aggression pact with DCFS—don't knock us, and we won't knock you" (*Chicago Tribune*, September 22, 1995).

Stressing the large monetary outlays going to DCFS as a result of the litigation also had a detrimental effect on the reform effort. In commenting on Schneider's resignation as the *B.H.* monitor, Dold disparaged the "effort to reform the Illinois Department of Children and Family Services through a federal consent decree. . . . Four years and nearly $4 billion later," he said, "there's not much to show for it" (*Chicago Tribune*, September 22, 1995). Continually repeating the charges of collusion between the ACLU and McDonald helped give legitimacy to the attacks from the politicians who frequently sought to further their own political agendas by attacking the department, the court that approved the consent decree, and the decree itself.

In assessing the political implications of *B.H.*, a number of respondents were concerned about the legislature's resentment of the court and the agency and, ultimately, the agency's clientele. Although most rejected the notion of a conspiracy between the plaintiffs and the defendant and dismissed the suggestion that the parties had collaborated with each other, a few expressed concern about the image of the decree as a "friendly settlement." Some suggested Wolf and Brody should have been "more confrontational" with the agency. They believed they were "too accommodating" and "too sensitive" to its problems, citing their willingness to meet with Tchen and DCFS officials behind closed chamber doors. Several respondents also noted that the decree poisoned the atmosphere for future efforts at systemic reform, predicting that, as a result of *B.H.*, the state would refrain from entering into any negotiated settlement agreements in the future.

Child Welfare Authorities

Despite the increased resources available to the agency, DCFS had been unable to comply with the decree's mandate to reduce the caseworker-to-child ratio by 1994. During this time as well, it was clear that the juvenile courts were severely strained and unable to cope with the demands on them. Within two years, however, there were signs that the child welfare system—DCFS and its counterpart, the juvenile courts—was beginning to function more efficiently and more effectively and would be able to meet the specified caseload ratio. By 1998, a number of these improvements were evident.

DCFS

On March 6, 1996, the governor's office issued a press release reporting that by FY 1997, DCFS would be in compliance with the caseloads ratios imposed by *B.H.* (Illinois Department of Children and Family Services 1996). Although the additional DCFS staff hired in response to the consent decree was partially responsible for the agency's achievement, the change in the agency's method of supervising the staff of the private agencies, thereby freeing up more DCFS personnel to take on cases, also contributed (Loftus 1998).[7]

Beginning around 1996, with fewer children entering the child welfare system, there were indications of a lessened demand for state child welfare services. As seen in appendix table 1, calls to the hotline dropped between FY 1995 and 1997. More important, as appendix table 2 shows, the number of children reported as abused or neglected during FY 1997 was 119,405, representing a substantial decrease from an all-time high of 139,718 two years earlier. Additionally, the number of "indicated" reports also declined in FY 1996 and 1997, as appendix table 3 demonstrates.

Because of the reduced demand, the department's burden began to lighten. Beginning in FY 1997, as illustrated in appendix table 4, the child welfare caseload started to decline. Although the drop was small between FY 1996 and 1997, it became more substantial the next year. As appendix table 5 indicates, the number of children placed in substitute care also grew more slowly from FY 1996 to 1997 than in previous years and even seemed to be decreasing from FY 1997 to 1998 (although there were still two months left in the fiscal year).

The change in conditions has several possible explanations. Wolf (1998) speculated that some of the decline in the child welfare caseload could be attributed to lower crack cocaine use and the improved economy. More concretely, Loftus (1998) pointed to the practice of performance contracting, referring to the contractual relationship between DCFS and private child welfare agencies, in which private agencies must meet predetermined standards for the delivery of services or risk losing their contracts with the state. Additionally, he claimed the agency's new, more efficient, approach to monitoring the work of the private agencies helped explain why the caseworker-to-child ratios had improved.

Assistant Public Guardian Charles Golbert (1998), however, was more skeptical and noted that the decline in DCFS's caseload is also attributable to legislation enacted in 1995. Known as the "Grandma law," it changed the definition of neglect so that certain categories of children were excluded from the caseload a priori.[8] Golbert believed the changed definition helped explain the decline in the agency's caseload.

Beginning in FY 1996, under the new definition of neglect, parental absence was not grounds for taking a child who had been safely living with a relative for more than a month, typically a grandmother (hence the name of the law), into state custody. Such children, who are deflected from DCFS custody and ineligible for foster care payments, are not referred to the juvenile courts and are not included in DCFS's caseload. These children may be served by Extended Family Service workers, if necessary, on a short-term basis.

DCFS was also making inroads in achieving permanency for children by dramatically increasing the rate of adoptions. According to McDonald, the number of children adopted in FY 1998 nearly doubled over the previous fiscal year: from 2,229 in FY 1997 to 4,293 a year later (Illinois Department of Children and Family Services 1998e, 1). Because of the changes in federal law and the new emphasis on adoptions, the state was receiving additional funds from the federal government by surpassing its adoption rate of 1,800 children (the average number of adoptions over the last three years). The state has also put pressure on the private agencies to permanently place six out of twenty-five children in their caseload or face not receiving reimbursement for additional foster children.

The agency's efforts to increase the adoption rates were in part facilitated by a package of state laws, labeled the Omnibus Permanency Initiative of 1997, that, among other provisions, mirrored the federal law requiring child welfare authorities to set permanency goals, including adoption, no longer than twelve months after the child is taken into care.[9] Subsequent permanency hearings were to take place in court every six months thereafter. The new law absolves the agency from providing family preservation services under certain circumstances and frees children for adoption more quickly than in the past by easing the rules for terminating parental rights.

Beginning in January 1997, DCFS launched another initiative, offering a new approach to permanency called "subsidized guardianships." This option, representing an intermediate position between adoption and foster care, also helped to lower the agency's caseloads. Subsidized guardianship was a partial response to the growing trend of placing children in the homes of relatives in the belief that a relative's home, in addition to providing the most "family-like setting" as required by IV-E, was psychologically beneficial to the child by helping maintain continuity between the family home and the foster care placement. According to the latest report by the Children's Defense Fund (1998, 68), the Department of Health and Human Services (HHS) estimated that nationally approximately one-third of the children in foster care live with relatives, an arrangement generically known as "kinship" care.

In discussing kinship care, Dana Burnell Wilson, program director for the Child Welfare League, emphasized that for children who "go to live with people they know, people they trust, their sense of trauma is lessened." She added that sending them to the homes of relatives "keeps children attached to a family, to a community and to a culture with which they are already familiar" (*Washington Post*, April 16, 1997).

Reflecting this increasing trend of kinship care, the Illinois Juvenile Court Act was amended to include "subsidized guardianship" as a permanency option, an alternative to adoption or return home. Perhaps more significantly, the agency received approval from HHS for a five-year pilot program to authorize the state's use of federal Title IV-E funds for children who lived under a guardianship arrangement.[10] Guardianships were not unique in the child welfare system; by 1996 ten states treated a guardianship as a permanent status, but none of these states were being reimbursed by the federal government for children placed in guardianship (Schwartz 1996, 470–71).

Although the family loses access to services in a subsidized guardianship situation, the guardians continue to receive a state subsidy, approximately the same amount as adoptive parents under the adoption assistance program of Title IV-E. With the state and the federal government sharing the cost of this program, DCFS had estimated the program would save $40 million over five years (*Chicago Tribune*, September 19, 1996).

Subsidized guardianships are available for children who have been in state custody for more than two years, in their current placement for more than one year, and unlikely to go home within the next year (Goerge and others 1997). On the basis of these standards, DCFS had estimated that in January 1996, about 10,160 children met the criteria for the new program (*Chicago Tribune*, January 16, 1996).

One of the advantages of a "subsidized guardianship" is that it permits children who do not return home to achieve permanency without necessitating adoption; it also allows relatives to retain financial assistance while removing the state's authority over them. Furthermore, relatives are frequently reluctant to adopt children in their extended family because, among other things, adoption requires that the parent's rights be terminated. In a "subsidized guardianship" the parents maintain visitation rights and the right to consent to adoption, allowing the guardians to avoid potential family conflicts. It also seems a more reasonable arrangement for those who see no need to adopt children to whom they are related and with whom they are already living (see Schwartz 1996).

When asked how DCFS had been able to improve its operations and finally achieve compliance with the decree, Loftus (1998) summarized the experiences of the preceding two years, succinctly stating, the agency is now "managing the exits and managing the entrances."

Juvenile Court

Although *B.H.* was aimed largely at reforming DCFS, the defects in a child welfare agency cannot be cured without addressing the problems of the juvenile court system. Perhaps not the primary offender, the juvenile courts must also be held accountable for the often lamentable treatment accorded to the children in the child welfare system.

In 1994 Cook County opened its new $58 million juvenile court building, increasing the number of courtrooms from thirteen to twenty-seven. The new facility was designed to accommodate the needs of the 40,000 families involved in child abuse and neglect proceedings (*Chicago Lawyer*, February 1997).

Then in 1995 the newly elected chief judge of the Cook County Circuit Court, Donald O'Connell, replaced the retiring Harry Comerford. O'Connell declared reorganization of the juvenile court, long considered in disarray, a top priority of his administration (McMurray, 1995). True to his word, in the first systemic change to occur in more than thirty years, O'Connell created the Juvenile Justice and Child Protection Department, transforming the juvenile court from a part of the county division of the circuit court into a department and placing it on an equal standing with the municipal and county departments. Within the new department, he created two divisions: the Juvenile Justice Division for delinquency cases and the Child Protection Division for abuse, neglect, and dependency cases. Each division was headed by its own presiding judge, with Salyers selected as head of the Child Protection Division.[11] Salyers's stated goal from the time of her appointment was to close all new files within two years (*Chicago Lawyer*, February 1997).

The need for court reform had been apparent for a long time. A study of juvenile court procedures from January 1, 1993, to March 1, 1996, found that, although the system had been improved, it still failed to meet the statutory timelines of P.L. 96-272.[12] Published by Chapin Hall in 1997, the report noted that the court was best able to meet the statutory guidelines at the beginning stages of the process, before the dispositional hearing, and least able to conform to the law in the latter, or postdispositional, phases. The court was most untimely with respect to holding permanency hearings, which were more likely to be continued, and continued for longer periods of time, than proceedings in the earlier stages (Merry and others 1997, 14–15).

In an attempt to streamline the operation of the court, Salyers successfully sought county funding for a two-year permanency planning project to begin in January 1996. The project had a number of goals: to conduct research on the court, to identify ways to close cases that no longer needed court supervision, to find ways to better orient parents and other participants to court procedures, to determine whether mediation was an effective step, and to develop pilot reform projects (Merry and others 1997, 10).

Designed to achieve permanency for children in a more timely fashion, the project ushered in a number of administrative changes according to Slater (1998), director of Policy Initiatives of the Permanency Project. First, there are extended temporary custody hearings, during which the parties, the attorneys, and DCFS child protection worker meet before the formal hearing to discuss the child's welfare and to draw up a preliminary plan for visitation. Second, approximately fifty-five days after the temporary custody hearing (before adjudication), the court holds a family conference to discuss the progress in the case. Although the judge is present, the meeting is held off the record, and the judge is more of a participant than an adjudicator. At the end of the session, a summary of the discussion is read into the record. Third, there is an effort to create staggered court calls, so the participants can have more certainty about the timing of the court hearings.

Thus, by the end of the decade, the child welfare authorities were at last responding to the wake-up call of *B.H.* and instituting several needed substantive and procedural changes. Although respondents expressed reservations about the wisdom of some of the policy changes—and it was too soon to predict whether they would lead to lasting improvements—even the most zealous critics seemed ready to admit that most of the changes were welcome, and the system, although not without its flaws, was finally moving in the right direction.

8   Child Welfare Reform

EVALUATING SYSTEMIC LITIGATION

This study has applied the five-part research model shown in chapter 1 to the federal class action suit known as *B.H.* Its aim was to elucidate the effects of institutional reform litigation on the Illinois child welfare system and to examine the role of the federal court in the child welfare policymaking process. By exploring each stage of the litigation in depth, it has been possible to delineate the events that occurred during the ten years of *B.H.* and to present a more accurate picture of the litigation as a whole. The portrait that emerged demonstrated that institutional reform litigation is a continuing, interactive process, with events in each phase affecting events in later phases and continual interaction among the actors involved, including the court, the parties, and nonlitigants.

The Five Stages of *B.H.*

The *B.H.* lawsuit was part of a rising tide of federal class action litigation against state and local child welfare agencies. It was prompted by increasing demands on the child welfare system and a refusal by, or inability of, government authorities to effectively police the delivery of child welfare services.

The Stimulus Phase

As past research has shown, lawsuits aimed at structural reform of public institutions are triggered by a variety of stimuli. *B.H.* was primarily motivated by the need to correct the widespread failures of the child welfare system within Illinois, evidenced by overburdened juvenile courts and an understaffed and underfunded child welfare agency. The decision of the American Civil Liberty Union (ACLU) to pursue systemic reform was based, in part, on the belief that the entire child welfare system was in crisis and that piecemeal litigation was insufficient to solve the myriad problems within it.

By 1988 a number of other factors had emerged to bolster the determination to seek federal relief for the conditions within the system. First, there was an increasingly engaged and professionalized child welfare community in the state, sparked by an active child welfare advocacy bar. Most of the attorneys dedicated to child welfare litigation were public interest lawyers, employed by nonprofit public interest law firms or government-funded or -subsidized legal services agencies. The leading members of this group were the lawyers from the ACLU, assisted by attorneys in a private law firm, the Legal Assistance Foundation of Chicago (LAF), and the Cook County Office of the Public Guardian (OPG).

Another important factor helping trigger the litigation was the growing trend of class action litigation against child welfare agencies around the nation, with the federal courts becoming more willing to place children in foster care within the ambit of the Fourteenth Amendment's substantive due process guarantees. Moreover, within Illinois, policies of the Department of Children and Family Services (DCFS) had been successfully challenged in previous state and federal court litigation, including two federal class actions suits that were aimed at correcting the agency's inattention to the needs of Spanish-speaking children and their families and its restrictive parental visitation policy. The litigation was also spurred by the persistent and negative media attention to DCFS, spotlighting its many shortcomings. Through special investigative reports and editorials, the press helped place agency reform on the policymaking agenda and helped prepare the public for the long and costly litigation that ensued.

Together these factors prompted Illinois child welfare advocates to seek the much-needed systemic relief through litigation in the federal courts.

The Accountability Phase

During this phase, the federal court for the Northern District of Illinois established the contours of the state's responsibilities to children in care. A successful lawsuit requires a convincing legal theory. Throughout the 1980s, child welfare litigants had been increasingly successful in persuading the lower federal courts that states were constitutionally liable for harm done to the children in their custody. Similarly, most courts also determined that state agencies receiving federal funds were bound by specified conditions in the 1980 federal child welfare statute. In assessing the limits of a state's accountability, the federal courts resolved that the rights of children in care outweighed the principle of state autonomy, and in doing so they firmly placed themselves in the path of future claims against failing child welfare agencies.

The class action suit, captioned *B.H. v. Johnson* after the lead named plaintiff—a seventeen-year-old foster child with the initials *B.H.*—was brought on behalf of the almost 20,000 children in the Illinois foster care system; the plaintiffs claimed that the state had defaulted in its duty to them. The defendant, technically the director of DCFS, was the state of Illinois.

The accountability phase of the litigation was devoted largely to analysis of the appropriate legal standards to use in evaluating the plaintiffs' claims. As in other areas of public law litigation where the litigants proffer relatively novel legal theories with little or no controlling authority within the circuit, the plaintiffs' first major challenge was to survive the state's motion to dismiss for failure to state a cognizable legal claim. In *B.H.*, a case that raised profound concerns about federalism, state fiscal autonomy, and the reach of the substantive due process doctrine, the plaintiffs forced the court to assess its own role in child welfare policymaking as well as the state's in determining the validity of their claim.

The plaintiffs were required to rebut the general principle that the state owed no constitutional duty of protection to its citizens and was therefore not responsible for any harm to them. Against the backdrop of the evolving substantive due process doctrine, the courts needed to decide whether to apply this general principle or, as most of them seemed inclined to do, to exploit the exception that had sprung up in situations involving a person in state custody or where the state has a "special relationship" with the victim.

The Adjudication Phase

The adjudication phase began with the court's preliminary ruling that the plaintiffs had cleared the bar of the state's motion to dismiss. Under Gordon Johnson's leadership, DCFS had initially responded to *B.H.* by challenging the legal basis of the plaintiffs' claims. After losing on that front, the state adopted a strategy of contesting liability and attempting to evade settlement talks. During Jess McDonald's brief tenure as director of the agency at the end of Jim Thompson's term as governor, the state entered into negotiations with the plaintiffs and, encouraged by Judge John Grady, the parties agreed on a settlement that eventually became the consent decree. In the decree, DCFS promised to institute reforms that all parties to the litigation regarded as essential.

The *B.H.* settlement was conditioned by a number of factors: nationally, the federal courts had signaled their willingness to allow children in state custody to pursue judicial remedies for relief of deficiencies in child welfare systems. Child welfare systems in Alabama and Washington, D.C., to name just two, were under orders to reform and operating under varying degrees of judicial supervision. Clearly, the tide of legal authority was turning against DCFS. More directly, the *B.H.* settlement negotiations were characterized by the judge's playing the simultaneous role of cheerleader and referee, intervening when necessary to ensure that the parties continued to try to achieve a fair and practicable resolution of the case. As the talks progressed, DCFS came under legal attack from other groups of plaintiffs seeking specified policy reforms, with the courts declining to dismiss those cases as well. Finally, an important aspect of the *B.H.* settlement was the testimony of leading national child welfare experts who were brought in to assess the state of the agency and make recommendations for change. Organized under the authority of the federal court, their efforts laid much of the groundwork for the consent decree.

The adjudication phase ended with judicial approval of a comprehensive consent decree, the most sweeping in the nation, in which the state promised to do better by its abused and neglected children.

The Implementation Phase

Because systemic reform necessitates a metamorphosis in the culture of the affected agency, the implementation phase of the litigation process is characterized largely by efforts to change agency norms and, ultimately, the behavior of its personnel. In the implementation stage of the *B.H.* litigation, the difficulty of reforming DCFS bureaucracy was compounded by worsening conditions of child abuse and neglect within the state, largely ineffective leadership within the agency throughout most of the implementation period, and budgetary uncertainty that threw its personnel policies into turmoil and threatened to undermine the agency's ability to conduct its business and plan effectively.

During this phase, DCFS operations were under further attack from litigants who had grievances with other, more narrowly defined, areas of agency policy. The resulting court orders and consent decrees affected the agency's ability to devote its resources to complying with *B.H.* Additionally, legal developments in state and national child welfare policy affected the agency's incentives to comply with the decree. On the one hand, events established that the trend toward judicial involvement in child welfare policymaking would continue as the lower courts limited the *DeShaney* decision to its facts and continued to fix liability on states for harm done to children in state custody. On the other hand, the Supreme Court's narrow view of the "reasonable efforts clause" that constituted the heart of the 1980 child welfare act severely jeopardized attempts to maintain judicial enforcement of federal child welfare law. Fortunately for the *B.H.* plaintiffs, the decree contained an exclusionary clause that had exempted it from a possible adverse ruling by the Supreme Court in the upcoming *Artist M.* case.

Despite the fears about judicial overreaching in institutional reform litigation, the *B.H.* judge responsible for supervising the agency's compliance with the decree was not inclined to play a very activist role. Grady conscientiously supervised the implementation process, but preferred to leave most of the details to the parties. Although he was committed to improving the agency and securing DCFS compliance with the decree, he also demonstrated awareness of the difficulties the agency faced in meeting its obligations under the decree. Grady was reluctant to intervene in the day-to-day decisionmaking of the agency, his restraint stemming in part from his view of the judicial role in institutional reform litigation. Perhaps a more activist judge might have been tempted to intervene further into agency policymaking—as some respondents desired—but Grady's approach was a balanced one. He was not afraid to exert the authority of the federal courts but, at the same time, recognized the limits of his role.

The final component of the implementation phase involved the appointment of the monitor to oversee compliance with the decree. Most observers were disappointed with the results of the monitoring activity, believing the monitor had not achieved the goals expected of him; yet few had concrete suggestions about how the monitor's effectiveness could have been improved.

By assiduously documenting the agency's deficiencies and focusing attention on its failure to comply with the decree, the monitor, not surprisingly, alienated some of DCFS personnel. At the same time his inability to propose innovative solutions for the agency's problems led others to question his usefulness. Most respondents acknowledged that the monitor and his staff were dedicated to their tasks and worked hard at them, yet they felt the monitoring process yielded little benefit for the litigation effort. They did not blame the monitor entirely for the department's failure to comply with the decree; many acknowledged that the comprehensive scope of this ambitious decree might have defeated the efforts of any monitor.

Although other studies of institutional reform litigation have suggested that a monitor working in concert with a judge can be instrumental in securing an agency's compliance with a decree, there is little evidence that the *B.H.* monitor, working with this judge, was a key agent in the reform effort.

The Response Phase

In reviewing the response stage, it is clear that the most concrete reaction to *B.H.* from state political leaders was the expansion of DCFS resources. Because of the consent decree, DCFS was accorded special treatment in the Illinois budgetary process. Unlike the years before *B.H.*, when its funding was always uncertain, after *B.H.*, DCFS's appropriations steadily rose, soon topping $1 billion as a result of some very large annual increases.

State legislators increasingly resented the judicial mandate to improve child welfare services and looked for opportunities to attack both DCFS and the courts. Rather than accepting responsibility for the virtual collapse of the child welfare system, they blamed the courts, the agency, and even, to some extent, DCFS's clientele for the agency's lamentable condition. Their suspicions about collusion between the American Civil Liberties Union (ACLU) and

DCFS led to legislation aimed at hindering state executive branch officials from entering into consent decrees in all institutional reform litigation.

The reaction to *B.H.* within the child welfare community was marked by dissension among the members of the child welfare bar, which erupted almost immediately after *B.H.* was filed. The relationship among the attorneys in the Illinois children's advocacy bar, fragile to begin with, was characterized by friction during almost every stage of the litigation process, but was especially evident during the implementation stage. Conflicts over personality differences and legal strategy led to charges and countercharges among the advocates, especially the plaintiffs' attorneys and the public guardian's office.

Personality conflicts aside, all sides believed in the superiority of their approach to child welfare and, ultimately, to reform. However, although they undoubtedly were sincere in their convictions that they represented the best interests of the state's abused and neglected children, their battles with each other might well have slowed down the implementation of the consent decree. Perhaps if they had not been diverted by their continual infighting, their energies could have been directed more effectively to furthering the agency's compliance with the decree.

Media attention to the deficiencies of the Illinois child welfare system in the late 1980s helped place child welfare reform on the public policy agenda; however, the media's role in the succeeding stages of the Illinois child welfare litigation was more mixed and not always constructive. As an unpopular government agency gobbling up an inordinate share of state resources, DCFS was always a convenient target for the media. The press also served as an outlet for state officials to grumble about increased appropriations arising from the litigation and to attack unpopular entities like the ACLU and the federal courts—as well as the omnipresent scapegoat, DCFS. While there were legitimate grounds for the press to criticize the agency for failing to live up to the promises made in the consent decree, the media made little effort to nurture the reform effort. Finally, although DCFS committed itself to reform in response to *B.H.*, its efforts were hindered by a succession of leadership changes and lingering budgetary uncertainty that created near-chaotic conditions in its personnel policies. By 1996, when most of the interviews were conducted, the agency still had not achieved full compliance with the consent decree.

Within a few years, however, there were visible signs of improvement in the agency and mounting evidence that it was changing in the direction of reform. An objective indicator of its progress was the lowered caseload ratio that conformed to the terms of the decree. Indeed, the agency seemed to go beyond the explicit demands of the decree by also taking on the challenge of trying to produce successful outcomes for children in substitute care.

In the wake of *B.H.*, the child welfare authorities also began to attack the grim conditions within the juvenile courts. Under the direction of a new chief judge who energized the entire system, additional judgeships were created, procedures were streamlined, a new system of hearing officers was instituted, and improvements in the physical plant were made as well. Thus, although *B.H.* was not aimed at reforming the juvenile courts, by directing attention to the deficiencies within DCFS, the litigation extended its beneficial effects to the juvenile court system as well.

While it might be extravagant to attribute all the positive changes within the system to *B.H.*, there is little doubt that the suit played a significant role in sparking the reforms that reverberated throughout the entire state child welfare system.

B.H. and Child Welfare Reform

In assessing the role of consent decrees in structural reform cases, Theodore Stein (1987, 159) noted, "It seems clear that [such] litigation has resulted in institutional reform." This study has demonstrated that while reforming public institutions is a complex process that requires a long-term perspective, the *B.H.* litigation "resulted in institutional reform" of the Illinois child welfare system.

Overall, when asked to appraise the effectiveness of systemic litigation in reforming government agencies, many of the respondents expressed views that were summarized by one of the judges, who said that litigation, by creating "intolerable pressure" on political bodies, can lead to institutional reform. "It keeps agencies on their toes," said another.

Weighing the usefulness of systemic litigation, Clark Peters (1998) asserted, "The threat of litigation is a nice club to have in your hands as you approach agencies." Charles Golbert (1998) called it a "critical tool to effectuate change in government bureaucracies that aren't going to change on their own." Even more forcefully, Thomas Geraghty (1997), of Northwestern University's Children and Family Justice Center, asserted that litigation is "sometimes the only way" to get state agencies to respond. Thus although, as Benjamin Wolf (1996) pointed out, a decree "does not change things from awful to wonderful," virtually every respondent acknowledged that litigation can produce systemic changes that the state is unlikely to initiate on its own.

Speaking of the difficulty of implementing child welfare reform following litigation, a decade ago Lowry (1988) had warned that securing a decree is only the first step in the process. These respondents agreed, pointing out that while litigation can amass resources for an agency, there is no guarantee that it can bring about the kind of changes necessary to improve the delivery of services. "Litigation doesn't make hard problems easy," said Wolf (1998). As another respondent put it, litigation might be "too lofty" to produce the practical changes needed to reform an agency. Calling it "one of the tools for reform," Michael O'Connor (1997), former president of the Illinois Caucus for Foster Children, warned that systemic reform litigation cannot cure all the system's ills. Michael Dsida (1996), the former assistant public guardian, explained that litigation "was not always successful in reshaping the institutional framework." Echoing his sentiment, another respondent suggested that although one could get "really positive results from lawsuits and decrees," the results could be imperiled by the difficulty of sustaining them during the implementation phase. And Diane Redleaf (1997) cautioned, "No litigation seeking systemic reform is as effective as plaintiffs' counsel want it to be."

Not surprisingly, respondents with DCFS ties expressed little enthusiasm about the benefits of systemic reform litigation. Although they admitted it served some worthwhile purposes, one termed such litigation "destructive"; another believed that it created even more problems than it solved; and one former DCFS official, conceding that it might be useful, characterized such litigation as "a pain in the rear." It requires "tremendous" expenditures of time to compile data and report to the judge and monitor and diminishes the ability of agency personnel to perform their jobs, said one respondent on DCFS side; another denounced it because "it saps the creative juices" from all parts of the agency.

When questioned about the effects of *B.H.* specifically, most respondents were generous in their praise of the litigation, yet less sanguine about concrete results it had achieved. Diane Geraghty's (1998) view that "*B.H.* brought about significant and meaningful change" was echoed in varying degrees by many. Indeed, the child welfare advocates interviewed for this study unanimously agreed that the *B.H.* litigation had been a catalyst for child welfare reform in Illinois. They pointed out that it had significantly enhanced DCFS resources and improved a number of critical areas of the Illinois child welfare system. In short, the respondents believed that *B.H.* focused attention on the agency in a way that no other litigation had, finally forcing the state to accept responsibility for the deficiencies of its child welfare system.

Although they recognized that *B.H.* had generated positive changes in the Illinois child welfare system, most respondents expressed concern about the slow rate of transformation within the agency. They pointed especially to its failure to achieve the decree's mandated reduction in the caseworker-to-child ratio—almost two years after the deadline had passed. But, as one judge noted, *B.H.* is not unique in this regard because compliance with a decree is always relative in large-scale institutional reform cases.

Overall, by 1996, five years into the life of the consent decree, most respondents believed that while *B.H.* could point to some accomplishments within DCFS, it was premature to declare victory over the child welfare system. While they variously blamed the agency, the attorneys, the judge, the monitor, and the politicians, most also believed that the nature of the litigation, especially its far-reaching aims, contributed to this state of affairs. They described *B.H.* as "massive," "complex," "awesomely huge," and, finally, perhaps too ambitious in attempting to "change the [agency's] culture." A few compared *B.H.* unfavorably with Alabama's *R.C.* decree. Although they acknowledged the latter had a more limited scope, they believed it had succeeded in ameliorating the worst conditions of the Alabama foster care system.

The respondents characterized *Norman* as the prototype of an effective decree. It had, they believed, largely accomplished its goal of giving families on the brink of homelessness a real chance at staying together. In contrast to *B.H.*, they said, the *Norman* decree was "focused" and had "narrow quantifiable goals" that were more easily achieved. One respondent explained that the *Norman* monitor was more effective than the *B.H.* monitor, in part, because there "was less room for attitudes [of the agency personnel] to have a negative impact," adding that it was also easier to identify the class members and provide resources to them. Some pointed to *Aristotle P.*, with its narrower goal of increasing the frequency of sibling visits among children in foster care, as a more efficacious litigation effort. Wenzel (1996), consultant to DCFS in *Hill*, contrasted the large numbers of children in the *B.H.* class to the smaller numbers in the *Hill* class, saying the limited size of the latter class produced "a better decree."

Murphy (1996) also faulted *B.H.* for taking a "scattershot approach," aimed too broadly at solving the myriad problems within the system. "Broad-based lawsuits do not work," he insisted. In his view, to be effective, litigation must focus on a discrete policy area. *Norman* was good, he said: "It was a one-issue lawsuit" and "easily monitored."

A suit for system-wide relief rarely results in total victory or defeat for either side. In 1996, when the bulk of the interviews were conducted, most respondents, reflecting their experiences with *B.H.*, were rather skeptical of the degree to which the litigation had succeeded in reforming the child welfare system. Within two years, however, there were indications that the litigation was beginning to fulfill the goal envisioned by Wolf of "chang[ing] bureaucracies and . . . giving caseworkers the tools . . . to do their job" (*National Law Journal*, June 27, 1994). Although it had been unable to meet the deadlines established in *B.H.*, DCFS seemed by 1998 to be making real progress toward satisfying the commitments it had made to the state's abused and neglected children in 1991. While it is difficult to know the extent to which *B.H.* was responsible for "chang[ing]" DCFS, in 1998 there was little dispute that the agency was performing at a higher level of efficiency, its staff members were more professional, and its leadership was more capable.

A second round of interviews with three individuals close to the litigation yielded a more positive view of the agency than was evident in the earlier interviews. Representing the opposing sides in *B.H.*, Wolf and Loftus agreed that there was greater cause for optimism about the Illinois child welfare system than there had been in the past—as recently as two years earlier.

Wolf (1998) pointed out that, while problems remained, at last DCFS was moving in the right direction in many ways. It was, he felt, "doing better" in working with intact families to keep children out of the child welfare caseload, in increasing adoption rates, and in supervising the work of the private agencies.

Loftus (1998) also attributed much of the credit for DCFS's improved record to its more effective supervision of the private social welfare agencies that are responsible for approximately 70 percent of the foster care population in Illinois.[1] He explained that he and Jess McDonald had sought to institute the "performance contracting" approach to these private contractors in 1994, when McDonald was reinstated as director of the agency; it had taken about a year, he said, to implement the change. Loftus claimed that the agency had met—and even surpassed—the requirements of the consent decree with more efficient monitoring of private agencies and a more aggressive approach to intact families that allowed it to reduce the rate of placement in substitute care and lower the caseload ratio. He was very proud of the agency's success in increasing the rate of adoptions, its innovative approach to "subsidized guardianships," and its accreditation by a national agency (only one of two states to have an accredited child welfare agency). Summing up, he believed there was a "huge improvement in all kinds of indicators."

Golbert (1998), whose responses were more restrained than Wolf's or Loftus's, conceded that some of DCFS's services had improved. Although he acknowledged that the child welfare caseload had declined and that the department was close to achieving the required caseload ratios, he was still concerned that, among other things, *B.H.*'s preclusive effect was hindering reform in other areas of the child welfare system. He was less sanguine than Loftus or Wolf about the agency's work with intact families, pointing out that the caseload numbers were down in part because the amended definition of "neglect" kept children out of the system. He granted that the agency was "working harder" at adoptions but considered it too soon to judge the effectiveness of "performance contracting" or "subsidized guardianships." In sum, he also believed that the agency had made advances, but felt that the reform effort was still incomplete.

Thus, although its progress was slower than many hoped, the child welfare system was clearly transformed in the ten years after *B.H.*'s filing. At the end of the *B.H.* decade, reform was evident in DCFS's use of better management techniques and its adoption of a number of innovative approaches to the delivery of child welfare services. It is clear that *B.H.* played a significant role in bringing about these results.

The Federal Courts and Child Welfare Policymaking

In the 1970s and 1980s, the nation's public interest bar increasingly sought to enlist the power of the federal courts to compel states to reform public institutions. In requiring the courts to weigh the extent of the state's obligation to the plaintiffs, these suits, mostly brought as class actions, expanded the judicial role in public policymaking and raised questions about federal court decrees that triggered a redistribution of state resources. Not surprisingly, states resisted demands for reform and attempted to curb the court's interference in their fiscal and managerial authority.

Reflecting in part their concern for state autonomy, states' rights advocates and judicial scholars challenged the propriety of the court's role in social policy reform. In particular, they questioned the court's ability to make determinations of liability and award proper relief as well as its capacity for overseeing the results of the changes it ordered. Others, less concerned with state autonomy, also raised questions about the court's effectiveness in carrying out social reform, suggesting that courts are essentially unable to implement such decisions.

Because they believed that the political process and piecemeal lawsuits were insufficient to solve the needs of their politically powerless clients—the state's abused and neglected children—in 1988, the Illinois child welfare advocates had turned to class action systemic litigation. With *B.H.*, the Illinois child welfare bar became part of a growing cohort of child welfare reform litigants in the federal courts, following in the footsteps of their colleagues a generation ago. Not surprisingly, the *B.H.* litigation led to similar charges of undue federal court intervention in the public policymaking process, particularly from state political leaders.

In determining that children in foster care have a constitutional and statutory right to safety, enforceable in a § 1983 cause of action, the federal courts helped ensure their continual involvement in the nation's child welfare systems. The story of *B.H.*, however, suggests that the court's involvement in child welfare policymaking, while crucial, was also circumscribed. Grady was, of course, *a* key player in the litigation, but he was by no means the *only* one, and perhaps not even the *most* important one.

Grady maintained a relatively low profile during the settlement process, limiting himself, for the most part, to creating an atmosphere conducive to settlement; he encouraged the parties to reach their own agreement and ultimately approved the settlement negotiated by them. Demonstrating his awareness of the complexities involved in administering a child welfare agency, Grady urged the plaintiffs to be realistic about the demands they made on DCFS. The final accord was a product of extensive negotiations between the parties, reflecting the recommendations of the child welfare experts.

During the implementation stage, Grady was aware of the need for flexibility in his supervisory role and was generally receptive to requests from both sides. "The need for such receptiveness," he explained, "is inherent in any long range institutional reform, where changing circumstances are the order of the day. The court," he added, "is favorably disposed toward things that work, and the parties should have no reason to think that any concrete, pragmatic proposal would be rejected" (*B.H. v. McDonald* 1997a, 4).

Thus, contrary to charges of judicial overreaching, the court was far from proactive in administering the state's child welfare system. Consistent with his judicial role, Grady presided over the settlement negotiations and supervised the implementation process, but never sought to dictate policy to DCFS administrators. Indeed, even when DCFS had failed to live up to the demands of the decree, Grady merely exhorted the agency to try harder to reach the goals outlined in the agreement.

The judges interviewed in this study rejected the view that because they had little knowledge of how to manage large bureaucracies, they should refrain from deciding systemic reform cases. While frank to admit they lacked expertise in child welfare policy, they pointed out that child welfare suits hardly represented their most difficult cases; as one judge noted, there is nothing inherently complex or unique about child welfare litigation. Furthermore, as a few indicated, judges can enlist experts to assist them. Calling them the "last of the generalists," Aspen (1996) explained that judges have access to additional resources through lawyers, expert witnesses, and law clerks.

Indeed, *B.H.* demonstrated that federal judges do not require specialized knowledge of public institutions to be effective decisionmakers in institutional reform cases. Grady was aware he lacked expertise in child welfare policy and recognized the importance of seeking assistance from others and following their advice. Relying on the experts in the field, he recognized that his judicial function did not require him to impose his own views of child welfare policy on the parties. That the court did not attempt to administer the child welfare system was more a tribute to its wisdom than its incapacity.

Although Grady's judicial posture may have been idiosyncratic, none of the other judges interviewed for this study—whether Carter, Reagan, Bush, or Clinton appointees—expressed any enthusiasm for involving himself in an institutional reform case. Shadur (1996), calling litigation the "least satisfactory approach" to solving the problems of society, explained that judges are forced into such cases because political leaders refuse to make unpopular decisions. Nordberg (1996) stressed that when engaged in such litigation, courts must ensure that there is a factual basis for claims that can lead to court orders against government bureaucracies.

Reflecting their concern about the appropriate limits of judicial involvement in a state's affairs, the judges were all cognizant of the problems inherent in judicial management of government agencies. Castillo (1996) pointed out that "courts are reluctant to order changes that make them administrators of agencies"; he added that judges should not have "day-to-day control of agencies" because it leads to resentment by all parties. Shadur (1996) emphasized that the court "can't and shouldn't micromanage institutions," suggesting that monitors were often useful in this regard.

There was unanimous agreement among these judges that they and their colleagues are aware of financial and administrative constraints on agencies when adjudicating institutional reform cases. They differed somewhat in the extent to which they believed they should be influenced by this knowledge. As Aspen (1996) noted, "The question is how sensitive they [judges] are to such things." Nordberg (1996) summarized the views of many by explaining that in deciding such cases, a "court must take the rights of the class into account, but also has to consider the functioning of the agency and the cost to taxpayers."

The judges—including those sometimes accused of manifesting insufficient respect for state budgetary autonomy—believed that courts should strive to avoid imposing costly remedies whenever possible. But they also denied that judges could or should excuse constitutional violations because of a state's funding constraints. "They [judges] have an obligation," Nordberg (1996) said, "to impose the law." After cautioning that judges must refrain from dictating to state legislatures, especially with respect to ordering expensive remedies, Plunkett (1996) nevertheless conceded that there are times when federal judges must decide that other factors are more important than state finances. Hart (1996) contended that while he remains cognizant of budgetary limitations on state agencies in deciding reform cases, once he determines the law, it is "really not [his] function" to be concerned about the state's ability to fund a decree or court order. "I don't care where the money comes from," another judge stated, adding, "That's not my province, not my problem."

At the same time, the judges were aware of constraints on their ability to force the bureaucracy to comply with a decree, most believing that leveling fines against an agency was only marginally effective in bringing about compliance.[2] Additionally, some judges believed that the fines, which were paid to the federal court, were a poor use of state resources.

The responses of these judges indicate that Grady is not unique among judges in maintaining a balance between a commitment to his judicial role and an awareness of the constraints on him. Faced with the same decisions, the other judges interviewed for this study would likely have reacted similarly.

The Courts and Institutional Reform Litigation

The story of *B.H.* provides little support for the charges made by Horowitz (1977) and others that courts seek to enlarge their policymaking role at the state's expense—with little ability to do so. The *B.H.* court performed its most important function at the outset of the case when it carried out its prescribed duty of adjudicating the plaintiffs' constitutional claims and, following the prevailing view of the circuits, refused to allow the state to evade its constitutional obligation to children in state custody.

After that, Grady did not impose a remedy in *B.H.*; the decree grew out of the interactions between the parties and was ratified by the state's chief executive. Nor did the court seek to administer the state's child welfare system or attempt to replace the agency's bureaucratic expertise with its own. The decree merely established the policy parameters (primarily determined by the agency leadership) in which state officials administered the system. Indeed, Grady always expressed an awareness of the challenges DCFS faced and the difficulty of meeting them; he never suggested that he could meet them more successfully. And finally, Grady's behavior in *B.H.* does not support the view that federal court judges are indifferent to state fiscal constraints. There is no evidence that the state ever presented a serious case for insufficient resources to fund DCFS reform effort. Moreover, Grady never ordered the state to appropriate funds for DCFS, nor did he ever interfere with the state's budgetary process. He did, of course, indirectly do so by obliging the state to meet its constitutional obligations to its abused and neglected children; his oath of office, however, left him with little choice in the matter.

Nor is there evidence to support the charge that agencies collude with plaintiffs to foster litigation to enhance their budgets. While DCFS clearly benefited from the revenue increases, the litigation was, on the whole, an unwelcome development for the agency leadership, forced to share its policymaking role with plaintiffs' lawyers and placed under the continual supervision of the court.

Similarly, *B.H.* also refutes the assertions that the constraints on the federal courts render them ineffective in producing social reform, making litigation a useless enterprise. On the contrary, this account of *B.H.* has shown that legal advocates can use the authority of the courts to mobilize resources on behalf of litigants who are unable to effect change through the normal political process. In a related vein, this study demonstrates that scholars must broaden their horizons beyond the confines of Supreme Court decisionmaking when assessing the role of the federal courts as a source of public policy change. As *B.H.* and other cases show, the child welfare reform litigators owed their victories to the lower court judges, who succeeded, for the most part, in avoiding the constraints imposed by the Supreme Court in *DeShaney* and *Artist M.*

In contrast to the claims made by some that courts are incapable of producing social reform, this study shows that federal court involvement was crucial in the child welfare policymaking process, playing an instrumental role in reforming the child welfare system. *B.H.* demonstrates that, by encouraging legal advocates and mobilizing public support, institutional reform litigation can ultimately spur policy change. And, although *B.H.* reveals the constraints on the federal courts, especially during the implementation stage, it also shows that the courts have learned to overcome some of these constraints. In short, *B.H.* confirms that structural reform litigation, with all its tribulations for courts and litigants, pays off.

Appendix

Appendix Table 1
Number of Calls to the Illinois Central Register,
Fiscal Years 1982–97

Fiscal year[a]	Number of calls[b]	Fiscal year[a]	Number of calls[b]
1982	111,736	1990	255,887
1983	118,739	1991	266,581
1984	129,452	1992	322,748
1985	167,610	1993	334,317
1986	181,548	1994	369,309
1987	186,219	1995	377,467
1988	206,428	1996	352,629
1989	233,241	1997	355,579

Sources: Illinois Department of Children and Family Services (1992, figure 2); Illinois Department of Children and Family Services (1998a, figure 1).

[a] The Illinois fiscal year begins on July 1 and ends on June 30.

[b] Calls include requests for information; reports may or may not lead to investigations.

Appendix Table 2
Number of Illinois Children Reported Abused or Neglected,
Fiscal Years 1987–97

Fiscal year[a]	Number of children reported	Percent change from previous fiscal year
1987	91,714	30.2
1988	94,086	2.6
1989	102,230	8.7
1990	103,420	1.2
1991	107,307	3.8
1992	130,562	21.7
1993	125,342	- 4.0
1994	136,312	8.8
1995	139,718	2.5
1996	125,220	-10.4
1997	119,405	- 4.6

Source: Illinois Department of Children and Family Services (1998a, table 1).

[a] The Illinois fiscal year begins on July 1 and ends on June 30.

Appendix Table 3

Number of Illinois Children Indicated for Abuse or Neglect, Fiscal Years 1987–97

Fiscal year[a]	Number of children indicated[b]	Percent change from previous fiscal year
1987	38,857	14.8
1988	41,329	6.4
1989	40,932	-1.0
1990	38,209	-6.7
1991	37,304	-2.4
1992	43,169	15.7
1993	42,220	-2.2
1994	49,536	17.3
1995	53,368	7.7
1996	44,754	-16.1
1997	42,251	-5.6

Source: Illinois Department of Children and Family Services (1998a, table 2).

[a] The Illinois fiscal year begins on July 1 and ends on June 30.

[b] An indicated report means an investigation of suspected child abuse or neglect has resulted in credible evidence that abuse or neglect occurred.

Appendix Table 4

Child Welfare Caseload of the Department of Children and Family Services (DCFS), Fiscal Years 1992–98

Fiscal year[a]	Number of cases[b]
1992	43,077
1993	47,802
1994	56,128
1995	66,438
1996	67,926
1997	67,001
1998	59,861

Sources: Illinois Department of Children and Family Services (1995, 3-1); Illinois Department of Children and Family Services (1998a).

[a] The Illinois fiscal year begins on July 1 and ends on June 30.

[b] Total family/child caseload.

Appendix Table 5

Number of Illinois Children Placed in Substitute Care, by Type of Care, Fiscal Years 1992–98[a]

Fiscal year[b]	Foster care	Relative foster care	Institutional care	Total substitute care
1992	11,109	15,004	3,429	29,542
1993	12,048	17,985	3,782	33,815
1994	13,861	22,631	4,669	41,161
1995	15,632	27,071	5,159	47,862
1996	17,476	28,034	4,709	50,219
1997	19,029	28,129	4,173	51,331
1998[c]	18,494	25,731	3,990	48,215

Sources: Illinois Department of Children and Family Services (1995, 4-1); Illinois Department of Children and Family Services (1998c).

[a] Excludes approximately 2,500–3,000 children placed out of the state.

[b] The Illinois fiscal year begins on July 1 and ends on June 30.

[c] FY 1998 data as of April 30, 1998.

Appendix Table 6

State Expenditures for *Norman* Population and Number of Recipients, by Monitor Reporting Period, 1991–94

Reporting period	State expenditures	Number of recipient families
7/1/91–12/31/91	$ 106,901	176
1/1/92–6/30/92	$ 235,279	431
7/1/92–12/31/92	$ 357,260	NA
1/1/93–6/30/93	$ 281,696	NA
7/1/93–12/31/93	$ 398,916	360
1/1/94–6/30/94	$ 349,905[a]	476
7/1/94–12/31/94	$ 475,785[a]	769
Total	$2,205,742	2,212

Source: Norman v. McDonald (1995).

Note: Totals calculated by author from available data.

[a] Data from estimates.

Appendix Table 7
Department of Children and Family Services (DCFS) Appropriations, Fiscal Years 1980–99

Fiscal year[a]	Amount appropriated ($ thousands)	Percentage increase
1980	164,143.5	—
1981	184,244.2	12
1982	186,510.2	1
1983	202,639.7	9
1984	215,027.3	6
1985	236,180.5	10
1986	261,351.9	11
1987	281,865.1	8
1988	307,569.7	9
1989	364,762.2	19
1990	427,906.1	17
1991	499,902.9	17
1992	588,777.1	18
1993	714,489.7	21
1994	854,381.6	20
1995	1,098,522.4	29
1996	1,221,046.6	11
1997	1,282,975.8	5
1998	1,341,422.8	5
1999	1,380,146.8	3

Source: Illinois Bureau of the Budget FY 1982–99.

Note: Annual percent increases calculated by author. FY 1980–FY 1991 amounts are identified as appropriated funds and other resources; FY 1992–FY 1998 amounts are identified as general revenue funds and other state funds, with federal funds excluded.

[a] The Illinois fiscal year begins on July 1 and ends on June 30.

Notes

Chapter 1

1. Individual damage suits, brought mostly in state courts on relatively narrow legal grounds, preceded the development of systemic litigation (Mushlin, Levitt, and Anderson 1986).

2. The Supreme Court curtailed the federal judiciary's authority to intervene in local taxing policy in *Missouri v. Jenkins*, 495 U.S. 33 (1990).

3. McCann (1994, 293) also examines the arguments of the "structuralists," who support the neorealists in their assessment of the courts and maintain as well that litigation reduces the ability of social movements to achieve their goals. This discussion is less relevant to child welfare litigation since there is no comparable social movement fueling this litigation.

4. "Substitute care is a social service provided for children who cannot live with their own parents" (Goerge 1990, 423).

5. Funded by the U.S. Department of Health and Human Services, this data archive of child welfare statistics in five states was created in 1986 by researchers at the Chapin Hall Center for Children at the University of Chicago. Complete from 1988 to 1993, the data set containing longitudinal data from the five states permits analysis of the duration of foster care and reentry into the foster care system for each child in the child welfare system (Goerge, Wulczyn, and Harden 1996, 13–14).

6. These percentage figures were calculated by the Children's Defense Fund (1998) on the basis of data collected by the American Public Welfare Association.

7. The New York and Illinois child welfare systems are both favorite targets of child welfare advocates; each was sued thirteen times in state *and* federal court during this time.

8. The Cook County Juvenile Court's Child Protection Division accounts for about 75 percent of the approximately 50,000 Illinois children in substitute care (Merry and others 1997, 1).

9. The Cook County Public Guardian's office is the only office of its kind in the nation, serving as guardian *ad litem* to the county's abused and neglected children and guardian to its disabled elderly (Murphy 1997, 68).

10. The respondents include nine federal court judges—two at the appellate level and seven at the district court level, including most of the district court judges who were involved in class action suits against DCFS; nine child welfare attorneys from private law offices as well as public interest law firms that represented plaintiffs in a variety of class action lawsuits; the Cook County Public Guardian and three assistant public guardians, including the supervisor of its special litigation unit; the director and executive deputy director of DCFS; three former DCFS

directors (one interviewed by telephone); DCFS's general counsel; the director, former director, and a staff member of DCFS's Office of Litigation Management; the former deputy director of Cook County DCFS; the special assistant attorney general serving as chief (outside) counsel for DCFS until 1996; the head of DCFS's Child Welfare Litigation Division in the Office of the Attorney General; the Inspector General of DCFS and two staff attorneys; two court-appointed monitors and two staff members; the director of Policy Initiatives of the Cook County Circuit Court Child Protection Division; the director of the Clinical Evaluation and Services Initiative of Cook County Juvenile Court; a co-manager of the Rule 706 Expert Panel; the director of the Children and Family Research Center of the University of Illinois; the director of the Family Centered Services Evaluation Project of the Children and Family Research Center of the University of Illinois; the associate director and a research associate of the Chapin Hall Center for Children at the University of Chicago; the director and assistant director of the Cook County Court Appointed Special Advocates; the executive director of Illinois Action for Children; the associate director of the Citizens Committee on the Juvenile Court; the chair of the Citizens Committee on the Juvenile Court; the senior projects director of Voices for Illinois Children; a former president of the Illinois Caucus for Foster Children; and two members of the Illinois General Assembly (one interviewed by telephone). Additionally, three respondents (one of the plaintiffs' attorneys, a DCFS official, and an assistant public guardian) were reinterviewed two years after their initial interviews to acquire a more long-term perspective on the progress of the child welfare reform effort in Illinois a decade after the lawsuit was filed. Effective January 1, 1993, the Child Welfare Litigation Division in the Office of the Attorney General was designated to serve as counsel for DCFS, replacing the private law firm representing the department in all matters other than *B.H.* The attorneys within the new division were designated as special assistant attorneys general (20 ILCS 505/9.8a).

11. These advocates, primarily attorneys, were associated with the Children's Defense Fund, the Children's Rights Project of the New York Civil Liberties Union, the Center for Mental Health Law, the Center for Law and Social Policy, the Center on Social Welfare Policy and Law, the American Bar Association Center on Children and the Law, the Children's Rights Project of the Legal Assistance Foundation of Chicago, the Youth Law Center, the National Center for Youth Law, and the Children's and Institutionalized Persons Project of the Roger Baldwin Foundation of the American Civil Liberties Union. There is some overlap between the two sets of respondents; three attorneys were interviewed for both projects.

12. The information gathered from these interviews was published in Mezey (1996).

13. Juvenile court judges from Lake, McHenry, Kane, and DuPage counties were interviewed; the excluded county was Will County. The results of these interviews were reported in Mezey (1995).

Chapter 2

1. Neglect reports constituted almost two-thirds (65 percent) of child maltreatment reports within Illinois (*Norman v. McDonald* 1995, 1).

2. See Caldwell, Bogat, and Davidson (1988) for discussion of research associated with explanations of child maltreatment and Fryer (1993, chap. 3) for discussion of research on factors associated with child maltreatment, including studies that focus on the parents' psychological disorders.

3. Some critics (for example, Besharov 1984) argue that because many of the reports of abuse and neglect are unsubstantiated, restrictions should be placed on reporting. Others (for example, Gelles 1996) counter that unsubstantiated reports are not necessarily false or invalid. In Gelles's view, they merely lack sufficient evidence to make a clear determination of whether the child was harmed.

4. Lowry has filed several child welfare lawsuits around the country, including major efforts against the New York City and Washington, D.C., child welfare authorities.

5. Another source of funding for programs serving abused and neglected children is the Social Services Block Grant, Title XX of the Social Security Act, established in 1975. By 1991, states were spending about half their Title XX allocations on child welfare services (Stein 1991, 45).

6. Schuerman and Littell (1995, 16), however, suggest that this phrase seems to place "the emphasis on planning rather than doing."

7. Ironically, as Testa and Goerge (1988, 1) note, because the federal government had stopped collecting state and county data on foster care in 1971, there were no reliable national data on the foster care system at the time the law was enacted.

8. The law required individual case plans to specify the services offered. The accompanying federal regulations to P.L. 96-272 listed an array of services that might be spelled out in case plans: for example, substance abuse counseling, temporary child care, psychological counseling, and parenting classes (Bufkin 1996/1997, 359).

9. A showing of reasonable efforts is one of eight factors that determine whether the state will receive federal reimbursement (Testa and Goerge 1988, 17 n. 2).

10. Foster care expenses for each child can range between $10,000 and $20,000 a year, including administrative costs (Herring 1995, 195).

11. Boyer (1995) notes that like any parents, courts and agencies have disagreements over how to achieve the best outcome for "their" children.

12. Some, such as Gelles (1996, 184 n. 1) differentiate between the terms "family preservation" based on the Homebuilders model, and "family reunification," using more traditional methods of keeping children in their families or returning them to their families after removal. That distinction is not made in this study unless specifically noted.

13. The Homebuilders program purportedly saves $2,331 per case (Stoesz and Karger 1996).

14. An Illinois version of Homebuilders was announced in November 1986. For the first six months, the program, labeled Family First, was supposed to be

staffed by eight caseworkers who would serve from 60 to 100 families. Caseworkers would work with two families at a time for a maximum of one month (*Chicago Tribune*, November 11, 1986). See Schuerman, Rzepnicki, and Littell (1994, chap. 1) for discussion of the Illinois program as well as examples of other family preservation programs.

15. The practice of concurrent planning has been an integral part of permanency planning in some states for quite a while; it was introduced in Washington in 1981 and designed for children who are unlikely to be returned home. In the Washington model, concurrent planning is implemented as soon as a child enters foster care (Sandt 1997).

16. The previous year Congress had tried to increase adoption rates by allowing tax benefits for adoptive parents.

Chapter 3

1. All tables are presented in the appendix.

2. Reports of abuse and neglect are screened by intake workers. According to Golbert (1998), the standard for determining whether to investigate a report can be analogized to a "motion to dismiss" standard; that is, accepting the report as true, does the action constitute abuse and neglect? If the answer is yes, a copy of the report is transmitted to the Division of Child Protection, which sends an investigator to determine whether the allegation is true.

3. See Gittens (1994) for a history of the early years of the Illinois child welfare system; the book broadly looks at policy toward dependent children, juvenile offenders, and disabled children.

4. 20 ILCS 505/1. DCFS was given responsibility for licensing private agencies and providing direct services that the private social welfare agencies were unwilling to perform, such as preventive services, child protection, and placement for minority children (Gittens 1994, chap. 3).

5. Today there is a long list of mandated reporters, including, for example, hospital administrators, school personnel, truant officers, child care workers, and dentists.

6. Beginning in January 1996, DCFS no longer had responsibility for children thirteen and older facing criminal charges.

7. 705 ILCS 405/2-9. The statute, 705 ILCS 405/2-7, defines "temporary custody" to include both "temporary protective custody" and "shelter care"; in either case, the child is removed from home. The terms "temporary custody" and "protective custody" are often (erroneously) used interchangeably, but more commonly "protective custody" is used when the child is removed from home at the initiative of a child protection worker or police officer, and "temporary custody" is used when DCFS is granted custody, or retains custody, at the judicial hearing. Taking a child into protective custody does not require prior approval from the juvenile court.

8. Although it rarely occurs, a state's attorney may file a petition with the juvenile court without DCFS's having removed the child from home.

9. 705 ILCS 405/2-10. This language was inserted throughout the bill (see Public Act 88-7), amending several sections of the Juvenile Court Act of 1987.

10. 20 ILCS 505/35.5(a).

11. When there is a conflict between the two, Illinois caselaw indicates that the child's best interests must prevail.

12. The duties of the guardian *ad litem* are discussed in 705 ILCS 405/2-17.

13. In Cook County, this attorney's primary duty often appears to be to defuse the juvenile court judge's periodic displays of anger and frustration at the agency and DCFS worker (Mezey 1995).

14. The role of the court-appointed special advocate is described in 705 ILCS 405/2-17.1.

15. The judge may extend this deadline by thirty days.

16. The adjudicatory hearing is discussed in 705 ILCS 405/2-21.

17. The dispositional hearing is discussed in 705 ILCS 405/2-22.

18. 705 ILCS 405/2-27.

19. Permanency review hearings are discussed in 705 ILCS 405/2-28.

20. The duties of hearing officers are discussed in 705 ILCS 405/2-28.1.

21. Despite the concerns about family preservation policy, most experts probably believe that returning children home to parents who are able to care for them represents the best outcome for the entire family, including the children.

22. Within the next few years, DCFS would enter into consent decrees pertaining to emergency housing provisions (*Norman v. Suter* 1991), permanency planning hearings (*Dana W. v. Ryder* 1993), and sibling placements and visits (*Aristotle P. v. Ryder* 1994); these cases are discussed in subsequent chapters.

23. The court dismissed the state claim.

24. Almost twenty years later, a federal court judge appointed Miller as receiver in the Washington, D.C., child welfare agency. On the basis of his record at DCFS, several respondents expressed amazement at his appointment in D.C.

25. The ACLU is the largest public interest law firm in the United States; it employs more than sixty staff attorneys, who, along with 2,000 volunteer attorneys, handle nearly 6,000 cases annually. According to its mission statement, its goal is to ensure that the Bill of Rights guards against unwarranted government intrusion into people's lives and to extend the protection of the state to groups of persons traditionally denied it (American Civil Liberties Union <http://www.aclu.org/library/pbp1.html> [20 May 1998]).

26. Schiff Hardin & Waite, in existence since 1864, is a firm with more than 200 attorneys; it is based in Chicago, with offices in Washington, D.C., New York, and Merrillville, Indiana (Schiff Hardin & Waite <http://www.schiffhardin.com/firm.html> [20 May 1998]).

27. One of the largest law firms in the world, Skadden, Arps (as the firm and its affiliates are collectively known) consists of more than a thousand attorneys in twenty offices worldwide, nine in the United States and eleven in Asia, Australia, Canada, and Europe (Skadden, Arps, Slate, Meagher & Flom <http://www.sasmf.com/market/index.htm> [20 May 1998]).

Chapter 4

1. The issue to consider in a motion to dismiss is not whether the plaintiffs can win, but whether they should be allowed to proceed to the merits of the case. All facts correctly pleaded in a complaint must be construed in the light most favorable to plaintiffs. The rule regarding 12(b)(6) motions is that the complaint "should not be dismissed for failure to state a claim unless it appears beyond doubt that the plaintiff can prove no set of facts in support of his claim which would entitle him to relief" (*Conley v. Gibson* 1957, 46).

2. Although the Eleventh Amendment immunizes states from suit, the Supreme Court allows individuals to sue state officials in their official capacities for prospective, that is, injunctive or declaratory, relief (see *Ex Parte Young* 1908; *Edelman v. Jordan* 1974; *Will v. Michigan Department of State Police* 1989).

3. The court dismissed their procedural due process and equal protection claims.

4. Cases such as this were made possible by the Supreme Court's decision in *Monell v. New York City Department of Social Services* (1978), which held that local governments are not immune from being sued under § 1983 for deprivation of constitutional rights. *Monell* reversed the Court's previous holding in *Monroe v. Pape* (1961) that local governments were immune from liability (see Kieffer 1984).

5. Although there are a number of unspecified liberty interests protected by the Constitution, perhaps the most important is the right to bodily integrity (*White v. Rochford* 1979, 383).

6. Akhil Reed Amar and Daniel Widawsky (1992) argue that the Thirteenth Amendment's ban on involuntary servitude applies to child abuse. They believe that a parent who mistreats a child violates the Thirteenth Amendment, and, unlike the Fourteenth Amendment, which is limited to state action, the Thirteenth applies to private action. Moreover, they claim, the language of the Thirteenth commands the state to take affirmative steps to abolish servitude, or, in this case, to protect the child when it knows of the abuse.

7. One exception was *Milburn v. Anne Arundel County Department of Social Services* (1989), where the Fourth Circuit exercised a narrow view of custody, holding that the state was not liable for injuries to a four-year-old child who had been *voluntarily* placed in foster care by his parents.

8. Over the next decade, a long line of cases discussing the availability of a § 1983 remedy in federal court followed (see, for example, *Wright v. Roanoke Redevelopment and Housing Authority* 1987; *Golden State Transit Corp. v. City of Los Angeles* 1989; and *Wilder v. Virginia Hospital Association* 1990).

Chapter 5

1. Grady also noted a Second Circuit ruling, *Society for Good Will to Retarded Children v. Cuomo* (1984), in which the court extended *Youngberg v. Romeo* (1982) to any person in state custody.

2. Grady also ruled that the children sued Johnson in his official capacity only and had properly alleged that he committed "the acts complained of with deliber-

ate indifference to plaintiffs' rights and did so pursuant to official policy or custom" (*B.H.* 1989, 1398).

3. In *Rufo v. Inmates of Suffolk County Jail* (1992, 392), a case involving a district court's modification of a consent decree, the Supreme Court said in dicta that "financial constraints may not be used to justify the creation or perpetuation of constitutional violations. . . ."

4. Eventually, amid procedural wrangling, including an interlocutory appeal to the Seventh Circuit, the parties reached a settlement in 1994 (*Aristotle P. v. Ryder* 1994). The decree is discussed in chapter 6.

5. In addition to the main class of plaintiffs, the court also certified a subclass that did not include children placed in homes under DCFS supervision by order of the juvenile court.

6. Only Subclass B alleged the due process violation. Shadur noted that he would have been required to dismiss the claim under *DeShaney* had the entire class (including those children remaining at home under protective order) alleged a due process violation.

7. On April 3, 1990, Shadur modified the injunction to require DCFS to provide data to the OPG showing its compliance with the order on a weekly basis. Following oral arguments in June, the appellate court ordered the district court to hold hearings to determine the status of DCFS's caseworker assignment plan at the time he issued the injunction. The district court issued its findings in July, and the appellate court affirmed in October.

8. The state's motion for rehearing and rehearing *en banc* was denied on December 20, 1990. The Supreme Court's decision in *Artist M.* is discussed in chapter 6.

9. The parties negotiated a new consent order approved by the court in October 1993 to resolve problems of implementation; this order included hiring more senior-level staff, setting caseload standards, and improving the contracting system with outside providers. For further information on the history and current status of the *R.C.* case, see Bazelon Center for Mental Health Law (1998).

10. The implementation of the *LaShawn A.* decree is discussed in chapter 6.

11. Although not the judge from whom Grady learned about this use of experts, another federal court judge, Alan Nevas, appointed a mediation panel consisting of a neutral party and a representative from each side in a suit against Connecticut's Department of Children and Families. After complex negotiations, the panel proposed a consent decree that was approved by the court following public hearings. As part of the implementation process, with oversight by the mediation panel, the parties produced a set of twelve manuals setting forth procedures, timetables, and substantive reforms; these manuals were subsequently incorporated into the consent decree (see *Juan F. v. Weiker* 1994).

12. While Grady made it clear that *B.H.* was not intended to preclude future state-law actions that dealt with different issues from *B.H.*, it was not clear which issues would be considered "different" enough. A number of subsequent actions brought by the OPG were dismissed on *B.H.* grounds (see *Katherine M. v. Ryder* 1993, 483–84).

Chapter 6

1. The data in the five-state Multistate Data Archive were updated to 1994, and a sixth state, Missouri, was added to the data set.

2. By 1995 private agencies were handling approximately 60 percent of the state's foster care program under contracts with DCFS (*State-Journal Register,* November 19, 1995).

3. In many of these cases, the courts were divided on the issue of the standard of conduct; some adopted the "deliberate indifference" standard used in prison cases and others the "professional judgment" standard used to determine the state's liability in cases involving injury to mentally ill patients. The former is a more difficult standard for plaintiffs to meet. Most courts, however, have failed to acknowledge that two standards exist or that courts are split on their use (see Kearse 1996).

4. The conferees noted that the provision for such a study was dropped for technical reasons only. Under the so-called "Byrd rule," extraneous matters are dropped from reconciliation bills.

5. The plaintiffs filed the first motion for contempt in December 1992; the second one was filed in March 1994.

6. Under the doctrine of pendent jurisdiction, a federal court *may* rule on state, or in this case, District of Columbia, claims even when the federal claims are dismissed. But under some circumstances, the state claims *must* be dismissed.

7. Although the first child welfare receiver, receivers were not unknown in the District. Earlier, another federal judge had placed the District's public housing authority into receivership (*Washington Post,* May 23, 1995).

8. The *Norman* Liaison in DCFS office can increase the amount to $1,200, and the Office of Litigation Management can raise it to $2,000 (Cheney-Egan 1997).

9. Funds paid to *Norman* beneficiaries come out of the state treasury.

10. In February 1995, the parties had jointly moved the court to extend the monitor's duties until February 15, 1997; the court lengthened the monitor's term only to February 15, 1996. The plaintiffs then moved to extend the term for two years starting in February 1996.

11. One respondent suggested that part of Grady's frustration stemmed from his disappointment in the monitor's efforts to secure the agency's compliance with the decree.

12. Rule 53 refers to "masters," not monitors. However, the terms were used interchangeably by the respondents, thus tending to obscure any functional differences between the two.

Chapter 7

1. 30 ILCS 105/40.

2. Murphy's attempts to intervene in the settlement negotiations are discussed by the Seventh Circuit in *B.H. v. Ryder* (1993).

3. Most respondents pointed out that he was too junior to have been given the responsibility for such an important case.

4. Joined by Goodwin, Easterbrook concurred in the opinion to express some additional thoughts about the pitfalls of systemic litigation against state agencies.

5. DCFS had successfully argued in *Katherine M. v. Ryder* (1993) that the *B.H.* decree precluded any subsequent state court litigation against the agency for systemic reform and that the class of plaintiffs who were in DCFS custody and "exposed to, suffered, or perpetrated sexual abuse" were a subclass of the *B.H.* class and therefore under the jurisdiction of the federal court.

6. Amanda Wallace was sentenced to life imprisonment without parole in July 1996. A little more than a year later, she committed suicide in her prison cell by strangling herself.

7. Private social welfare agencies, such as Catholic Charities or Lutheran Children's Services, are responsible for almost three-quarters of the Illinois children in foster care. According to Loftus (1998), in Cook County, about 75 percent of the foster care population is in the private sector; in downstate Illinois, about 60 percent is in private hands. These agencies work under contract with DCFS and are required to place a certain percentage of children in permanent status; failure to perform risks future contracts with the state.

8. This law was introduced at DCFS's initiative on March 1, 1995. Amending 20 ILCS 505/7, it was quickly passed by the legislature and signed by the governor, taking effect on July 1, 1995. Related to the changed definition of "neglect," the legislation also included the controversial "Home of Relative Reform Plan" or HMR Reform. HMR Reform created a second tier of benefits for children who remained in the homes of relatives who were not licensed as foster parents. The lower payment was pegged to the Illinois "standard of need," a average of $252, making it higher than welfare benefits and almost a hundred dollars less than the average foster care benefit of $350. In large part adopted as a budget-cutting device, under the plan DCFS would merely have to make up the difference between public aid benefits and the standard of need, about $75 a child.

The LAF challenged HMR Reform in federal district court on procedural grounds, claiming it violated due process by not giving relatives an adequate opportunity to become licensed as foster parents; they also alleged it contravened Title IV-E as well as an almost twenty-year old Supreme Court ruling on relative foster care (*Miller v. Youakim* 1979), in which the Court held that states were required to provide foster care benefits to children living with relatives as long as the children met the eligibility standards under Title IV-A.

In *Youakim v. McDonald* (1995), the court enjoined DCFS from putting the plan into effect and ordered the agency to continue paying relatives the full foster care payments until they had an opportunity to become licensed if they wished (see Goodwin 1996/1997). After the proper transitional period, DCFS was permitted to institute the lower payments to unlicensed foster parents.

9. House Bills 66 (P.A. 90-27) and 165 (P.A. 90-28), signed by Edgar on June 25, 1997, composed the Permanency Initiative of 1997. The legislation took effect on January 1, 1998.

10. According to Loftus (1998), Delaware was the first state to get such a waiver from HHS, but Illinois was the first large state.

11. In the counties surrounding Cook, juvenile court judges are responsible for adjudicating all matters involving juveniles, including abuse and neglect, delinquency, termination of parental rights, and adoption.

12. The study was funded by a federal grant: the Omnibus Budget Reconciliation Act of 1993 authorized HHS to provide grants to state supreme courts to allow them to study and improve the way in which states implement Titles IV-B and IV-E of P.L. 96-272. The Illinois Supreme Court designated the Citizens Committee on the Juvenile Court Support Fund to oversee the grant, and it, in turn, contracted with Chapin Hall to conduct the study and submit a report. The citizens committee chose to concentrate the study in Cook County.

Chapter 8

1. According to Loftus (1998), about 75 percent of the Cook County and 60 percent of the downstate foster care population are served by private agencies, subject to DCFS authority.

2. Shadur (1996) had imposed a civil contempt fine of $1,000 a day against the Cook County Board of Commissioners, not as punishment, but solely to induce them to comply with his order to reduce overcrowding at the Cook County Jail. As he noted, however, as soon as he imposed the fine, the board appropriated the money to pay it for a full year, indicating that it did not intend to comply with his order within any reasonable time. Approximately nine months (and about $270,000) later, Shadur vacated the balance of the fine, recognizing that it was futile to continue it. The fine turned out to be ineffective, he said, because the board simply paid it rather than taking action to comply with his order.

References

Allen, MaryLee, Carol Golubock, and Lynn Olson. 1983. Guide to the Adoption Assistance and Child Welfare Act of 1980. In *Foster Children in the Courts*, edited by Mark Hardin. Boston: Butterworth Legal Publishers.

Amar, Akhil Reed, and Daniel Widawsky. 1992. Child Abuse as Slavery: A Thirteenth Amendment Response to *DeShaney*. *Harvard Law Review* 105: 1359–85.

American Bar Association. 1993. *America's Children at Risk: A National Agenda for Legal Action*. Washington, D.C.: American Bar Association.

Anderson, Lloyd C. 1983. The Approval and Interpretation of Consent Decrees in Civil Rights Class Action Litigation. *University of Illinois Law Review,* no. 3 (summer): 579–632.

———. 1986. Implementation of Consent Decrees in Structural Reform Litigation. *University of Illinois Law Review,* no. 3 (summer): 725–78.

Appell, Annette R. 1997. Protecting Children or Punishing Mothers: Gender, Race, and Class in the Child Protection System. *South Carolina Law Review* 48: 577–613.

Aronow, Geoffrey F. 1980. The Special Master in School Desegregation Cases: The Evolution of Roles in the Reformation of Public Institutions through Litigation, *Hastings Constitutional Law Quarterly* 7: 739–75.

Barth, Richard P. 1998. Abusive and Neglecting Parents and the Care of Their Children. In *All Our Families: New Policies for a New Century*, edited by Mary Ann Mason, Arlene Skolnick, and Stephen D. Sugarman. New York: Oxford University Press.

Bazelon Center for Mental Health Law. 1998. *Making Child Welfare Work*. Washington, D.C.: Bazelon Center for Mental Health Law.

Berger, Raoul. 1977. *Government by Judiciary: The Transformation of the Fourteenth Amendment*. Cambridge: Harvard University Press.

Besharov, Douglas J. 1984. Malpractice in Child Placement: Civil Liability for Inadequate Foster Care Services. *Child Welfare* 63: 195–204.

Boyer, Bruce. 1995. Jurisdictional Conflicts between Juvenile Courts and Child Welfare Agencies: The Uneasy Relationship between Institutional Co-Parents. *Maryland Law Review* 54: 377–431.

———. 1996. Ethical Issues in the Representation of Parents in Child Welfare Cases. *Fordham Law Review* 64: 1621–54.

Bufkin, Michael J. 1996/1997. The "Reasonable Efforts" Requirement: Does It Place Children at Increased Risk of Abuse or Neglect? *University of Louisville Journal of Family Law.* 35: 355–78.

Bussiere, Alice. 1985. Federal Adoption Assistance for Children with Special Needs. *Clearinghouse Review* (October): 587–99.

Caldwell, Robert, G. Anne Bogat, and William S. Davidson II. 1988. The Assessment of Child Abuse Potential. *American Journal of Community Psychology* 16: 609–24.

Canon, Bradley C. 1998. The Supreme Court and Policy Reform: *The Hollow Hope* Revisited. In *Leveraging the Law: Using the Courts to Achieve Social Change*, edited by David A. Schultz. New York: Peter Lang.

Canon, Bradley C., and Charles A. Johnson. 1999. *Judicial Policies: Implementation and Impact*. 2d ed. Washington, D.C.: Congressional Quarterly.

Chayes, Abram. 1976. The Role of the Judge in Public Law Litigation. *Harvard Law Review* 89: 1281–1316.

Children's Defense Fund. 1998. *The State of America's Children Yearbook*. Washington, D.C.: Children's Defense Fund.

Chilton, Bradley Stewart. 1991. *Prisons under the Gavel: The Federal Takeover of Georgia Prisons*. Columbus: Ohio State University Press.

Clinton, Bill. 1997. Statement of the President. *White House Press Release* <http://www.pub.whitehouse.gov/uri-res/12R?urn:pdi//oma.eop.gov.us/1997/11/19/2.text.1> (10 December 1997).

Colvin, Stacy Marie. 1992. *LaShawn v. Dixon*: Responding to the Pleas of Children. *Washington and Lee Law Review* 49: 529–57.

Conrad, John P. 1989. From Barbarism toward Decency: Alabama's Long Road to Prison Reform. *Journal of Research in Crime and Delinquency* 26: 307–28.

Cooper, Phillip. 1988. *Hard Judicial Choices: Federal District Court Judges and State and Local Officials*. Oxford: Oxford University Press.

Cortner, Richard C. 1968. Strategies and Tactics of Litigants in Constitutional Cases. *Journal of Public Law*. 17: 287–307.

Costin, Lela B., Howard Jacob Karger, and David Stoesz. 1996. *The Politics of Child Abuse in America*. New York: Oxford University Press.

Craig, Conna, and Derek Herbert. 1997. *The State of the Children: An Examination of Government-Run Foster Care*. Dallas: National Center for Policy Analysis.

Crouch, Ben M., and James W. Marquart. 1989. *An Appeal to Justice: Litigated Reform of Texas Prisons*. Austin: University of Texas Press.

Dorne, Clifford K. 1997. *Child Maltreatment: A Primer in History, Public Policy, and Research*. 2d ed. Guilderland, N.Y.: Harrow and Heston.

Easterbrook, Frank H. 1987. Justice and Contract in Consent Judgments. *University of Chicago Legal Forum* 1987: 19–41.

———. 1991. Civil Rights and Remedies. *Harvard Journal of Law & Public Policy* 14: 103–11.

Effron, Alan. 1988. Federalism and Federal Consent Decrees against State Governmental Entities. *Columbia Law Review* 88: 1796–1820.

Eisenberg, Theodore, and Stephen C. Yeazell. 1980. The Ordinary and the Extraordinary in Institutional Litigation. *Harvard Law Review* 93: 465–517.

English, Abigail, and Madelyn DeWoody Freundlich. 1997. Medicaid: A Key to Health Care for Foster Children and Adopted Children with Special Needs. *Clearinghouse Review* 31: 109–31.

First, Curry. 1989. "Poor Joshua!" The State's Responsibility to Protect Children from Abuse. *Clearinghouse Review* 23: 525–34.

Fiss, Owen. 1979. Foreword: The Forms of Justice. *Harvard Law Review* 93: 1–58.

Frye, Lisa. 1993. *Suter v. Artist M.* and Statutory Remedies under Section 1983: Alteration without Justification. *North Carolina Law Review* 71: 1169–1205.

Fryer, George E., Jr. 1993. *Child Abuse and the Social Environment.* Boulder: Westview.

Galanter, Marc. 1974. Why the 'Haves' Come Out Ahead: Speculation on the Limits of Legal Change. *Law and Society Review* 9: 95–160.

Garbarino, James, and Kathleen Kostelny. 1993. Public Policy and Child Protection. In *Children at Risk in America*, edited by Roberta Wollons. Albany: State University of New York Press.

Gelles, Richard. 1996. *The Book of David: How Preserving Families Can Cost Children's Lives.* New York: Basic Books.

Gibeaut, John. 1997. Nobody's Child. *American Bar Association Journal* 83 (December): 44–51.

Gittens, Joan. 1994. *Poor Relations: The Children of the State in Illinois, 1818–1990.* Urbana: University of Illinois Press.

Glazer, Nathan. 1975. Toward an Imperial Judiciary. *Public Interest* 41: 104–23.

———. 1978. Should Judges Administer Social Services? *Public Interest* 50: 64–80.

Goerge, Robert M. 1990. The Reunification Process in Substitute Care. *Social Service Review* 64: 422–57.

Goerge, Robert M., and Fred H. Wulczyn. 1990. *Placement Duration and Foster Care Reentry in New York and Illinois: Volume I.* Chicago: Chapin Hall Center for Children at the University of Chicago.

Goerge, Robert M., Fred H. Wulczyn, and Allen W. Harden. 1996. New Comparative Insights into States and Their Foster Children. *Public Welfare* 54: 12–26.

Goerge, Robert M., and others. 1997. *Adoption, Disruption, and Displacement in the Child Welfare System, 1976–94.* Chicago: Chapin Hall Center for Children at the University of Chicago.

Golden, Renny. 1997. *Disposable Children: America's Child Welfare System.* Belmont, Cal.: Wadsworth.

Goodwin, Michael. 1996/1997. Case Note. *University of Louisville Journal of Family Law* 35: 641–48.

Gordon, Linda. 1994. *Pitied but Not Entitled: Single Mothers and the History of Welfare.* New York: Free Press.

Graglia, Lino. 1976. *Disaster by Decree: The Supreme Court's Decisions on Race and Schools.* Ithaca: Cornell University Press.

Haar, Charles M. 1996. *Suburbs under Siege: Race, Space, and Audacious Judges.* Princeton: Princeton University Press.

Handler, Joel. 1978. *Social Movements and the Legal System.* New York: Academic Press.

Hansen, Chris. 1994. Making It Work: Implementation of Court Orders Requiring Restructuring of State Executive Branch Agencies. In *Child,*

Parent, and State: Law and Policy Reader, edited by S. Randall Humm and others. Philadelphia: Temple University Press.

Harriman, Linda, and Jeffrey D. Straussman. 1983. Do Judges Determine Budget Decisions? Federal Court Decisions in Prison Reform and State Spending for Corrections. *Public Administration Review* 43: 343–51.

Hartnett, Mary Ann. 1991. *Judicial Review of Children in Substitute Care*. Chicago: Chapin Hall Center for Children at the University of Chicago.

Herring, David J. 1995. Exploring the Political Roles of the Family: Justifications for Permanency Planning for Children. *Loyola University Chicago Law Journal* 26: 183–209.

Horowitz, Donald. 1977. *The Courts and Social Policy*. Washington, D.C.: Brookings.

———. 1983. Decreeing Organizational Change: Judicial Supervision of Public Institutions. *Duke Law Journal*: 1265–1307.

Illinois Bureau of the Budget. FY 1982–FY 1998. *Illinois State Budget*. Springfield, Ill: Bureau of the Budget; also at <http://www.state.il.us/budget/tables/418.htm>

Illinois Department of Children and Family Services. 1992. *Annual Report: Executive Statistical Summary*. Springfield, Ill.: Department of Children and Family Services.

———. 1995. *Annual Report: Executive Statistical Summary*. Springfield, Ill.: Department of Children and Family Services (December 1995).

———. 1996. *Press Release: DCFS Budget Keeps Commitment to Abused Children; Boosts Funding for Adoptions by 25 Percent*. <http://www.state.il.us/gov/press/dcfs.htm> (29 May 1998).

———. 1998a. *Annual Report: Executive Statistical Summary*. Illinois Department of Children and Family Services. <http://www.state.il.us/dcfs/cant3.htm> (2 October 1998).

———. 1998b. *"Early History of Illinois Child Welfare Services Leading to the Creation of the Department of Children and Family Services."* <http://www.state.il.us/dcfs/swhistry.htm> (9 October 1998).

———. 1998c. *Annual Report: Executive Statistical Summary*. <http://www.state.il.us/dcfs/live1.pdf> (2 October 1998).

———. 1998d. *Annual Report: Executive Statistical Summary*. <http://www.state.il.us/dcfs/cwel1.pdf> (2 October 1998).

———. 1998e. *Press Release: Governor Announces Record High Numbers of Adoptions for Illinois Foster Children*. <http://www.stat.il.us.dcfs/nradptgv.htm> (9 October 1998).

Kearse, Brendan. 1996. Abused Again: Competing Constitutional Standards for the State's Duty to Protect Foster Children. *Columbia Journal of Law and Social Problems* 29: 385–410.

Kelly, Brenda L. 1994. Protection of Foster Children: A Constitutional Duty Anchored in a State's Choices? In *Child, Parent, and State: Law and Policy Reader*, edited by S. Randall Humm and others. Philadelphia: Temple University Press.

Kemerer, Frank R. 1991. *William Wayne Justice: A Judicial Biography*. Austin: University of Texas Press.

Kempe, C. Henry, and others. 1962. The Battered Child Syndrome. *Journal of the American Medical Association* 181: 17–24.

Key, Lisa E. 1996. Private Enforcement of Federal Funding Conditions under Section 1983: The Supreme Court's Failure to Adhere to the Doctrine of Separation of Powers. *University of California—Davis Law Review* 29: 283–353.

Kieffer, Maureen P. 1984. Child Abuse in Foster Homes. *Saint Louis University Law Journal* 28: 975–92.

Kingdon, John. 1984. *Agenda, Alternatives, and Public Policies*. New York: HarperCollins.

Kirp, David L., and Gary Babcock. 1981. Judge and Company: Court-Appointed Masters, School Desegregation, and Institutional Reform. *Alabama Law Review* 32: 313–97.

Kluger, Richard. 1976. *Simple Justice*. New York: Alfred A. Knopf.

Kohler, Mary. 1977. To What Are Children Entitled? In *The Children's Rights Movement: Overcoming the Oppression of Young People*, edited by Beatrice Gross and Ronald Gross. Garden City, N.Y.: Anchor Books.

Kulla, Roland, and Phyllis Richards. 1991. *Children's Social Services in Metropolitan Chicago: Volume III*. Chicago: Chapin Hall Center for Children at the University of Chicago.

Levine, Murray. 1986. The Role of the Special Master in Institutional Reform Litigation: A Case Study. *Law & Policy* 8: 275–321.

Levine, Murray, and David Perkins. 1997. *Principles of Community Psychology*. 2d ed. New York: Oxford University Press.

Lindsey, Duncan. 1994. *The Welfare of Children*. New York: Oxford University Press.

Lowe, Alexandra Dylan. 1996. New Laws Put Kids First. *American Bar Association Journal* May: 20–21.

Lowry, Marcia Robinson. 1988. Derring-Do in the 1980s: Child Welfare Impact Litigation after the Warren Years. In *Protecting Children from Abuse and Neglect: Policy and Practice*, edited by Douglas J. Besharov. Springfield, Ill.: Charles C. Thomas.

McCann, Michael W. 1994. *Rights at Work: Pay Equity Reform and the Politics of Legal Mobilization*. Chicago: University of Chicago Press.

McMurray, Scott. 1995. The Hard Case of Patrick Murphy. *Chicago Magazine* April: 82–125 (scattered).

Merry, Sheila M., and others. 1997. *Timeliness and Delay in the Cook County Juvenile Court Child Protection Division*. Chicago: Chapin Hall Center for Children at the University of Chicago.

Mezey, Susan Gluck. 1983. Judicial Interpretation of Legislative Intent: The Role of the Supreme Court in the Implication of Private Rights of Action. *Rutgers Law Review* 36: 53–89

———. 1988. *No Longer Disabled: The Federal Courts and the Politics of Social Security Disability*. Westport, Conn.: Greenwood.

———. 1995. The Illinois Child Welfare System: Survey of Juvenile Court Judges. Unpublished report, Center for Ethics, Loyola University, April 11, 1995.

———. 1996. *Children in Court: Public Policymaking and Federal Court Decisions.* Albany: State University of New York Press.

Murphy, Patrick. 1997. *Wasted: The Plight of America's Unwanted Children.* Chicago: Ivan R. Dee.

Mushlin, Michael B. 1984. Unsafe Havens: The Case for Constitutional Protection of Foster Children from Abuse and Neglect. In *Child, Parent, and State: Law and Policy Reader*, edited by S. Randall Humm and others. Philadelphia: Temple University Press.

Mushlin, Michael B., Louis Levitt, and Lauren Anderson. 1986. Court-Ordered Foster Family Care Reform: A Case Study. *Child Welfare* 65: 141–54.

Myers, John, E.B. 1992. *Legal Issues in Child Abuse and Neglect.* Newbury Park, Cal.: Sage.

Nakamura, Robert T., and Frank Smallwood. 1980. *The Politics of Policy Implementation.* New York: St. Martin's.

National Center for Youth Law. 1995. *Foster Care Reform Litigation Docket.* San Francisco: National Center for Youth Law.

———. 1998. *Foster Care Reform Litigation Docket.* San Francisco: National Center for Youth Law.

Nelson, Barbara. 1984. *Making an Issue of Child Abuse.* Chicago: University of Chicago Press.

Note. 1980. Judicial Intervention and Organization Theory: Changing Bureaucratic Behavior and Policy. *Yale Law Journal* 89: 513–37.

Oren, Laura. 1990. The State's Failure to Protect Children and Substantive Due Process: *DeShaney* in Context. *North Carolina Law Review* 68: 659–731.

Petit, Michael R., and Patrick A. Curtis. 1997. *Child Abuse and Neglect: A Look at the States.* Washington, D.C.: Child Welfare League of America.

Pine, Barbara. 1986. Child Welfare Reform and the Political Process. *Social Service Review* 60: 339–59.

Pressman, Jeffrey and Aaron Wildavsky. 1984. *Implementation.* Berkeley: University of California Press.

Preston, Lee. 1991. The House Focuses on the Home. *Illinois Bar Journal* 79: 578–82.

Preston, Scott J. 1996. "Can You Hear Me?": The United States Court of Appeals for the Third Circuit Addresses the Systemic Deficiencies of the Philadelphia Child Welfare System in *Baby Neal v. Casey. Creighton Law Review* 29: 1653–1710.

Rabkin, Jeremy. 1989. *Judicial Compulsions: How Public Law Distorts Public Policy.* New York: Basic Books.

Reidinger, Paul. 1988. Why Did No One Protect This Child? *American Bar Association Journal* 74 (December): 48–51.

Robison, Susan. 1990. *Putting the Pieces Together: Survey of State Systems for Children in Crisis.* Denver: National Conference of State Legislatures.

Rosenberg, Gerald. 1991. *The Hollow Hope: Can Courts Bring about Social Change?*

Chicago: University of Chicago Press.

———. 1998. Knowledge and Desire: Thinking about Courts and Social Change. In *Leveraging the Law: Using the Courts to Achieve Social Change*, edited by David A. Schultz. New York: Peter Lang.

Rosenberg, Janet, and William R. F. Phillips. 1982. The Institutionalization of Conflict in the Reform of Schools: A Case Study of Court Implementation of the PARC Decree. *Indiana Law Journal* 57: 425–49.

Ryan, Kevin. 1993. Stemming the Tide of Foster Care Runaways. *Catholic University Law Review* 42: 271–311.

Sandt, Claire. 1997. Concurrent Planning: Changing How You Do Business for Foster Children. *Child Law Practice* 16: 150–54.

Scheingold, Stuart. 1981. *The Politics of Rights Revisited*. In *Governing through Courts*, edited by Richard Gambitta, Marlynn May, and James Foster. Beverly Hills: Sage.

Schuerman, John R. 1997. *Best Interests and Family Preservation in America: A Discussion Paper*. Chicago: Chapin Hall Center for Children at the University of Chicago.

Schuerman, John R., and Julia H. Littell. 1995. *Problems and Prospects in Society's Response to Abuse and Neglect*. Chicago: Chapin Hall Center for Children at the University of Chicago.

Schuerman, John R., Tina L. Rzepnicki, and Julia H. Littell. 1994. *Putting Families First: An Experiment in Family Preservation*. New York: Aldine de Gruyter.

Schultz, David A., and Stephen E. Gottlieb. 1998. Legal Functionalism and Social Change: A Reassessment of Rosenberg's *The Hollow Hope*. In *Leveraging the Law: Using the Courts to Achieve Social Change*, edited by David A. Schultz. New York: Peter Lang.

Schwartz, Meryl L. 1996. Reinventing Guardianship: Subsidized Guardianship, Foster Care, and Child Welfare. *Review of Law and Social Change* 22: 441–82.

Sedlak, Andrea, J., and Diane D. Broadhurst. 1996. *Executive Summary of the Third National Incidence Study of Child Abuse and Neglect*. Washington, D.C.: U.S. Department of Health and Human Services.

Sheldon, Jill. 1997. 50,000 Children Are Waiting: Permanency Planning and Termination of Parental Rights Under the Adoption Assistance and Child Welfare Act of 1980. *Boston College Third World Law Journal* 17: 73–100.

Shotton, Alice C. 1989–90. Making Reasonable Efforts in Child Abuse and Neglect Cases: Ten Years Later. *California Western Law Review* 26: 223–56.

Silberman, Deanna. 1991. *Chicago and Its Children: A Brief History of Social Services for Children in Chicago: Volume I*. Chicago: Chapin Hall Center for Children at the University of Chicago.

Sinden, Amy. 1994. In Search of Affirmative Duties toward Children under a Post-*DeShaney* Constitution. In *Child, Parent, and State: Law and Policy Reader*, edited by S. Randall Humm and others. Philadelphia: Temple University Press.

Skoler, Daniel L. 1991. A Constitutional Right to Safe Foster Care? Time for the Supreme Court to Pay Its I.O.U. *Pepperdine Law Review* 18: 353–81.

Smith, Leo. 1992. Reducing State Accountability to the Federal Government: The *Suter v. Artist M.* Decision to Dismiss Section 1983 Claims for Violating Federal Fund Mandates. *Wisconsin Law Review* 1992: 1267–97.

Special Project. 1978. The Remedial Process in Institutional Reform Litigation. *Columbia Law Review* 78: 784–929.

Stein, Theodore. 1987. Issues in the Development, Implementation and Monitoring of Consent Decrees and Court Orders. *Saint Louis University Public Law Review* 6: 141–59.

———. 1991. *Child Welfare and the Law.* New York: Longman.

Stein, Theodore J., and Gary David Comstock. 1987. *Reasonable Efforts: A Report on Implementation by Child Welfare Agencies in Five States.* Washington, D.C.: American Bar Association.

Stoesz, David, and Howard Jacob Karger. 1996. Suffer the Children: How the Government Fails Its Most Vulnerable Citizens—Abused and Neglected Kids. *Washington Monthly*, June.

Taggart, William A. 1989. Defining the Power of the Federal Judiciary: The Impact of Court-Ordered Prison Reform on State Expenditures for Corrections. *Law and Society Review* 23: 241–71.

Tatara, Toshio. 1997. "U.S. Child Substitute Care Flow Data and the Race/Ethnicity of Children in Care for FY 95." *VCIS Research Notes*, no. 13 (March). Washington, D.C.: American Public Welfare Association.

Testa, Mark. 1985. *Child Welfare in Sociological and Historical Perspective.* Chicago: Chapin Hall Center for Children at the University of Chicago.

Testa, Mark, and Robert M. Goerge. 1988. *Policy and Resource Factors in the Achievement of Permanency for Foster Children in Illinois.* Chicago: Chapin Hall Center for Children at the University of Chicago.

Tjaden, Patricia G., and Nancy Thoennes. 1992. Predictors of Legal Intervention in Child Maltreatment Cases. *Child Abuse & Neglect* 16: 807–21.

Tucker, Cathleen, and Paul Blatt. 1994. *DeShaney* and Child Welfare Reform. In *Child, Parent, and State: Law and Policy Reader,* edited by S. Randall Humm and others. Philadelphia: Temple University Press.

U.S. Department of Health and Human Services. 1997a. *Child Maltreatment 1995: Reports from the States to the National Child Abuse and Neglect Data System.* Washington, D.C.: U.S. Department of Health and Human Services.

———. 1997b. "Protecting the Well-Being of Children." <http://www.acf.dhhs.gov/programs/opa/facts/chilwelf.htm> (19 June 1998).

Vondra, Joan I. 1993. Childhood Poverty and Child Maltreatment. In *Child Poverty and Public Policy,* edited by Judith A. Chafel. Washington, D.C.: Urban Institute.

Vose, Clement E. 1959. *Caucasians Only: The Supreme Court, the NAACP, and the Restrictive Covenant Case.* Berkeley: University of California Press.

Welling, Sarah N., and Barbara W. Jones. 1988. Prison Reform Issues for the Eighties: Modification and Dissolution of Injunctions in the Federal Courts. *Connecticut Law Review* 20: 865–94.

Welsh, Wayne N. 1995. *Counties in Court: Jail Overcrowding and Court-Ordered Reform.* Philadelphia: Temple University Press.

Wexler, Richard. 1995a. The Children's Crusade. *Chicago Reader* 24 March: 9–19 (scattered).

———. 1995b. *Wounded Innocents: The Real Victims of the War against Child Abuse.* New York: Prometheus.

Whittaker, James K. 1994. Foreword. In *Putting Families First: An Experiment in Family Preservation,* edited by John R. Schuerman, Tina L. Rzepnicki, and Julia H. Littell. New York: Aldine de Gruyter.

Williams, Alexander, Jr. 1991. Court-Ordered Prison Reform—An Argument for Restraint. *Howard Law Journal* 34: 559–66.

Wilton, Timothy. 1982. Legitimacy in Social Reform Litigation: An Empirical Study. *University of Michigan Journal of Law Reform*: 189–217.

Wood, Robert, ed. 1990. *Remedial Law: When Courts Become Administrators.* Amherst: University of Massachusetts Press.

Wulczyn, Fred H., and Robert M. Goerge. 1992. Foster Care in New York and Illinois: The Challenge of Rapid Change. *Social Service Review* 66: 278–94.

Wulczyn, Fred H., Allen W. Harden, and Robert M. Goerge. 1997. *An Update from the Multistate Foster Care Data Archive: Foster Care Dynamics, 1983–1994.* Chicago: Chapin Hall Center for Children at the University of Chicago.

Yackle, Larry. 1989. *Reform and Regret: The Story of Federal Judicial Involvement in the Alabama Prison System.* New York: Oxford University Press.

Yarbrough, Tinsley E. 1981. *Judge Frank Johnson and Human Rights in Alabama.* University: University of Alabama Press.

Zalman, Marvin. 1998. Juricide. In *Leveraging the Law: Using the Courts to Achieve Social Change,* edited by David A. Schultz. New York: Peter Lang.

Reported Opinions

Archie v. City of Racine, 847 F.2d 1211 (7th Cir. 1988).

Aristotle P. v. Johnson, 721 F.Supp 1002 (N.D.Ill. 1989).

Artist M. v. Johnson, 726 F.Supp. 690 (N.D.Ill. 1989).

Artist M. v. Johnson, 917 F.2d 980 (7th Cir. 1990).

B.H. v. Johnson, 715 F.Supp 1387 (N.D.Ill. 1989).

B.H. v. McDonald, 49 F.3d 294 (7th Cir. 1995) (1995b).

B.H. v. Ryder, 984 F.2d 196 (7th Cir. 1993).

B.H. v. Ryder, 856 F.Supp. 1285 (N.D.Ill. 1994) (1994a).

Bates v. Johnson, 1989 U.S. Dist. Lexis 7658 (N.D.Ill. 1989).

Bates v. Johnson, 901 F.2d 1424 (7th Cir. 1990).

Black v. Beame, 419 F.Supp. 599 (S.D.N.Y. 1976).

Bowers v. DeVito, 686 F.2d 616 (7th Cir. 1982).

Brown v. Board of Education, 347 U.S. 483 (1954).

Child v. Beame, 412 F.Supp. 593 (S.D.N.Y. 1976).

Conley v. Gibson, 355 U.S. 41 (1957).

Cort v. Ash, 422 U.S. 66 (1975).

Daniels v. Williams, 474 U.S. 327 (1986).

Del A. v. Edwards, 1988 U.S. Dist. LEXIS 1604 (E.D.La. 1988) (1988a).

Del A. v. Edwards, 855 F.2d 1148 (5th Cir. 1988) (1988b).

Del A. v. Edwards, 862 F.2d 1107 (5th Cir. 1988) (1988c).

Del A. v. Edwards, 867 F.2d 842 (5th Cir. 1989).

Del A. v. Roemer, 1990 U.S. Dist. LEXIS 10639 (E.D.La. 1990).

Del A. v. Roemer, 777 F.Supp. 1297 (E.D.La. (1991).

DeShaney v. Winnebago County Department of Social Services, 812 F.2d 298 (7th Cir. 1987).

DeShaney v. Winnebago County Department of Social Services, 489 U.S. 189 (1989).

Doe v. Bobbitt, 665 F.Supp. 691 (N.D.Ill. 1987).

Doe v. Bobbitt, 698 F.Supp. 1415 (N.D.Ill. 1988).

Doe v. Bobbitt, 881 F.2d 510 (7th Cir. 1989).

Doe v. Lambert, 1988 U.S. Dist. LEXIS 3384 (N.D.Ill. 1988).

Doe v. New York City Department of Social Services, 649 F.2d 134 (2d Cir. 1981).

Doe v. New York City Department of Social Services, 709 F.2d 782 (2d Cir. 1983).

Edelman v. Jordan, 415 U.S. 651 (1974).

Estate of Bailey v. County of York, 768 F.2d 503 (3d Cir. 1985).

Estelle v. Gamble, 429 U.S. 97 (1976).

Ex Parte Young, 209 U.S. 123 (1908).

Fox v. Custis, 712 F.2d 84 (4th Cir. 1983).

Golden State Transit Corporation v. City of Los Angeles, 493 U.S. 103 (1989).

Harlow v. Fitzgerald, 457 U.S. 800 (1982).

Harpole v. Arkansas Department of Human Services, 820 F.2d 923 (8th Cir. 1987).

Hobson v. Hansen, 327 F.Supp. 844 (D.D.C. 1971).

Jackson v. City of Joliet, 715 F.2d 1200 (7th Cir. 1983).

Jensen v. Conrad, 747 F.2d 185 (4th Cir. 1984).

Joseph and Josephine A. v. New Mexico Department of Human Services, 575 F.Supp. 346 (D.N.M. 1982).

Juan F. v. Weiker, 37 F.3d 874 (2d Cir. 1994).

K.H. v. Morgan, 914 F.2d 846 (7th Cir. 1990).

Katherine M. v. Ryder, 254 Ill. App. 3d 479, 627 N.E.2d 42 (1st App. Dist. 1993).

L.J. v. Massinga, 838 F.2d 118 (4th Cir. 1988) (1988a).

L.J. v. Massinga, 699 F.Supp. 508 (D.Md. 1988) (1988b).

LaShawn A. v. Barry, 69 F.3d 556 (D.C. Cir. 1995).

LaShawn A. v. Dixon, 762 F.Supp. 959 (D.D.C. 1991).

LaShawn A. v. Kelly, 990 F.2d 1319 (D.C. Cir. 1993).

LaShawn A. v. Kelly, 887 F.Supp. 297 (D.D.C. 1995).

Lesher v. Lavrich, 632 F.Supp. 77 (N.D.Ohio 1984).

Lesher v. Lavrich, 784 F.2d 193 (6th Cir. 1986).

Lynch v. Dukakis, 719 F.2d 504 (1st Cir. 1983).

Lynch v. King, 550 F.Supp. 325 (D.Mass. 1982).

Maine v. Thiboutot, 448 U.S. 1 (1980).

Martinez v. California, 444 U.S. 277 (1980).

Meador v. Cabinet for Human Resources, 902 F.2d 474 (6th Cir. 1990).

Mendez v. Rutherford, 655 F.Supp. 115 (N.D.Ill. 1986).

Middlesex County Sewerage Authority v. National Sea Clammers Association, 453 U.S. 1 (1981).

Milburn v. Anne Arundel County Depart of Social Services, 871 F. 2d 474 (4th Cir. 1989).

Miller v. Youakim, 440 U.S. 125 (1979).

Missouri v. Jenkins, 495 U.S. 33 (1990).

Monell v. New York Department of Social Services, 436 U.S. 658 (1978).

Monroe v. Pape, 365 U.S. 167 (1961).

Norfleet v. Arkansas Department of Human Services, 796 F.Supp. 1194 (E.D. Ark. 1992).

Norfleet v. Arkansas Department of Human Services, 989 F.2d 289 (8th Cir. 1993).

Norman v. Johnson, 739 F.Supp 1182 (N.D.Ill. 1990).

Norman v. McDonald, 930 F.Supp. 1219 (N.D.Ill. 1996).

Pennhurst State School and Hospital v. Halderman, 451 U.S. 1 (1981).

Roe v. Wade, 410 U.S. 113 (1973).

Rosado v. Wyman, 397 U.S. 397 (1970).

Rubacha v. Coler, 607 F.Supp. 477 (N.D.Ill. 1985).

Rufo v. Inmates of Suffolk County Jail, 502 U.S. 367 (1992).

Ruiz v. Estelle, 503 F.Supp. 1265 (S.D.Tex. 1980).

Scrivner v. Andrews, 816 F.2d 261 (6th Cir. 1987).

Society for Good Will to Retarded Children v. Cuomo, 737 F.2d 1239 (2d Cir. 1984).

Spence v. Staras, 507 F.2d 554 (7th Cir. 1974).

Suter v. Artist M., 503 U.S. 347 (1992).

Taylor v. Ledbetter, 818 F.2d 791 (11th Cir. 1987).

United States v. Carolene Products, 304 U.S. 144 (1938).

United States v. City of Parma, 494 F.Supp. 1049 (N.D.Ohio 1980).

Vermont Department of Social and Rehabilitation Services v. United States Department of Health and Human Services, 798 F.2d 57 (2d Cir. 1986).

White v. Rochford, 592 F.2d 381 (7th Cir. 1979).

Wilder v. Virginia Hospital Association, 496 U.S. 498 (1990).

Will v. Michigan Department of State Police, 491 U.S. 58 (1989).

Winston v. Children and Youth Services, 948 F.2d 1380 (3d Cir. 1991).

Wright v. Roanoke Redevelopment and Housing Authority, 479 U.S. 418 (1987).

Wyatt v. Stickney, 325 F.Supp. 582 (M.D.Ala. 1971).

Youakim v. McDonald, 926 F.Supp. 719 (N.D.Ill. 1995).

Youngberg v. Romeo, 457 U.S. 307 (1982).

Yvonne L. v. New Mexico Department of Human Services, 959 F.2d 883 (10th Cir. 1992).

Consent Decrees

Aristotle P. v. Ryder (1994) No. 88 C 7919, March 11, 1994.

Bates v. Johnson (1986) No. 84 C 10054, April 3, 1986.

B.H. v. Suter (1991) No. 88 C 5599, December 20, 1991.

Burgos v. DCFS (1977) No. 75 C 3974, January 14, 1977.

Dana W. v. Ryder (1993) No. 90 C 3479, March 25, 1993.

G.L. v. Zumwalt (1983) No. 77-0242-CV-W-4, March 21, 1983.

Hill v. Erickson (1994) No. 88 CO 296, January 3, 1994.

Joseph and Josephine A. v. New Mexico Department of Human Services (1983) No. Civ. 80-623JB, September 23, 1983.

L.J. v. Massinga (1987) No. JH-84-4409, July 27, 1987.

Norman v. Suter (1991) No. 89 C 1624, March 28, 1991.

R.C. v. Hornsby (1991) No. 88-H-1170-N, December 18, 1991.

Reid v. Suter (1992) No. 89 J 61956, May 20, 1992.

Court Orders

B.H. v. Johnson (1990a) No. 88 C 5599, *Order to Appoint Expert Witnesses.* August 31, 1990.

B.H. v. Johnson (1990b) No. 88 C 5599, *Order Regarding Expert Witnesses.* October 26, 1990.

B.H. v. McDonald (1997a) No. 88 C 5588, *Order.* January 22, 1997.

B.H. v. McDonald (1997b) No. 88 C 5599, *Agreed Order Modifying Consent Decree.* April 7, 1997.

Lynch v. King (1981) CA No. 78-2152-K, *Memorandum and Order.* June 9, 1981.

R.C. v. Hornsby (1989) No. 88-D-1170-N, *Memorandum Opinion and Order.* April 19, 1989.

Documents

Aristotle P. v. McDonald (1997) No. 88 C 7919, January 29, 1997, *Joint Motion for Entry of Agreed Order Regarding Consent Decree.*

B.H. v. McDonald (1995a) No. 88 C 5588, *Joint Memorandum in Support of the Parties' Motion for Entry of Agreed Order Regarding Consent Decree.*

B.H. v. McDonald (1996a) No. 88 C 5588, *Children Objectors' Memorandum in Support of Objections to the Proposed Agreed Order.*

B.H. v. McDonald (1996b) No. 88 C 5588, *Joint Memorandum in Support of Agreed Supplemental Order.*

B.H. v. McDonald (1996c) No. 88 C 5599, *Letter from the Office of the Inspector General to Judge John Grady.*

B.H. v. Ryder (1994b) No. 88 C 5599, *Monitor's Report from January 1, 1993 to December 31, 1993.*

Bates v. Johnson (1984) No. 84 C 10054, *Complaint.*

Bates v. Johnson (1987) No. 84 C 10054, *Motion for Contempt.*

Bates v. Suter (1991a) No. 84 C 10054, *Motion for Entry of Order For Supplemental Relief Pursuant to Contempt Judgment.*

Bates v. Suter (1991b) No. 84 C 10054, *Agreed Order for Supplemental Relief.*

Burgos v. DCFS (1975) No. 75 C 3974, *Complaint.*

Burgos v. DCFS (1976) No. 75 C 3974, *Decision on Pending Motions.*

Burgos v. DCFS (1987) No. 75 C 3974, *Motion for Contempt.*

Norman v. McDonald (1995) No. 89 C 1624, *Sixth Monitoring Report from January 1, 1994 to December 31, 1994.*

R.C. v. Hornsby (1988) No. 88-H-1170-N, *Complaint.*

Interviews and Observations

Aspen, Marvin. 1996. Interview with author, 8 May.

Biehl, Julie. 1996. Interview with author, 23 May.

Brody, Michael. 1996. Courtroom observation, 2 October.

Castillo, Ruben. 1996. Interview with author, 19 July.

Cheney-Egan, John. 1997. Interview with author, 21 August.

Dsida, Michael. 1996. Interview with author, 11 March.

Geraghty, Diane. 1998. Interview with author, 22 October.

Geraghty, Thomas. 1997. Interview with author, 9 September.

Gieseke, Gaylord. 1996. Interview with author, 13 September.

Golbert, Charles. 1996. Interview with author, 29 April.

———. 1998. Interview with author, 23 November.

Grady, John. 1996a. Interview with author, 10 June.

———. 1996b. Courtroom observation, 2 October.

Hart, William. 1996. Interview with author, 30 September.

Heybach, Laurene. 1996. Interview with author, 10 May.

Lehrer, Robert. 1997. Interview with author, 18 August.

Loftus, Joseph. 1998. Interview with author, 9 November.

McDonald, Jess. 1996. Interview with author, 23 February.

Monahan, Joseph. 1996. Interview with author, 3 October.

———. 1997. Letter to author, 23 September.

Morsch, Mary Sue. 1996. Interview with author, 9 May.

Murphy, Patrick. 1996. Interview with author, 10 April.

Nordberg, John. 1996. Interview with author, 10 May.

O'Connor, Michael. 1997. Interview with author, 16 September.

Ostro, Ginger. 1996. Interview with author, 7 June.

Peters, Clark. 1998. Interview with author, 30 October.

Plunkett, Paul. 1996. Interview with author, 27 June.

Redleaf, Diane. 1997. Interview with author, 9 July.

Ryder, Sterling. 1996. Interview with author, 19 June.

Schmiedel, Peter. 1996. Courtroom observation, 2 October.

Schneider, Joseph. 1996. Interview with author, 30 April.

Shadur, Milton. 1996. Interview with author, 26 April.

Slater, Peggy. 1998. Interview with author, 20 January.

Smith, Jeanine. 1996. Interview with author, 22 May.

Tchen, Christina. 1995. Interview with author, 22 December.

Wells, Susan. 1998. Interview with author, 18 December.

Wenzel, Charlotte. 1996. Interview with author, 15 May.

Wolf, Benjamin. 1996. Interview with author, 3 July.

———. 1998. Interview with author, 2 November.

Index of Names and Subjects

Illinois Better Government Association, 54
Illinois Catholic Conference, 59, 62
Illinois Caucus for Foster Children, 162
Illinois Child Care Association, 59, 112
Illinois Department of Children and Family Services (DCFS), 7, 11, 13, 14, 32, 37, 39–42, 134; abuse and neglect investigations by, 42, 43, 113; agency culture in, 109–14, 158, 163; and consent decrees, 13, 16, 48–53, 93, 104, 107, 108, 114, 122–26, 127–33, 137–38, 157, 158–59, 162, 163, 179n. 22; and emergency shelters, 113–14; funding of, 17, 41, 42, 50, 58, 59, 60–61, 64, 112–13, 114, 124, 134–36, 149, 152, 159, 160, 168; Inspector General for, 43, 144; jurisdiction of, 41–42; and monitors, 11, 16, 106, 108, 123–24, 129, 130–33, 159, 163, 182nn. 10, 11; origins of, 41–42; and permanency, 45, 46, 124; and private agencies, 54, 150–51, 164, 178n. 4, 182n. 2, 183n. 7, 184n. 1; and settlements, 92–94, 104, 137–39, 157–58; and Spanish-speaking families, 48–50, 156; systemic change in, 155–56, 157, 161–65; visitation policy of, 50–53, 94–95, 125–26, 156
Illinois Humane Association, 54
Institutional reform litigation, 1–4, 6–12, 17, 161–62, 163, 166, 169; and bureaucratic change, 109–14; and child welfare systems, ix–x, 1, 7–8, 11–12, 15, 17, 35–38, 48–53, 63, 86–87, 94, 155–56, 157, 161, 162, 165–69; and consent decrees, 1–2, 3, 9, 10, 11, 36–37, 85, 91, 92, 98–100, 104–7, 111, 114, 119, 126, 128–29, 138–39, 142, 159, 160, 162; models of, 8–12, 16–17; and monitors, 119, 120, 130–31, 159, 163, 182n. 12; and prison systems, 1, 2, 3, 6, 7, 9, 128, 130, 134; and receivers, 1, 101, 119–22, 182n. 7;

and serving agency interests, 134–35, 137–39; settlements of, 88, 91–94, 95, 98–100, 101, 102, 104, 106–7, 110, 126, 137–39; and state policymaking authority, 2–3, 17, 88, 96, 128, 134, 136–39, 156, 165, 167, 168

Jenner & Block, 56
Jewish Children's Bureau, 123
Johnson, Charles, 11
Johnson, Frank, 2
Johnson, Gordon, 50, 54, 59, 60, 61, 63, 64, 65, 93, 157, 180n. 2
Jones, Barbara W., 91, 92, 128
Jones, Ernestine, 121
Justice, William Wayne, 2
Juvenile courts, Illinois, 11, 14, 33, 39, 42–47, 55, 109, 147, 151–54, 161, 175n. 8, 178nn. 7, 8, 184n. 11; adjudicatory hearing in, 44, 45, 46, 154, 179n. 16; and attorneys, 43, 44–45, 46, 47–48; and "best interests of the child," 43, 45, 46, 148–49; dispositional hearing in, 45, 124–25, 179n. 17; hearing officers in, 46, 179n. 20; permanency review hearing in, 45, 46, 179n. 19; temporary custody hearing in, 43, 44, 154; and termination of parental rights, 46, 151–53, 184n. 11

Kane, Denise, 43, 125, 144
Karger, Howard Jacob, 28, 177n. 13
Kearse, Brendan, 21, 80, 182n. 3
Keaton, Robert, 82
Kelly, Brenda L., 29
Kemerer, Frank R., 6
Kempe, C. Henry, 22–23
Kennelly, Barbara, 33
Key, Lisa E., 25
Kieffer, Maureen P., 35, 180n. 4
Kingdon, John, 14
Kirp, David L., 127, 130
Kostelny, Kathleen, 20
Kluger, Richard, 2
Kohler, Mary, ix
Kulla, Roland, 41

Lago, Jim, 58, 71
La Rabida Children's Hospital and
  Research Center, 102
Legal Aid of Western Missouri, 36
Legal Assistance Foundation (LAF),
  47, 48–53, 55, 93, 97–98, 122,
  123, 125, 131, 146, 156, 183n. 8
Lehrer, Robert, 55, 131, 143, 145
Levine, Murray, 109, 110, 130, 135,
  147
Levitt, Louis, 1, 37, 175n. 1
Liederman, David, 29
Lindsey, Duncan, 21
Littell, Julia H., 12, 31, 32, 43, 94,
  112, 135, 177n. 6, 178n. 14
Loftus, Joseph, 131, 140, 144, 146,
  150, 153, 164, 183nn. 7, 10, 184n.
  1
Lowe, Alexander Dylan, 27, 30
Lowry, Marcia Robinson, 22, 35, 36,
  110, 161, 177
Loyola University Chicago, 102;
  ChildLaw Center at, 55, 146
Lutheran Children's Services, 183n. 7
Lutheran Social Services, 103

Madigan, Michael, 60, 112
Manion, Daniel, 97
Marovich, George, 98
Marquart, James W., 6, 7
Martinez, Bob, 29
Maryland Legal Aid Bureau, 84
McCann, Michael W., 5, 175n. 3
McDonald, Jess, 59, 93, 111–12, 131,
  136, 137, 138, 143, 145, 149, 157,
  164
McManus, Ed, 112
McMillen, Thomas, 49
McMurray, Scott, 33, 57, 58, 141,
  148, 153
Media, 10, 11, 17, 53–55, 59, 61, 134,
  137, 138, 141–42, 146–49, 156,
  160
Mental Health Law Project, 99
Merry, Sheila M., 33, 109, 154, 175n.
  8
Mezey, Susan Gluck, 5, 6, 44–45, 80,
  109, 147, 176nn. 12, 13, 179n. 13
Mikva, Abner, 119

Miller, George, 28
Miller, Jerome, 54, 63, 120–21, 179n.
  24
Monahan, Joseph, 103, 104, 131
Mondale, Walter, 23
Monitors, 10, 100, 119, 120, 159; and
  B.H., 11, 16, 106, 108, 129, 130–
  33, 163, 182n. 10; and *Norman,*
  123–24, 133, 163
Moorman, Ronald, 59
Moran, James, 56
Morsch, Mary Sue, 131
Moynihan, Daniel Patrick, 24
Murphy, Patrick, 20, 27, 30, 40, 47–
  48, 53–54, 57–58, 95, 124, 139–42,
  144, 148, 163, 175n. 9, 182n. 2
Mushlin, Michael B., 1, 21, 37, 175n.
  1
Myers, John E. B., 23

Nakamura, Robert T., 109, 147
National Association of Counsel for
  Children, 117
National Association of Counties, 117
National Center for Policy Analysis,
  13
National Center for Youth Law, ix, 13
National Commission on Child
  Welfare and Family Preservation,
  35
National Commission for Prevention
  of Child Abuse, 61
National Conference of State Legisla-
  tors, 117
National Council of Juvenile and
  Family Court Judges, 117
National Governors Association, 117
National League of Cities, 117
Nelson, Barbara, 23
Neo-legal realists, 5
Nevas, Alan, 181n. 11
New Orleans Legal Assistance
  Corporation, 85
New York Civil Liberties Union, 36,
  37, 85, 100
Nordberg, John, 121, 167
North American Council on Adopt-
  able Children, 29
Northwestern University, 122;

Substitute care, 12, 13, 14, 20–22, 24, 25, 26, 27, 31, 33, 34, 35, 40, 42, 44, 45, 55, 80, 109, 150–53, 160, 164, 175n. 4; and foster care drift, 21–22, 24, 25, 35; and foster parents, 45, 65, 106, 113, 127, 183n. 8; and kinship care, 45, 152; and subsidized guardianship, 151–53, 164; and temporary custody, 42, 43, 45

Suter, Sue, 111, 118

"Suter Fix," 118

Systemic litigation. *See* Institutional reform litigation

Taggart, William A., 134

Tatara, Toshio, 21

Tchen, Christina, 56–57, 116, 122, 138, 145, 149

Terry, Cleo, 113

Testa, Mark, 24, 177nn. 7, 9

Thoennes, Nancy, 18

Thompson, Jim, 57, 58, 59, 60, 63, 64, 93, 94, 111, 157

Tjaden, Patricia G., 18

Tucker, Cathleen, 31, 35

U.S. Children's Bureau, 23, 29, 121

U.S. Congress, 19, 24, 25, 26, 28, 29, 34, 42, 80, 81, 82, 91, 95, 96, 117, 118, 119

U.S. Department of Health and Human Services (HHS), 15, 18, 23, 25, 26, 29, 80, 90–91, 96, 117–18, 152, 175n. 5, 183n. 10, 184n. 12; and National Center on Child Abuse and Neglect (NCCAN), 18, 19, 23; and National Child Abuse and Neglect Data system (NCANDS), 18, 19

U.S. Solicitor General, 117

U.S. Supreme Court, 3, 4–5, 7, 13, 57, 66–67, 78, 80–81, 83, 91, 95, 97, 105, 114, 115, 116, 117–18, 119, 121, 122, 141, 158, 169, 181nn. 3, 8, 183n. 8

University of Illinois, Champaign-Urbana, 102, 143, 144; Children and Family Research Center at, 143–46

Voices for Illinois Children, 13, 110, 143, 146

Vondra, Joan I., 19

Vose, Clement E., 2

Wallace, Joseph, 17, 32, 33, 43, 114, 147–49

Welling, Sarah N., 91, 92, 128

Wells, Susan, 144–46

Welsh, Wayne N., 6, 7, 9, 10

Wenzel, Charlotte, 121, 125, 163

Wexler, Richard, 20, 21, 28, 30, 31, 32, 141, 148

Whittaker, James K., 12

Widawsky, Daniel, 180n. 6

Wildavsky, Aaron, 109

Williams, Alexander, Jr., 3

Williams, Ann, 94–95

Williams, Walter, 147

Wilson, Dana Burnell, 152

Wilton, Timothy, 110

Wolf, Benjamin, 32, 55–56, 57, 58, 59, 61, 64, 86, 94, 113–14, 140, 141, 145, 146, 149, 150, 161, 163, 164

Wood, Robert, 9, 10

Wright, Skelly, 2

Wright, Susan Webber, 115

Wulczyn, Fred H., 12, 39, 40, 109, 175n. 5

Yackle, Larry, 6, 7

Yarbrough, Tinsley E., 6

Yeazell, Stephen C., 3

Youth Law Center, 117

Zalman, Marvin, 5

Index of Cases